THE BEST OF NOLA

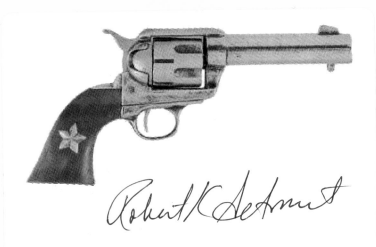

OUTLAWS AND LAWMEN OF THE OLD WEST:
THE BEST OF NOLA

INTRODUCTION BY CHUCK PARSONS,
EDITOR, NOLA *QUARTERLY*

EDITED BY ROBERT K. DEARMENT

OUTLAW-LAWMAN RESEARCH SERIES
VOLUME V
LIMITED TO 1,000 COPIES

NOLA
NATIONAL ASSOCIATION FOR OUTLAW-LAWMAN
HISTORY, INC.

IN AFFILIATION WITH THE
UNIVERSITY OF WYOMING
LARAMIE, WYOMING

Outlaws And Lawmen of the Old West: The Best of Nola; introduction by Chuck Parsons; edited by Robert K. DeArment.
p. cm.--(Outlaw-lawman research series: v. 5)

Includes bibliographic references and index.
ISBN 0-935269-29-0
1. Outlaws--Western biography. 2. Peace officers--Western
Biography. 3. Frontier and pioneer life--Western. 4.Western history.
5. Crime history.

Published by NOLA

Distributed by True West Publishing, LLC • 6702 E. Cave Creek
Road, Cave Creek, Arizona 85331

Cover design by Daniel Harshberger
Cover art by Bob Boze Bell

In affiliation with the University of Wyoming, Laramie, Wyoming

CONTENTS

EDITOR'S NOTE

It was interesting and enjoyable going back through the NOLA publications of the last quarter century to select outstanding articles for inclusion in this book and to write brief biographical sketches of the authors. Through membership in NOLA it has been my privilege to know all of those whose work is represented in these pages and a finer group of people will not be found anywhere. Originating in all parts of the country (and England as well), spanning several generations, from diverse home and educational backgrounds, and following many different career paths, they are linked together by a single common bond, an avid interest in the gunfighters, outlaws and lawmen of the Old West and a desire to know the true history of that unique period in which they lived. Through their research and writing each has contributed greatly to our knowledge of this era. Sadly, four of those whose work appears in these pages—C.L. Sonnichsen (1901-1991), Nellie Snyder Yost (1905-1992), Philip J. Rasch (1909-1995), and Jim Browning (1921-1999)—have since passed on, and to their memory this volume is respectfully dedicated.

Robert K. DeArment
Sylvania, Ohio
2000

INTRODUCTION

The National Association for Outlaw and Lawman History, Inc. (NOLA) was formed in 1974 to provide an organization for western history enthusiasts with a special interest in outlaws and lawmen. Most of the original founders had a particular interest in Butch Cassidy, the Sundance Kid, and the Wild Bunch, and the articles in the early NOLA publications reflect that narrow attention. But as the organization grew, new members, researching other facets of the genre, widened the scope to include articles on outlawry throughout the entire West during the second half of the nineteenth century.

The first NOLA publication was a *Newsletter* that appeared in the spring of 1975. It contained news of the first annual convention, called "the Rendezvous," to be held at Brown's Park; a single book review; the announcement of a $5,000 donation to NOLA by Pinkerton's, Inc.; a list of members; sketches of the fifteen members of the board of directors; and articles on Butch Cassidy's survival after his reported death in Bolivia and Wild Bill Hickok's last gunfight in Abilene, Kansas. This *Newsletter* was in fact a combination of what would become two separate publications, the *Newsletter* and the *Quarterly*. The *Newsletter* contained articles about members and news of western-related activities and events of interest to members. Appearing in the *Quarterly* were historical articles and book reviews.

The first *Quarterly*, published in the summer of 1977, still contained *Newsletter* material. Beginning in the spring of 1978, however, two separate publications appeared.

Through the years the goals of the *Quarterly* publication have remained constant: to make available articles of high quality, well researched and written, on the history of gunfighters, outlaws and lawmen in the Old West. Contributions have come mainly, but not exclusively, from members of NOLA.

A NOLA member who contributed greatly to the Quarterly as well as numerous other periodicals was Philip J. Rasch, who joined the organization in 1975. Before his death in 1995 Dr. Rasch conducted original research and wrote and published more than 160 "papers," as he called them, on frontier violence. Most of his work dealt with his favorite subject, Billy the Kid and the Lincoln County War, but, especially, in his later years, he ventured into other areas of study. Many of his pieces appeared in obscure publications, difficult to find. In 1994 the NOLA board of directors approved the concept of publishing Dr. Rasch's articles in book form. The first three volumes, *Trailing Billy the Kid* (1995), *Gunsmoke in Lincoln County* (1997), and *Warriors of Lincoln County* (1998) comprise a trilogy of Rasch's work on the Lincoln County War. A fourth edition, *Desperadoes of Arizona Territory*, was published in 1999. All have been edited by Robert K. DeArment, who also edited this volume.

To help celebrate NOLA's twenty-fifth anniversary, the NOLA board of directors at its February 1999 meeting, authorized publication of a book containing many of the outstanding articles which have appeared in the *Quarterly* over the years. Secretary Rick Miller, board member Robert K. DeArment and I were assigned to select the "Best of the NOLA *Quarterly*."

In the selection process weight was given to the following considerations, in no particular order: evidence of original research by the author; the article's contribution to historical knowledge; the author's bona fides in the field; the extent of the author's contribution to NOLA's goals, either in a leadership role or by article submissions; and the diversity of subject matter in the final book.

The articles selected provide information, much of it new, on gunfighters and outlawry in Arizona, Oklahoma, California, Kansas, Missouri, Montana, New Mexico, Texas and Wyoming, a vast area of the frontier West. featured are many popular western notables: John Wesley Hardin, Wild Bill Hickok, Billy the Kid, Butch Cassidy, Buffalo Bill Cody, Teddy Roosevelt, the James Gang, the Wild Bunch, and the Earps and Clantons, but other stories concern less well-publicized, but still fascinating, frontier figures. Together they represent some of the best that has appeared in the pages of the NOLA *Quarterly* during the last quarter century.

CHUCK PARSONS
QUARTERLY EDITOR
LULING, TEXAS,
2000

John Boessenecker

Born in San Francisco in 1953, John Boessenecker became interested in frontier history at an early age and sold his first article to a western magazine at age fifteen. After graduation from San Francisco State University in 1975 with a degree in history and eight years service as a police officer, he attended University of California's Hastings College of the Law in San Francisco and was admitted to the California bar in 1985. He has published many articles on frontier crime and law enforcement in a number of national and regional publications. The University of Oklahoma Press has published four of his books: *Badge and Buckshot: Lawlessness in Old California* (1988), *The Grey Fox: The True Story of Bill Miner, Last of the Old Time Bandits* (with Mark Dugan 1992), *Lawman: The Life and Times of Harry Morse, 1835-1912* (1998) and *Against the Vigilantes: the Recollections of Dutch Charley Duane* (1999). A fifth book, *Gold Dust and Gunsmoke: Tales of Gold Rush Outlaws, Gunfighters, Lawmen, and Vigilantes* (1999) was published by John Wiley & Sons, Inc. John has been a frequent speaker on western documentary programs produced for television on PBS and the History Channel. He is married to Marta S. Diaz, a Superior Court judge, and the couple have two children. He is an avid collector of Old West memorabilia. When not researching and writing western history, he practices law in the field of probate, trust and estate litigation.

HARRY MORSE VS. JUAN SOTO:
A Visit to the Site of California's
Most Famous Outlaw-Lawman Gunfight
•
By John Boessenecker
NOLA *Quarterly*, April-June 1998.

In 1968, at the age of fifteen, I read Joseph Henry Jackson's *Bad Company* (1949) and was enthralled by the accounts of the book's hero, Harry Morse, pioneer sheriff of Alameda County, California. Like most boys, I had been raised on television westerns. I especially enjoyed those about real lawmen of the Old West: Wyatt Earp, Wild Bill Hickok, and Bat Masterson. But living in California, I believed that one would have to travel to Tombstone or Dodge City to find a place where frontier lawmen shot it out with dangerous outlaws. Jackson's book showed me that such lawmen and desperadoes once rode and fought only miles from where I lived in the San Francisco Bay Area. That fact fired my imagination. I determined to learn all that I could about this aspect of California history. But I soon discovered that very little had been written about California outlaws and lawmen, and much of what had been published was wrong. My interest in the frontier resulted in my earning a Bachelor's degree in history and led me to research in primary source materials to learn the truth about lawlessness in frontier California.

I first wrote a magazine story about Sheriff Morse which was published in 1972. I conducted research on him only sporadically until 1985, when I completed the manuscript for my first book, *Badge and Buckshot: Lawlessness in Old California*, which was published by the University of Oklahoma Press in 1988. Beginning in 1985 I devoted as much time and energy as possible to tracking down the details of Morse's life and career. The result of my efforts is *Lawman: The Life and Times of Harry Morse, 1835-1912* (University of Oklahoma Press, 1998), which is the first full-length biography of a frontier California sheriff.

Harry N. Morse was one of the greatest of the western lawmen. He was sheriff of Alameda County, California, from 1864 until 1878, and head of the Morse Detective Agency in San Francisco from 1878-1906. As sheriff he was famous for breaking up the outlaw bands of central California. Among countless hair-raising exploits, he killed the noted bandits Narato Ponce and Juan Soto, and tracked down bandido chieftain Tiburcio Vasquez in one of the Old West's longest manhunts. Later, as the foremost private detective on the West Coast, he captured Black Bart (Charles E. Boles), America's greatest stage robber, and played a principal role in many of the most important criminal cases of his time.

Harry Morse's greatest exploit was his duel to the death with bandit chieftain Juan Soto on May 10, 1871, high in the Coast Range in the rugged, isolated mountains south of Pacheco Pass. This was the most famous outlaw-lawman gunfight of the California frontier and is considered by gunfighter aficionados one of the Old West's classic shoot-outs.

In brief, the story began on the night of January 10, 1871, when Juan Soto, a notorious robber and ex-convict, accompanied by two unidentified compadres, held up the Thomas Scott store near Sunol in Alameda County. They shot and killed the clerk, Otto Ludovisi, and escaped on horseback. Harry Morse made a long search for the killers but could not find them. He became convinced that two of them were Juan Soto and his close friend and fellow bandit, Bartolo Sepulveda, and both were indicted for murder.

Five months later Sheriff Morse was invited by Nick Harris, sheriff of Santa Clara County, to take part in a manhunt for Juan Soto in the Coast Range. Harris had received a tip that Soto was hiding out in the Sausalito Valley, in the mountains a dozen miles south of Pacheco Pass. On May 8, 1871, Morse and Harris rode out of San Jose at the head of a heavily armed, nine-man posse. They spent two days riding through the mountains in an effort to find the remote valley.

Harry Morse, circa 1870. *Author's Collection*

Finally, on the morning of May 10, the posse crossed a ridge adjacent to St. Mary's Peak and looked down on several small adobes. They were the homes of herders who grazed cattle and sheep in the valley and surrounding mountains. Morse divided the posse, taking Theodore Winchell to the nearest adobe and sending Harris and the rest of the posse to search the other houses.

Morse and Winchell rode up to a rock corral behind the adobe where a Mexican was working. Morse asked for a drink of water, and the man, unsuspecting, invited them into the adobe. As the sheriff stepped inside, he got the shock of his life. Juan Soto sat at a table directly in front of him, surrounded by both male and female companions. Morse jerked his six-gun and ordered Soto to raise his hands, but the burly outlaw sat motionless. Several times he ordered Winchell to handcuff Soto, but Winchell lost his nerve and fled outside, leaving Morse to fend for himself.

Quickly two of Soto's band seized Morse, while the bandit chieftain leaped to his feet and struggled to draw his pistols, which were buttoned beneath a soldier's overcoat. Morse jerked his six-gun loose and fired; the bullet tore off Soto's hat. Morse broke free and ducked out the door with the enraged bandit, revolvers in each hand, close behind. As the sheriff raced toward the rear of the adobe, Soto opened fire on him at close range. Morse dropped to the ground and the bullet passed harmlessly over his head. Morse fired back, then leaped to his feet and sprinted for his horse. Four times this happened, and each time Sheriff Harris, who was racing to Morse's aid, thought that his friend had been killed. Morse's last shot struck Soto's pistol and rammed the barrel into his face, stunning him.

While Soto raced back into the adobe to rearm, Sheriff Morse reached his horse and grabbed his rifle, a Winchester Model 1866 carbine. Moments later Juan Soto emerged from the adobe, a five-shooter clutched in each fist and a third in his belt. He ran to his horse, hitched to a large oak tree west of the house. But the animal spooked and Soto headed toward another horse 200 yards north.

Sheriff Morse called for the outlaw to surrender but Juan Soto ignored the command. At a range of 150 yards Sheriff Morse put a rifle ball through the desperado's right shoulder. Badly wounded and desperate to kill his pursuer and escape, Soto turned and charged headlong at Harry Morse. Sheriff Harris, who by now had joined Morse, fired once with his Spencer rifle but missed. As Soto closed to 100 yards, Harry Morse fired again. The heavy slug tore off the top of the outlaw's head. Morse took $80 in coin from Soto's pockets and gave it to an old woman to bury the body.

Morse's ability to dodge Soto's pistol fire at close range and his deadly marksmanship in twice hitting an armed, running opponent at ranges of more than 100 yards did not escape the notice of the press. The gunfight, coupled with numerous other exploits, firmly established his reputation as the most famous lawman and manhunter on the Pacific Coast. The following year, after Morse captured the notorious Procopio Bustamante (nephew of legendary bandit Joaquin Murrieta), Eastern news papers picked up the story. Ned

Buntline (E.Z.C. Judson), who met the Alameda sheriff during a temperance lecture in 1868, took notice and made Harry Morse the hero of a dime novel story, *Red Dick, The Tiger of California*. The sheriff was embarrassed that he was the subject of blood and thunder fiction. (And incidentally, although Harry Morse is the only real lawman that Ned Buntline wrote a dime novel about, no one has ever suggested that he gave Morse a "Buntline Special" six-shooter. That makes one wonder why he would have given such a weapon to Wyatt Earp, particularly when there is no evidence that Buntline ever met Earp, or for that matter, even knew who Earp was.)

Juan Soto's compadre, Bartolo Sepulveda, was present at the gunfight but managed to escape. Several years later he surrendered to Morse and was twice convicted of murder, first being sentenced to death and then to life imprisonment. It turned out that Sepulveda was innocent and that Harry Morse had used highly questionable methods to secure his conviction in court. But that is another story.

As a youth I wondered whether the adobe where Morse encountered Juan Soto still existed. Years later I learned that the adobe was the headquarters of the Pfeiffer Cattle Company, and that although a second story had been added, it was still standing. Intermittently for a number of years I attempted to find someone who knew where the adobe was. I finally learned its general location from a historian in Los Banos, who provided me with a topographical map upon which he marked its approximate location. But he did not know how to get there. After several more years of periodic checking I was able to learn that the adobe was very difficult to get to, and that the rough jeep trails leading to it were all on private land and were blocked by locked gates.

Finally my friend Phil Hudner, a past president of the Society of California Pioneers and a partner in the San Francisco law firm of Pillsbury, Madison & Sutro, learned of my quest and told me that he might be able to help. Phil is a descendant of a pioneer family which survived the ill-fated Donner Party and settled in Hollister, San Benito County. Phil had visited the Pfeiffer adobe as a boy, more than forty years ago, but could not remember exactly where it was or how to get to it. However, he knew of Al Pfeiffer of Hollister whom he thought might be related to the family which had owned the adobe for many years. Phil also knew Mitt French, the manager of the huge Quien Sabe Rancho, whom he called and got permission to cross the ranch to the Pfeiffer holdings.

Through Phil I contacted Al Pfeiffer and was delighted to learn
that he owned the Pfeiffer adobe and cattle ranch and would be
happy to let us visit and show us around. The only problem was that
the trip was a long one, a two-and a-half hour, nineteen-mile, bone-
jarring journey on rough jeep trails, through a long series of locked
gates. We would never find it without a guide and Al Pfeiffer would
not be able to take us. He would be at the adobe, working on the
spring roundup and shipping cattle to market. Mitt French solved
the problem by assigning one of his men, Sam Robinson, to drive
Phil Hudner and me in a four-wheel-drive truck.

Phil and I drove to Hollister on the morning of May 8, 1997, 126
years almost to the day of the fatal gunfight. We met Sam Robinson
at the first locked gate, miles southeast of town. We bundled into the
cab of his truck and started into the mountains. The Pfeiffer Ranch
is so isolated that even Sam, who had worked at the Quien Sabe for
fourteen years, had never been there. About half of the trip was
across Quien Sabe holdings and Sam knew the way. But when we
passed through the last gate, he had only general directions and we
got lost several times as the road petered out and turned into something even less than a jeep trail.

The country was so remote that we never laid eyes on another
human on the trip except for Al Pfeiffer. Wildlife was abundant. We
saw deer and two coyotes, one chasing a fawn up a mountainside.
We also spotted half a dozen wild boars. These are prized by
hunters and are very elusive and seldom seen. Yet the country was
so isolated that three wild boars, wading in a creek across the trail
and unused to humans, did not bother to run. Instead they lazily
watched us as we drove by. A few miles farther on Sam had to honk
his horn to force another boar out of our way.

Two hours of bouncing and bone shaking brought us to what
looked like an old wooden shack with a tin roof. Nearby was an old
barn, and opposite the shack a small spring. The place was vacant,
without a soul in sight. Here the road reached a dead end, and we
turned to retrace our path. Later we learned that this was not a wood
shack at all, but the Alvarado adobe, its walls and roof covered with
wood and tin which have ably protected its thick adobe walls. In
1871 this was the headquarters of such noted outlaws as Tiburcio
Vasquez, Procopio Bustamante, and Juan Soto.

Now we were thoroughly lost We decided to keep heading north,

in the general direction of where we believed the Pfeiffer adobe
was. We tried to spot St. Mary's Peak, but incorrectly identified several high promontories instead. After several miles on meandering,
boulder-strewn cattle trails we approached a small band of cattle
near a heavily wooded creek. This was a hopeful sign. Following a
rocky trail, we forded the creek and headed up the arroyo to the
high ground on the other side. The trail turned into a rough dirt
road. Following it, we finally came in sight of a two-story house at
the edge of a large meadow. A lone, pointed peak was behind. This
was the Pfeiffer adobe, and behind it, St. Mary's Peak. Al Pfeiffer
came out to greet us. He rarely gets visitors and was eagerly awaiting our arrival.

The house turned out to be a typical California adobe. It was built
in the 1850s and has a porch in front, what used to be a lean-to for
cooking in the back, and two-and-a-half foot thick walls. A second
story had been added in the 1880s. The house had been owned by
Al's uncle, Heini Pfeiffer, since about 1914 and has been in the family ever since. The sheet metal roof and wood siding over the adobe
walls have protected the old building well from the elements.

To the rear of the house is a crumbling rock corral, where Morse
and Winchell tied their horses. In front of the adobe is a large meadow. Here, about fifty yards directly in front of the adobe, is the spot
where Juan Soto died. At the rear of the adobe is where Soto and
Morse fought their celebrated pistol duel. Forty yards west of the
adobe is an ancient oak tree where Juan Soto's horse was tied.
Several barns and outbuildings have been added since 1871, but otherwise the ranch is much the same as it was when Morse fought
Soto there.

I stood on the spot where Juan Soto first faced Morse in the front
room of the adobe, and in the place near the rock corral where
Morse fired the long shot which ended the bandit's life. Al Pfeiffer
showed us the spot where Juan Soto was buried, under a cottonwood tree , about fifty yards east of the house. The story of the gunfight was well known to him, and had been passed down through
the Pfeiffer family over the years. I had brought along a diagram of
the gunfight scene which was published in the *Alameda County
Gazette* in 1871, and we walked over the ground carefully, reenact-
ing the fight and photographing everything. Al did not know all the
particulars of the fight and was fascinated when I explained the

details—who stood where, what types of guns were used, what was said by the combatants. Al was particularly pleased that I brought with me the prize of my western collection—Morse's inscribed Model 1866 Winchester carbine that he used to kill Juan Soto. Each of us was photographed holding the rifle in front of the old adobe.

Like many western buffs, I have made visits to scenes of some of the great gunfights of the Old West: the O.K. Corral in Tombstone, Blazer's Mill, and Lincoln, New Mexico, the TA Ranch in Johnson County, Wyoming, the Blevins house in Holbrook, Arizona. But none of them fascinated me as much as our visit to the Pfeiffer adobe. Phil Hudner and I were the first visitors to the adobe to retrace Morse's movements and walk over the exact ground where the gunfight had taken place. That was a treat I shall long savor and will never forget.

Larry K. Brown

A fifth generation professional writer, Larry K. Brown was born in 1936 at Grand Island, Nebraska. After earning a Bachelor of Arts degree in journalism from the University of Nebraska in 1960, he served twenty years in the U.S. Air Force as an Information/Public Affairs officer. During and after his military career he continued his education, earning a Master's degree in Public Relations from Boston University, post-graduate credits in Mass Communication at the University of Oklahoma, and graduate credits in historical studies at the University of Texas at Dallas. He worked as a public relations-mass communication executive in the petroleum industry before joining the staff of the American Heart Association (AHA) in 1986. The following year he moved to Cheyenne, as the Executive Director, AHA-Wyoming, Inc. Since 1993 he has devoted full time to research and writing, with emphasis on early Western criminal history. He has written five books and many magazine articles featuring Western history, as well as fictional short stories. Wyoming Writers, Inc. honored his first book with its "Western Horizon Award," and Cambridge University Press included the book's text in its computerized lexicon, designed to assist students learning English as a second language. Brown has also scripted programs for NBC-TV's *Today* and ABC-TV's *Prime Time Sunday* shows. He makes speaking engagements for the Wyoming Council for the Humanities and Wyoming Arts Council. He is the father of four grown children.

SHOOT OUT THE OLD YEAR
·
By Larry K. Brown
NOLA *Quarterly*, July-September 1997

No angels sang when "Big Toe" Grace Bicktold and Frank [Francis] Howard met in July 1893 at Dixon, Wyoming, but they got along better than many Snake River Valley's residents. Their physical intimacy, however, waited until the following month. And then, when the blacksmith offered her a full-time bed at his cabin, the prostitute of some seventeen years refused.

Her independence waned that September, however, when she clashed with Jess, a brother of William A. "Mike" Dunbar, owner of the saloon where Grace lived and made it her business doing pleasure with the customers. Faced with either finding a new home or leaving town on the next stage, she recalled Howard's offer and sought him out that same evening at his room.

"I guess by the look of things," she lamented, "they will fire me in the morning...he [Jess] is mad at me and I can't get along with him...I am kind of afraid of him and I want to get that room if I can." Despite her plight, they struck no deal.[1]

Just before daylight, Grace returned and told Howard that Dunbar, indeed, sacked her and again asked his help. This time he agreed. Borrowing a five dollar gold piece from his boss, D.C. Jones, owner of a general store, Howard immediately visited his landlord's agent and rented the other half of his cabin for two dollars a month. He also bought a small cook stove for four dollars and offered Grace an irrefutable deal: free food and fixin's for her if she cooked for him. She concurred, paid her first month's $2.00 rent, and moved her belongings into Howard's back room.[2]

Helping the soiled dove feather her new nest, the bar owner Dunbar gave her a bedstead and quilts in exchange for the money she claimed he owed her. With those furnishings and a mattress gift from Howard, Grace was back in business, literally as well as figuratively.

Regarding Howard, she said, "He made me a good support while I was living with him; [we] was the best of friends." But despite his generosity and the sex they shared during the next two months, Grace considered him no more than a "very intimate friend." Never a lover, she said. That role fell to Charley Horn, a cowboy she had met several years earlier at the Rawlins, Wyoming, brothel in which she earned her keep. One evening, five or six drunken railroaders called on her during one of the cowpoke's frequent visits. "Charley told them to go," she bragged, "and they all jumped on him...He pulled his gun, however, and cleaned out the whole lot."[3]

About 1891, Horn had followed Grace to the Snake River Valley and joined J.C. Cane's L-7 cattle outfit, but the cowpuncher soon further tarnished his reputation at the bars in nearby Dixon by regularly trading his pay for "bug juice."

Only God knows when Grace and Horn resumed their relationship, but the proverbial beginning of the end came Christmas eve 1893 when, shortly after dark, Grace entered Howard's chamber and introduced him to her Horn. Returning to her room through the door that connected their quarters, Howard recalled,

> They had—I didn't count the bottles, but she said they had five bottles of beer; on the table was a bottle of beer that was opened, and a small black—probably a pint bottle as near as I can tell with some sweet wine, and some stronger liquor mixed in with it...We all drank a glass of beer apiece I think.[4]

As their blood warmed to the alcohol and the men swapped lies, bored Grace slipped out in search of something—someone—more interesting. Discovering her absence, thick-tongued Horn mused, "I wonder where Grace is gone? I wish she would come back; this is a

Frank Howard shot to death an L-7 cowboy, Charley Horn, following a dispute over the charms of "Big Toe" Grace Bicktold, the lover neither man wished to share. *Wyoming Division of Cultural Resources.*

pretty way to go out and leave a man when I made arrangements to come and stay with her tonight."

When his new drinking buddy offered no explanation, Horn left and looked for her at Dunbar's. But Howard followed his instincts and uncertain feet to Ivey's saloon. Through a streaked window, he saw her flit around the corner of the bar like a roach in flight from light. Believing she went to the back door, he raced to the rear of the building. After unsuccessfully searching the alley, he returned to the saloon and found her inside playing the piano. Ivey and customer

Bert Marshall stood nearby. This time, however, she remained seated when he approached.

"Charley Horn wants you to come home," he demanded.

"I don't give a damn if he does," she replied; "I am going to have a good time tonight."

Cowed by her stubbornness, Howard returned to his cabin and told Horn about Grace's decision. Together, Horn and the smithy staggered off again in search of their lady friend. As they neared Ivey's saloon, Horn suggested, "You go to the front door and see if she is there; if she slips out the back door I will catch her."

Entering the bar, Howard found a garrulous Grace sitting on the floor with her back to the door, shooting craps for drinks with a customer named Ira Whitaker. Shocked by her unusually liquored up condition, Howard chastised, "This is a pretty thing for you to be doing; a pretty situation for you to be in, flat here on the floor. Come and go home, Grace."

"I don't have to go," she shot back.

"You've got to go home," insisted Howard, as he slipped his arms around her waist; "Horn wants you."

As he picked her up off the floor, Whitaker swung his fist at him, and Grace slipped from Howard's grasp when they both crashed to the floor.

Moments later, Horn stormed into the room with his pistol drawn and stepped over Howard, still entangled with Grace. When Whitaker fled the room, the drunken cowpoke turned on Ivey, the armed proprietor, but Grace broke loose, threw herself between the two, and grabbed the front of Horn's coat.

"We don't want any fuss here[,] Charley," she cried.

As their anger passed, Horn pocketed his pistol and joined a game of cards while Ivey returned his gun to the shelf beneath the bar. Howard, in turn, left the saloon and went home alone. Later that night he heard Grace and Horn come back to her room.[5]

As the winter of 1893 flew in on November's wings, lonely Howard probably pined for Grace's warmth, but once his bed cooled from her absence, he lost patience with her carousing and caterwauling. Five days after the fateful run-in at Ivey's, their sour relationship went from bad to worse.

Well, I had got disgusted with the noise that was made in her end of the room; I couldn't sleep nights; she generally sat up all night, and I had to work and I had to sit up all night—to tell the truth I was worn out so I was not able to work scarcely, losing so much sleep...I told her this thing would not do; I could not stand it any longer; I wanted to sleep; I told her I was disgusted with this thing and she would have to get out of the house.[6]

But free-spirited Grace adamantly refused his demands. Despite their disagreement, a good night's sleep made Howard contrite, so the following afternoon he offered her a sleigh ride. But she refused, so he again demanded she leave. When she angrily invoked Horn's help, the disgusted smithy countered by pulling his stove from her room before locking the door that linked their lives. Chilled and fretful, the bawd rushed to Dunbar's, where she found Horn in the back room.

"I have no more stoves than nothing in the world...What do you think about anything like that?" she bemoaned.[7]

"That's all right[,] I guess," he said; "if it's his stove let him have it; don't quarrel about it; don't say anything about it; I will get you another and that will settle it."

With his paramour reassured, Horn went to Emerson's store and bought another stove.[8] As laborers installed it in her room, Howard's muffled voice called through the partition.

"Grace, you needn't mind putting up the stove. You don't want to put no stove up there at all, you will have to take it down in the morning."[9]

When Horn later returned to Grace's room with a load of wood for the new heater, she told him of Howard's latest threats. "Very well," Horn reassured; "if Howard tries to take it down[,] I will be at the taking down."[10]

That night, Howard heard Grace's and Horn's voices:

I think they were, as near as I could tell, right opposite where my stove was in my room; probably close to their stove...I think it was along in the evening, probably quite late [about 9:00 or 10:00 p.m.]...She was talking to him saying something [sic] about my taking the stove out of the house and wanting her to get out...I think she said she didn't know what she would do if she had to get out of there.[11]

Horn replied, "You don't have to, because [I'll] fix that God damned blacksmith...I will do him up if he undertakes to put you out of the house, or anyone else."[12]

The next evening, as Howard made his way along a soft dirt path to his cabin, he heard a voice call from behind.

"Hey!"

Howard stopped, turned, and recognized the shadowy figure.

"What are you trying to put Grace out of the house for?" demanded Horn.

Risking an argument with a man whom he considered "under the influence of liquor," Howard replied, "I am not trying to put her out myself; I was trying to get papers to put her out. I'm disgusted with her."

"You had better let her alone, you God damned son of a bitch; you have been fooling with her long enough," the cowboy threatened. His little finger toyed with the trigger of a pistol that played in his palm. "You better let Grace alone," insisted Horn, "or I will put daylight through you...The best thing you could do would be to leave town," Horn warned as he turned and walked toward Grace's room.[13]

Late the following afternoon, Howard went to Ivey's saloon in search of protection. He forgot to carry the rifle from his cabin and worried about returning unarmed, because Horn might be at Grace's place. Upon finding Bert Marshall in the bar, Howard called him aside, explained his fears, and asked for a gun. When Marshall refused, Howard fortified himself with a drink and left the saloon. Upon seeing Constable Phil Lefler and his wife riding back into Dixon, Howard welcomed the couple.

"How do you do? You're pretty near froze[;] you better come...and have a drink."

Accepting the blacksmith's invitation, the trio headed for Dunbar's saloon for some liquid heat. As they walked, the blacksmith confided,

"I want to talk to you about a little matter; I don't know how it will strike you...I want you to throw Grace out of the house."

Not without "legal papers," explained Lefler.[14]

Determined to rid himself of Grace, Howard went in search of his friend and boss, D.C. Jones, who also served as the Dixon Precinct's justice of the peace. He found Jones at Ivey's saloon and asked him to issue Grace an eviction notice. She "was carrying on rough and drinking and carousing around and keeping him awake," he said, and he wanted her out of his cabin. But New Year's Eve comes but once a year, so Jones happily begged off until the next day— January 1, 1894. Regrettably, although the justice's decision bought him time, Howard bought bullets.[15]

Charles F. Perkins, a local ranchman and store owner, recalled that Howard came to his shop shortly after leaving Jones.

> We were closing up store [about 8:30 p.m.]," he said, "and [Howard] wanted to know if I had any cartridges, I think 45-70; I told him I thought I had; I found one box; he said he wanted two or three boxes; he was going hunting in the morning; I could only find one box; he bought that and paid for it.

After adding a can of sardines and a piece of tobacco to the order, Howard picked up his purchases and left the store.[16] He returned to Ivey's saloon, hoping for the loan of a weapon that Cyl Chick once offered. Not finding Chick there, however, the increasingly desperate Howard braved the dark and raced to the blacksmith's shop where he found Jones's cumbersome twelve-pound Sharp's rifle. Now armed, Howard returned safely to his room and retrieved his own big bore rifle and cartridge belt.[17]

At eight o'clock p.m. on New Year's Eve 1893, Horn arrived at Grace's place, where they planned shooting the old year out and the new year in. After chatting for about an hour, they heard a rap at the door. Grace laid aside the vest on which she sewed buttons and Horn got up from the bed. After cautiously slipping a brown-handled six-shooter into his waistband,[18] he donned his coat before greeting their guest, "Mrs. Shirl," who returned a load of clean laundry. After the wash woman left, Horn again removed his coat as Grace returned to her chair at the mending table.[19]

Fifteen minutes later, the profile of a man carrying a rifle caught Grace's eye as he passed her south window. Not more than two minutes later, a shot near the cabin startled the couple.

"Douse the glim[,] Grace[,] and look out," directed Horn. Stepping to the south door, he cautiously opened it to a clear, moonless night. The light from Grace's lamp silhouetted his body. As Grace moved to his side, she saw a familiar face bathed in light that beamed from Dunbar's saloon and reflected off the bright snow.

"My God, it's Howard," she said. Her lover silently grasped the

door frame with his right hand and leaned toward the darkness. Just
as he eased his bare head past the jam, a gun shot slammed his body
back into the room. Bits of gore and gray matter flecked the floor,
as blood pooled beneath his hair. Horn's dull eyes stared blankly at
the ceiling while his bent, limp arms framed his face like those of a
grotesque ballet dancer. A pistol lay near his right hand. His feet
rested near the threshold.[20]

Rushing to the mortally wounded man's side, Grace raised and
held him in her arms while begging unsuccessfully that he speak.
After laying his body back on the floor, she turned to the door just
as Howard rushed past a nearby coal shed. As soon as she recovered
from her shock, she ran to Dunbar's saloon and shouted, "Come
quick! Howard has shot and killed Horn, I think!" Continuing to
Whitaker's saloon, she found Constable Phil Lefler playing cards.
After telling him of the crime, he tossed his chips in his hat and left
them on the bar.

"Take them," he said, "and keep them until I come back."

Before following the crowd back to her room, Grace sent word to
the L-7 ranch to alert Horn's boss, J.C. Cane, and friends about the
shooting. Only then did she rejoin her dying lover and hold his hand
until he died minutes later without speaking.[21]

In the meantime, Constable Lefler searched unsuccessfully in the
darkness for the murderer. Early the next morning, however, the
lawman and his posse of Ed Leggett, Ed Smizer, and John Smart
finally struck the suspect's trail.[22]

After fleeing town on foot, Howard went northwest for less than a
mile along the snow-blown road. He then turned south and struck
the divide between Four Mile and Willow Creeks, walking on the
east side of the ridge so the wind drifted over his trail. Continuing
on for six or seven more miles, he found himself near Livingston's
ranch where "I stopped," he said, "and rested probably once or
twice standing up," before crossing the creek at Perkins's bridge.
His passing through small herds of cattle helped obliterate his trail
until he crossed Timberlake Gulch just above Hinman's placer
claims, then headed southwest through a small draw and into Pole
Gulch.

Freeman Scott caught and joined the posse at Four Mile Creek.
Although they temporarily lost Howard's trail there, it appeared
again a couple of miles downstream, where the murderer left the

ridge and continued south along the stream. Closing in on their prey, members of the posse separated with deputy Leggett going up the east side of Pole Gulch. Smart and Smizer followed the trail in the ravine while Lefler and Scott took the west side.[23]

Howard, resting near the top and at the end of that same draw, suddenly sighted his pursuers. Oblivious of his danger, Lefler advanced up the opposite side and into rifle range as Howard rose up from a half-kneeling position and drew a bead on the one-armed constable. The blast of his rifle barrel in the sunlight attracted the attention of Leggett on the same side of the gulch with Howard. The deputy instantly raised his gun to his shoulder and called for Howard's surrender or death. Smizer and Smart, still at the bottom of the gulch, caught sight of Howard about the same time and seconded Leggett's demands. Surrounded and outgunned, the felon surrendered. About 10:00 a.m., the posse relieved him of his weapons[24] and ammo belt with about twenty-five rounds of ammunition.

"You have got yourself into a nice box now, haven't you?" said Lefler.[25]

"I expect so," mused the weary Howard.

"What did you want to kill that man for?" asked the constable.

"It wasn't me, it was whisky," lamented the blacksmith.

"Did you know you had killed him?"

"No," Howard acknowledged, but "when [I shoot], something falls"[26]

Following a brief rest, Lefler and his posse turned their horses towards Dixon, arriving there with Howard about midnight.[27] The following Monday afternoon, Justice Jones heard his old employee Howard's case before the constable took his captive to Rawlins, where he locked him in Carbon County's jail.[28]

A week prior to the May term of the Third Judicial District Court, the court assigned the Merritt and Smith law firm (H.D. Merritt and Geo. C. Smith) to defend the indigent, accused murderer. Finally, on Thursday morning, May 31, 1894, Howard's case came before Judge Jesse Knight in the Carbon County courtroom. Selecting a jury took up most of that day. The next morning, Carbon County Attorney and Prosecutor D. H Craig called to the stand Grace Bicktold, whose reputation for truthfulness was more brittle than her virtue. Although Grace claimed, "I never knew there was any trouble between them," she acknowledged under cross-examination that Howard threatened "to get even with his rival."[29]

Regarding the circumstances surrounding the shooting, Howard offered this explanation:

> I heard a noise and heard two persons, from the noise...I saw Horn...He opened the door and stepped out [on the porch]...As near as I can tell from what I can remember, he had one foot on the door step, and maybe both feet; I am not positive about that; if I am not mistaken very much he had his left hand on the door frame.

According to the blacksmith, the cowboy had a pistol in his right hand,

> when he came to the door...[and] kind of raised the gun up...and when he brought [it] down for business on me, I...was moving when I shot; I went right past the corner...I was probably five feet from the corner of the building.

After the shot, Howard said,

> I went right on; I might say I run—the next thing to it; I went around the corner and went in the door, or just reached the door, possibly stepped in one step; my other gun [the .45-70 caliber rifle for which he purchased bullets earlier that day] laid on the work bench close to the door.

Carrying both rifles, Howard ran north up the street. The Court examined additional witnesses throughout that Friday. Following supper the next evening, the court heard the lawyers' respective closing arguments. Minutes later, the jurors received their final instructions from the judge and deliberated from about midnight until they reached their decision at 7:00 a.m. Two and a half more hours elapsed, however, before Judge Knight returned to the crowded courtroom. And it took a few minutes more before jury foreman H. A. Kirk announced the verdict: "Murder in the First Degree."

The following Friday—June 8—calm, but pale Howard returned to the court for sentencing and heard the judge set his execution for the following November 23. Howard, who claimed, "He was prepared for anything," sat without flinching throughout the brief process before marching out of the courtroom "with a firm and steady tread."[31]

While serving his last days in the Carbon County jail, Howard and some fellow prisoners unsuccessfully tried escaping on Thursday, February 15, with the help of a case knife, which they nicked into a saw. After severing lock bolts on an outside entrance to their cage and disguising the deed with brown paint scraped from the wall behind a stove, they planned a "French leave." Fellow prisoner John Hayes, however, foiled their escape by "peeping" to jailer Rubio Rivera.[32]

About a week before Howard's execution, Governor John E. Osborne granted the condemned man a two-week reprieve while he investigated the case. After reviewing a transcript of all evidence and again listening to case summary arguments by the defense attorneys, the governor refused clemency.[33]

Finally, faced with the reality of the noose and pressured for the truth, Howard shared information about his origin and background. Born about 1851 at Hazel Green, Wisconsin, he and his parents moved to Illinois and, at the age of about fourteen, he learned the blacksmith trade. Three years later [about 1868], they moved to Iowa where the seventeen-year-old plied his trade. He also worked on a farm until 1877 when he continued on to Jefferson County, Colorado, where he "went prospecting and mining." He labored, too, briefly as a Union Pacific railroad detective before being arrested at Ogden, Utah, for forging "an order on the R.R Paymaster and disposing of it to a well known businessman in Rawlins."[34]

Arriving in Wyoming about 1892, Howard said, "I run an engine at [Frank H.] Kelsey['s], the first place I went to work after I came here." Not long after, he "went down on the Savoy [creek] and took up a claim there...That winter I was trapping; the snow was too deep to stay on the ranch," so he moved to Dixon and went to work for Jones in July 1893."[35]

In the meantime, in preparation for Howard's execution, Sheriff Jens Hansen supervised construction of a scaffold on the east side of the Carbon County courthouse. High fencing prevented uninvited views by the curious general public.[36]

Finally the fateful day—December 7, 1894—arrived as Howard awoke at 6:00 a.m. after spending a fitful night sleeping in his everyday clothes. After picking up a breakfast of toast, eggs, and coffee, his spiritual advisor, Father M. Ternes, arrived and administered the Catholic sacrament of confession. A big drink of whiskey helped calm his nerves after the religious ritual. Then, at 9:30 a.m., Sheriff Hansen's wife came by to wish "good-bye" to the appreciative Howard. An hour later, Sheriff Hansen and his men took him from his cell and led him to the jailer's room from where he stepped through an open window and onto the scaffold, where he greeted the invited guests with a pleasant "good morning." As the sheriff and deputy Joseph P. Rankin strapped his arms and legs, Howard's lips spoke a silent prayer.[37]

"Have you anything to say, Howard?" asked the sheriff.

"All I have to say is that I die without any fear, firmly believing in the Holy Catholic church. I ask all who I may have ever injured to forgive me, as I believe God has, and I offer my life for any crime I may have committed. I thank you all." Then, with his eyes toward heaven, he asked that "God have mercy on my soul."[38]

After Howard embraced his priest for the last time, Sheriff Hansen pulled the traditional black execution hood over the condemned man's head, masking his flushed face. Then, without another moment's delay, the sheriff stepped back quickly and tripped the trap that dropped Howard exactly six feet and eleven inches below the floor of the scaffold, snapping his neck upon impact.

Seven minutes passed before Doctor James Carter, unable to detect a pulse, pronounced the murderer dead. Soon thereafter, the undertaker carried away the body to his morgue.

Poor, star-crossed Howard, whose failure at love resulted in two deaths—his and his rival,—Horn—found a home the following Sunday—December 9—at the cemetery on the north side of Rawlins. Hopefully, the angels, who failed to herald his romance with Grace, discovered their voice in time to welcome him home.[39]

NOTES

1 Grace Bicktold's and Frank Howard's Testimonies, *State of Wyoming v. Frank Howard*, Third Judicial District, Carbon County Court Criminal Case #339, 31 May 1894, pp.1-47,163-198.

2 Ibid., also "Murder at Dixon," *The Journal*, Rawlins, Wyoming, January 6, 1894, p.3 (5-6). Howard leased his front (east) room in July 1893 from Thomas Livingston for $3.00 per month. Livingston served as landlord, Rigg's agent in that deal, and subsequently rented the back (west) room to Howard for an additional $2.00. The two-room building previously was

Rigg's saloon. Howard later testified that $10.00 was the only money he received from Grace, who apparently believed she had bartered her sex for rent.

3 Ibid. Grace once said Horn was a "good man for his size; that whenever he got into a racket it took a pretty good man to handle him." Despite Grace's categorization, Howard considered the cowboy "a medium sized man."

4 Ibid.

5 Ibid.

6 Ibid.

7 Ibid.

8 J.C. Cane's Testimony, *State of Wyoming v. Frank Howard*, Third Judicial District, Carbon County Court Criminal Case #339, 31 May 1894, pp. 227-229. Cane said Horn borrowed money from him to buy the replacement stove for Grace.

9 Grace Bicktold's and Frank Howard's Testimonies, op. cit.

10 Ibid.

11 Ibid.

12 Ibid.

13 Ibid.

14 Ibid., also Frank Howard's, Phil Lefler's, and Bert Marshall's Testimonies, *State of Wyoming v. Frank Howard*, Third Judicial District, Carbon County Court Criminal Case #339, 31 May 1894, pp. 83-91, 163-198. According to Howard, Lefler didn't help evict Grace because the constable didn't like him and he didn't trust the lawman.

15 D.C. Jones's Testimony, *State of Wyoming v. Frank Howard*, Third Judicial - District, Carbon County Court Criminal Case #339, 31 May 1894, pp. 100-130.

16 Grace Bicktold's, Frank Howard's, . Charles F. Perkins's, and D.C. Jones's Testimonies, *State of Wyoming v. Frank Howard*, Third Judicial District, Carbon County Court Criminal Case #339,31 May 1894, pp. 1-47, 72-76, 163-198; also Inquest Testimony by Charles F. Perkins re Charles Horne, 1 January 1894. According to Jones, Howard sold his sleigh the same day Grace refused his ride and apparently used that money to purchase bullets for his weapon.

17 Grace Bicktold's and Frank Howard's Testimonies, op. cit.

18 J.C. Cane's Testimony, *State of Wyoming v. Frank Howard*, Third Judicial District, Carbon County Court Criminal Case #339, 31 May 1894, pp. 227-229. Cane reiterated what several had said, that Horn did not nor-

mally carry a weapon either on the ranch or when he went to town. The afternoon of the murder,—however, Ed Smizer, who was visiting from the 4-Mile ranch in Colorado, gave Horn a pistol and insisted he carry it because "I think Smizer was afraid there might be some trouble come up; he knew Howard was kind of stuck on Grace."

19 Grace Bicktold's and Frank Howard's Testimonies, *State of v. Frank Howard*, Third Judicial District, Carbon County Court Criminal Case #339, 31 May 1894, pp. 1-47, 163-198, also "Particulars of a [?] Murder—The Coroner's Inquest," *The Republican*, Rawlins, Wyoming, 11 January 1894, p. 8 [3-4].

20 Grace Bicktold's, Frank Howard's, John Baker's, and D.C. Jones's Testimonies, *State of Wyoming v. Frank Howard*, Third Judicial District, Carbon County Court Criminal Case #339, 31 May 1894, pp. 1-47, 100-130, 163-198; also "Murder at Dixon," *The Journal*, Rawlins, Wyoming, 6 January 1894, p. 3 (5-6). According to Jones, the death bullet carved its path across the casing of the south side window before striking its victim in the head. "The bullet entered a little past the center of the head to the left, and came out right along in there—busted out quite a whole [sic] where it came out; it came out between the eye and the ear; I don't think it was as far back as the ear; it busted out here, a little to the right of the top of the head...the ball entered the forehead pretty near the hair, a little bit to the left of the side...and came out a little bit to the right of the top of the head on a line nearly between the eye and the ear." Although Grace denied Horn went armed to the door, Baker, who "was the first, or one of the first to reach [Horn's] body," found the body and revolver as described here.

21 Ibid; also "Particulars of a [?] Murder—The Coroner's Inquest," op cit.; "Murder at Dixon," *The Journal*, Rawlins, Wyoming, 6 January 1894, p. 3 (5-6); Inquest Testimony re Charles Horn, 1 January 1894 Witnesses claimed Horn lived for approximately an hour to an hour and a half after being shot. According to testimony provided during the inquest over which Justice Jones presided, the bullet struck Horn in the center of his forehead before "passing just under the skull and out over the right ear, tearing away a piece of the skull nearly two inches long and an inch wide where it came out."

Horn was buried on 3 January 1894 at the "Reader burial ground...and although the day was cold and blustery, quite a number of friends followed his remains to the grave. He had a great many friends among the cowboys."

According to an article in the Rawlins, Wyoming, *Republican* entitled "Particulars of a [?] Murder—The Coroner's Inquest," p. 3 (3-4), "Rather a strange coincidence is the fact that within four months two men who have been stopping at the ranch of J.C. Kane have been murdered and the Christian name of each was Charley and each of them was shot with a 45-70 rifle." Evidence suggests, however, that although the newspaper reporter assumed that Howard shot Horn with his .45-70 caliber rifle, Howard, in fact, had used Jones's .44-70 caliber weapon.

22 "Murder at Dixon," *The Journal*, Rawlins, Wyoming, 6 January 1894, p. 3 (5-6); also Transcript of Docket in Case of *State of Wyoming v. Frank Howard* in Justice Court of D.C. Jones, Justice of the Peace, Rawlins, Wyoming, I January 1894. Grace was arrested because of her peculiar relationship in the situation. Unable to post the required $500 bond, she remained in jail during the rest of January 1 and the following day until friends Lydie M. and S.L. Willis posted bail, and she was released on January 3.

23 Ibid.

24 One was a 45-70 and the other was a .44 caliber weapon.

25 Constable Phil Lefler's Testimony *State of Wyoming v. Frank Howard*, Third Judicial District, Carbon County Court Criminal Case #339, 31 May 1894. pp. 83-91. Lefler, who admitted under cross-examination that he had once served about six months in Denver's jail, but never convicted for horse stealing, said Pole Gulch runs into the Four Mile ranch.

26 "Murder at Dixon," *The Journal*,, Rawlins, Wyoming, 6 January 1894, p. 3 (5-6). Although Lefler claimed that Howard blamed "whisky" for the crime, no one else testified to having seen either Howard or Horn drink to excess or act drunk the day of the shooting.

27 "Murder at Dixon," *The Journal*, Rawlins, Wyoming, 6 January 1894, p. 3

28 "Murder at Dixon," *The Journal*, Rawlins, Wyoming, 6 January 1894, p. 3 (5-6); also Constable Phil Lefler's Testimony, *State of Wyoming v. Frank Howard*, Third judicial District, Carbon County Court Criminal Case #339, 31 May 1894, pp. 83-91; "Particulars of a [?] Murder— The Coroner's Inquest," op. cit.

29 Grace Bicktold's and Frank Howard's Testimonies, *State of Wyoming v. Frank Howard*, Third Judicial District, Carbon County Court Criminal Case #339, 31 May 1894, pp. 1-47, 163-198; also "District Court News," *The Journal*, Rawlins, Wyoming, 26 May 1894, p. 3 (7); 'Murder in the First Degree," *The Daily Leader*, Cheyenne, Wyoming, 5 June 1894, p. 3 (4)

30 Frank Howard's Testimony, op. cit.

31 "Frank Howard Doomed," *The Republican*, Rawlins, Wyoming, 11

June 1894, p. 1 (1); also [no title], *The Republican*, op. cit., p. I (5); "Sentenced to Death," *The Journal*, Rawlins, Wyoming, 9 June 1894, p. 3 (5); "Murder in the First Degree," *The Daily Leader*, Cheyenne, Wyoming, 5 June 1894, p. 3 (4). The jury included H.A. Kirk (foreman), plus John M. Delany, J. S. Allen, C. Hastings, Wm. McCarty, Harry Franklin, Frank Kennedy, John Kurtz, O.C. Smith, E. Henderson, Barney Fitzpatrick, and W.S. Cox.

32 "Preparing for a Jail Break," *The Republican*, Rawlins, Wyoming, 22 February 1894, p. I (2); also "A Desperate Gang," *The Journal*, Rawlins, Wyoming, 17 February 1894, p. 3 (5). The other prisoners included "two men held for murder, Howard and Morrison, the two horse thieves, Brown and Hittle, the forger and embezzler, Emil Eidelhoff, the two petty forgers, Lucas and Christmas, and Wm. Phillips, the coon who carved the Hanna yellow gal." Hittle, who provided the knife-file, was believed to have obtained the blade from friends permitted to visit him at the jail. Although safely locked in their cells at night, they did the filing during the day while they had access to the corridor. They planned to escape at night, however, by using three heavy ash bed slats to spring the door enough to get out.

33 "Execution Postponed," *Rawlins Republican*, Rawlins, Wyoming, 22 November 1894, p. I (1); also [no title], *Rawlins Republican*, Rawlins, Wyoming, 29 November 1894, p. 1 (3); also "Howard Will Hang," *The Journal*, Rawlins, Wyoming, 17 November 1894, p. 3 (7); [no title], *The Journal*, Rawlins, Wyoming, I December 1894, p. 3 (2); "Howard Must Swing," *The Daily Leader*, Cheyenne, Wyoming, 2 December 1894, p. 3 (3).

34 "Local Brevities," *Carbon County Journal*, Rawlins, Wyoming, 19 June 1880, p. 4 (2); also "The Law Obeyed," *Rawlins Republican*, Rawlins, Wyoming, 13 December 1894, p. I (1). Howard did not publicly disclose information about his past until briefly before his execution even though there were several prominent individuals in the area who also claimed Hazel Green as their previous home Among those were "Postmaster Magor of Rawlins; Thomas Magor of Baggs; Jude Allen of Medicine Bow, and the Tregonings of Laramie." According to the newspaper account of Howard's execution, "Some of them were old neighbors of Howard's folks, yet he did not divulge his identy [sic] until the last. Through the trial and all his trouble, he was without friend or a cent of money, and he seemed to want it so."

35 Grace Bicktold's, Frank Howard's, Andres N. Boner's Testimonies, op. cit. Frank H. Kelsey, who lived about ten miles from Dixon, testified that he had known Howard when he was living in Colorado about 1883. When he

moved to Wyoming two years later, Howard "followed about seven years later." It is believed that when Howard referred to the "Savoy," he was talking about Savery Creek on which there also was a village named Savery. And, although the exact time period is not known, Boner testified Howard had worked for him, too, "for a short time." Included in Carbon County Criminal Court records of J.P. Hawley, Justice of the Peace, in which William J. Smith filed a 12 June 1880 complaint charging that a "Frank Howard," on or about 11 June 1880 gave him [Smith] a "written order on the Paymaster of [the]...Union Pacific Railroad Company" for $60 which Smith honored and paid. A criminal warrant was also issued on 12 June, but additional records regarding the case or its settlement have not been found by the author. It has not been confirmed that the Frank Howard in this case is the same man who later shot and killed Charley Horn.

36 "Executive Postponed," Rawlins Republican. Rawlins, Wyoming, 22 November 1894, p. I (1); also "Howard's Expiation," *The Daily Leader*, Cheyenne, Wyoming, 8 December 1894, p. 3 (3) The gallows was the same as that which had been used on 26 February 1888 in Rawlins for the execution of Benjamin "The Bad Man From Bitter Creek" Carter. Carter was convicted for murdering James Jefferies, who shared his tent during a cattle roundup in Carbon County on 4 October 1886.

37 "The Law Obeyed," *Rawlins Republican*, Rawlins, Wyoming, 13 December 1894, p. I (1); also "Howard's Expiation," *The Daily Leader*, Cheyenne, Wyoming, 8 December 1894, p. 3 (3) "Chas. F. Howard Hanged," *The Daily Leader*, Cheyenne, Wyoming, 7 December 1894, p. 3 (3). Father Ternes was the pastor of St. Joseph's Catholic Church. Twenty to twenty-five people witnessed Howard's execution, including Sheriff Ward of Evanston and Attorney Palmer of Rock Springs. The rope used for the execution was a half-inch, four-strand that had been tested with 170 pounds of deadweight before the execution.

38 Ibid.

39 Ibid.; also "Howard Expiation," *The Daily Leader*, Cheyenne, Wyoming, 8 December 1894, p. 3 (3); "Chas. F. Howard Hanged," *The Daily Leader*, Cheyenne, Wyoming, 7 December 1894, p. 3 (3). According to the latter source, Howard "had not, so far as known, a single relative.

Jim Browning

James Albert "Jim" Browning was born in Paulding County, Georgia, in 1921. Raised in Douglas County, he attended public school there and was valedictorian of his high school graduation class at Douglasville, Georgia. His advanced education at West Georgia College was interrupted by World War II and he spent three and a half years in the U.S. Army Air Corps. After the war he attended the University of Georgia at Athens where he earned a Master's Degree in Chemistry, was elected to the Phi Beta Kappa Honor Society, and taught for four years. In 1950 he accepted a position as Professor of Chemistry at The Citadel, The Military College of South Carolina, at Charleston. He taught there for thirty-six years and retired in 1987 with the status Professor Emeritus. Long a student of Old West history, he spent his summers traveling, visiting the scenes of historical events and searching out and photographing the grave sites of Western figures, especially outlaws and lawmen. He drove over 300,000 miles and took more than 34,000 slides of old forts, ghost towns, and graves. In 1993 his research became available to the public with the publication of *Violence Was No Stranger*, a guide to the grave sites of over a thousand famous and infamous Old West characters. An earlier book, *The Western Reader's Guide*, a bibliography of Western non-fiction magazine articles published between 1953 and 1991, has become a valuable tool for Western history researchers. On February 4, 1999, Jim Browning passed on, losing a long fight with prostate cancer.

WHO WAS BILLY WILSON?
·
By Jim Browning
NOLA *Quarterly*, Summer 1990

F ollowing the "five day battle" in Lincoln, New Mexico, which climaxed the bloody Lincoln County War, a group of young men formed a loose association with Billy the Kid and moved throughout New Mexico and the Texas panhandle stealing and selling horses and cattle, and, in general, trying to protect themselves from the minions of the law led by Pat Garrett and others. Among this group were men such as Charlie Bowdre, Tom O'Folliard, Dave Rudabaugh, Doc Scurlock, Henry Brown, Tom Pickett, Fred Waite, and Billy Wilson. Brown, Scurlock, and Waite soon moved on to other fields.

The fame of Billy the Kid has resulted in dozens of books and thousands of articles devoted to the exploits of the young outlaw. Several members of the Kid's gang have also received much attention. Books have been written on Rudabaugh and Brown, and magazine articles have appeared on Pickett, O'Folliard, Bowdre, and Scurlock. Probably the least known of the associates of the Kid is Billy Wilson, whose real name was David L. Anderson.

Keleher [1] makes some mention of Wilson, and O'Neal [2] and Thrapp [3] also devote some space to him. The most comprehensive work to date is an article by Philip J. Rasch in the *West Texas Historical Association Yearbook* for 1958.[4] Dates from published sources pertaining to Wilson's birth and death rarely agree.

Part of the confusion arises from the fact that early writers researched the name "William Wilson" rather than "David Anderson" for background information, not realizing that William or Billy Wilson was an alias used by Anderson for only a short time. The existence of several William "Billy" Wilsons, who were moving through the Texas-New Mexico-Arizona area during the same time period, caused further confusion.

One William Wilson was legally hung in Lincoln, New Mexico, on August 2, 1875, for the murder of Robert Casey.[5] Another of the same name was a buffalo hunter from Dodge City, Kansas, who also worked the Texas panhandle. He passed through New Mexico and later was a cowboy for the Aztec Land and Cattle Company (the Hashknife Outfit) near Holbrook, Arizona. After leaving the Hashknife, this William Wilson and two others were hung by vigilantes near the Mogollon Rim in the fading days of the Pleasant Valley War.[6]

In an attempt to learn more about Wilson's life this writer has made four trips to Sanderson, Texas, where Wilson (there known as D.L. "Doc" Anderson) was killed, and to Brackettville, where he was married and later buried. Several individuals, some of whom had known Anderson, furnished valuable information about his later life.[7] Marriage and death records as well as census records for 1860, 1870, 1880 and 1890 further clarify certain aspects of his life.

David Anderson was the fourth of eight children born to George and Mary Anderson in Braceville, Trumball County, Ohio. George and Mary were both born in Ireland. David's birthday was always celebrated on November 23, which is undoubtedly correct, but the year of his birth is uncertain. Thrapp gives 1861, O'Neal gives 1862, and his headstone gives 1860. All of these appear to be in error based on census records. The 1860 U.S. census for Trumball County, Ohio, gives his age as 5; the 1870 census gives 12; and the 1880 census lists 21 as his age. To further complicate matters, the 1900 census for Pecos County, Texas, states that he was born in November of 1852 and gives his age as 47.[8] When he appeared in New Mexico, he was believed to be about 18 years of age. Actually he was closer to 25. His small stature (5 feet 5 inches, 135 pounds) allowed him to pass for a much younger age. Until a birth certificate can be located, the most probable year of birth appears to be somewhere between 1852 and 1856.

David's parents were farmers and, although the children worked hard, they received a fairly good education. However, farm life never appealed to young David. While in his early twenties, he left home and, a short time thereafter, found himself in Texas. In his later years he would tell friends that he left home to become a cowboy. As far as is known, he never returned to Ohio.

News of the Lincoln County War and the escapades of Billy the Kid spread through Texas and young Anderson could not resist the lure of excitement and adventure. By late summer of 1880, he had moved into the Lincoln County, New Mexico, area. In an effort to protect the family name in Ohio, David decided to take up an alias. He had two older brothers, William (called Billy), who was five years his senior, and Wilson, who was four years older. He borrowed his two brothers' first names and became known in New Mexico as William (Billy) Wilson.[9]

Wilson's stay in New Mexico has been fairly well documented. He purchased a livery stable in White Oaks, but after a short period of time he sold it to a man named West who paid for it with several $100 bills. When he cashed one of the bills at the Dolan store in Lincoln and others at the store of Jose Montaño, they were found to be counterfeit. A warrant for Wilson's arrest was issued and he decided to hide out along the Pecos River with the Kid and other members of the gang.

In late November of 1880, The Kid and Wilson exchanged gunfire with a posse but managed to escape. The next day the two, along with Dave Rudabaugh, were trapped in the ranch house of Jim Greathouse by the posse. After James Carlyle, a member of the posse, was killed during the night, the trio again managed to escape in the darkness. Some three weeks later, Wilson, the Kid, and others fought a running battle with Sheriff Pat Garrett's posse. Tom O'Folliard was killed but the others once more escaped.

Finally, at a place called Stinking Springs, on a cold snowy December 23, 1880, Garrett's posse was successful in the capture of the Kid, Wilson, Rudabaugh, and Tom Pickett. Charlie Bowdre had been killed a few hours prior to their surrender.

Wilson was eventually tried on the charge of passing counterfeit money, convicted, and sentenced to twenty-five years imprisonment. Later he was "allowed" to escape from prison at Santa Fe and he returned to Texas where he once again became David L. Anderson.

Having never lost his desire to be a cowboy, Anderson worked on several ranches near the Rio Grande. Since he was still wanted on the counterfeiting charges in New Mexico, he chose a remote and lightly populated area near Sanderson, Texas, the Mexican border only a short distance away.

Tiny Dryden, twenty miles to the east, and Fort Stockton, sixty-five miles to the northwest, were Sanderson's nearest neighbors.

Anderson was working for the C. Wright and Cauthers Cattle Company when he received an appointment to the U.S. Customs Service at Eagle Pass, Texas.[10] The G.H. & S.A. Railroad took him from Sanderson eastward to the little railroad junction of Spofford where it was necessary to take a small branch line south to Eagle Pass. The Spofford station was run by Robe[r]t J. Fitzmaurice and his wife, Mary. While waiting at Spofford for the train south, Anderson met the twenty-two year old daughter of the Fitzmaurice's, Margaret or "Maggie" as she was called. A whirlwind courtship resulted in their marriage on September 1, 1889. J.M. Malmartek, D.M.J., conducted the services in the St. Mary Magdalena Catholic Church in Brackettville, Texas.[11]

Shortly after the marriage, Anderson was transferred to Langtry, Texas, where Judge Roy Bean was still living.[12] The couple spent some two years at Langtry before David decided to leave the customs service and reenter the cattle business. He took a job as manager of the large T5 Ranch owned by the Hoosier Brothers of Kansas City. The ranch was headquartered about twenty-five miles north of Dryden at Independence Springs on Independence Creek. By 1895, Anderson had saved a little money, bought a few cattle, and registered them under the Circle Bar M brand.[13]

And then what he feared for some ten years happened. He was recognized as Billy Wilson. For a time it appeared he might have to return to New Mexico and serve the remainder of his sentence. New Mexico Territorial Governor W.T. Thornton, who had been Anderson's lawyer when he was tried on the counterfeiting charge, appealed to the U.S. Attorney General for aid in getting a presidential pardon for Anderson. More than twenty letters were written in his behalf by such men as Pat Garrett, Judge L. Bradford Prince (who had sentenced Anderson), and James J. Dolan.[14] On July 25, 1896, President Grover Cleveland signed the pardon that made Anderson a free man.[15]

Anderson continued to manage the T5 for several years and, when the owners decided to sell out their holdings in 1905, he bought the last few head of cattle and had the T5 brand transferred to his name. A few months afterwards, on October 4, 1905, a daughter, Ella Mae J. Anderson, was born. She was to be their only child. David continued in the cattle business until 1914, when the family moved to Sanderson. He ran for sheriff of Terrell County and was elected on November 10, 1914.[16] He was very popular with everyone, particularly the children, for whom be always had a kind word. His friends called him "Doc", but where he picked up this nickname is unknown.

Tuesday, June 4, 1918, started out as any other day in the little town of Sanderson, Texas, but it was to be "Doc" Anderson's last day on earth. A cowboy, Ed Valentine, had just been fired from his job on the Bow and Arrow Ranch by the owner, "Rufe" Murrah, who kept Valentine's saddle in settlement for a debt the cowboy couldn't pay.[17] Valentine then went into Sanderson and began drinking in the Harrell Saloon. In a drunken rage later in the evening, he ran everyone out of the saloon, threatening to shoot them if they didn't leave. He fired several shots which were returned by the citizens of the town.

A telephone call was made to "Doc" Anderson, who came immediately. Thinking he had nothing to fear from Valentine, whom he knew, the sheriff entered the side door to the saloon and called on Ed to throw down his gun and talk over the situation. Instead, Valentine opened fire and four bullets struck the lawman, killing him almost instantly.

Deputy Bob Gatlin was notified at Dryden and immediately came into town. Borrowing a .30-30 rifle and some shells from a merchant, Gatlin stationed himself across the street in a pool room where he had a view of the saloon. When Valentine appeared at a window, the deputy fired a single shot which entered his chest just below the collar bone, killing him instantly.

At the inquest held early the next morning, Anderson was described as of fair complexion, about 60 years of age, about five feet five inches tall, and weight approximately 135 pounds. One of Valentine's shots had struck Anderson's pistol and had almost torn off the sheriff's thumb. One bullet struck the elbow, ranged upward and came out in the upper arm. Another bullet entered the right side about six inches below the armpit, and the fourth ball went through the left shoulder, ranged through the breast, and came out near the left nipple.[18]

Valentine was described as of fair complexion, about thirty-six years of age, about five feet eight inches tall, and weighing about 160 pounds. Death came from a rifle ball which entered his left side below the collar bone and lodged in his body.[19]

A coroner's jury was selected, composed of A.R. Kelley, A. Girois, J.A. Rogers, G. Mussey, J.C. Hukinson, and Newt Taylor. The coroner was V.I. Cargile. The jury found "...that Ed Valentine came to his death while resisting arrest for the killing of D.L. Anderson, Sheriff of Terrell County, and further find that Bob Gatlin killed him in performance of his duty and was justified in doing so."[20]

Anderson's body was taken to Brackettville, Texas, where his funeral was held in the Catholic Church. He was buried in the St. Mary Magdalena Catholic Cemetery in a plot where his wife's parents, Robert and Mary Fitzmaurice, had been buried.

Ed Valentine had come to Sanderson from Fort Stockton. He was the second of ten children born to John and Maggie Valentine. John, who was born in Germany in February of 1833, came to the United States in 1878 and moved to Texas a short time afterward where, at the age of 45, he married his wife, Maggie, who was only 20. He was a janitor for the Pecos County courthouse until shortly before his death.[21] Maggie took her three youngest children with her to Sanderson and brought her son's body back to Fort Stockton where be was buried in East Hill Cemetery beside his father, John, and brother, Oswin, a veteran of World War I.

Anderson's wife, Maggie, died October 20, 1948, and their daughter, Ella Mae, who never married, died on July 19, 1970. Both are buried in the plot beside "Doc."

Bob Gatlin, the deputy who killed Ed Valentine, operated a ranch a few miles south of Dryden for a number of years. The ranch is still in existence and is operated by Gatlin descendants. After having lived in Del Rio, Texas, for many years, Bob suffered a massive stroke in 1943 which resulted in his being completely paralyzed until his death on January 26, 1946.[22] He was buried in the Del Rio Cemetery.

Notes

1 Keleher, William A., *Violence in Lincoln County, 1869-1881.* Albuquerque: University of New Mexico Press, 1957.

2 O'Neal, Bill, *Encyclopedia of Western Gunfighters.* Norman: University of Oklahoma Press, 1979.

3 Thrapp. Dan L., *Encyclopedia of Frontier Biography.* Glendale: The Arthur H. Clarke Company, 1988.

4 Rasch, Philip J., "Amende Honorable—The Life and Death of Billy Wilson." *West Texas Historical Association Year Book*, Vol. 34 (1958), 97-111.

5 Keleher, William A., *Violence in Lincoln County,* 17-19.

6 Letter to author from Robert H. Carlock, president, Aztec Land and Cattle Company, Limited, Mesa, Arizona, December 19, 1988. Mr. Carlock is gathering material for a history of the "Hashknife Outfit."

7 Personal interviews with Sanderson residents: Ervin Grigsby, Mrs. W.H. Savage, Noel S. Stirman, Dalton Hogg, and Mrs. E.E. Parley. Mr. Grigsby and Mrs. Savage were classmates of Ella Mae Anderson. Mr. Stirman is director of the Terrell County Historical Commission. Mr. Hogg, now retired, served as sheriff of Terrell County for sixteen years. Mrs. Fuley is with the Terrell County Museum.

8 U.S. Census Records, Trumball County, Ohio, for 1860, 1870, and 1880, and Pecos County, Texas, for 1900 and 1910.

9 U.S. Census Records, Trumball County, Ohio, for 1860 and 1870.

10 *Terrell County, Texas—Its Past—Its People.* Sanderson, Texas: Terrell County Heritage Commission, 1978, 249.

11 Marriage Record Book #2, 175, Kinney County, Texas.

12 *Terrell County, Texas—Its Past—Its People*, 249-250.

13 Ibid., 100.

14 Keleher, William A., *Violence in Lincoln County, 1869- 1881.* 323-324.

15 National Archives and Record Administration, Office of Pardon Attorney (Record Group 204), Volume P, Washington, D.C., *Billy Wilson alias D.L. Anderson*, case no. 42, offense: passing counterfeit money. A copy of this document is in the files of the author.

16 *Terrell County, Texas—Its Past—Its People*, 201.

17 Ibid., 555.

18 Record of Inquests, Book 12, 34. Terrell County Museum, Sanderson, Texas.

19 Ibid., 40.

20 Ibid., 39.

21 U.S. Census Records, Pecos County, Texas for 1900 and 1910.
22 *Terrell County, Texas—Its Past—Its People*, 392-395.

Don Cline

Don Cline was born in San Benito, Texas, in 1931. He attended four colleges and served in the U.S. Marine Corps. After marriage he moved to New Mexico where he and his wife raised five children. They now have seven grandchildren. An expert and instructor in the martial arts, Cline held the state championship in judo. Always athletic, he participated in the Senior Citizen Olympics and set the record for distance throw for baseball and frisbee. He also held the state record for frisbee distance throw and second place for baseball distance toss. Since 1994 he has suffered from a rare affliction called Complex Regional Pain Syndrome which developed after a double knee replacement, but he still manages to give judo and karate demonstrations. He has written since 1959 and has published more than fifty articles, as well as poetry. He once received an honorable mention in the Golden Spur awards of the Western Writers of America. He is the author of two books: *Alias Billy the Kid: the Man Behind the Legend*, and *Antrim & Billy*.

CITY CONSTABLE
HANGED FOR MURDERS
•
By Donald Cline
NOLA *Quarterly*, Autumn 1984

O f the many killers in the Old West, New Mexico had more than her share; many were infamous but most never achieved historical prominence. Such was the case with City Constable Milton J. Yarbery of Albuquerque. Milt Yarbery was unusual because he wore a badge and paid for his murders in a most unusual and bizarre manner.

According to news accounts, Yarbery was born in Walnut Ridge, Randolph County, Arkansas, circa 1848. He was thirty-five years old at the time of his execution and had a tall, lean body that seemed to roll in a shambling gait when he walked. He had keen, grey eyes and sported a sparse, black mustache that made his poorly developed head appear even smaller. His shoulders were thin and stooped. His overall physical impression left much to be desired.

People who knew him said his mental powers were insufficiently developed for he was unable to discern between a legal and an illegal act. Yarbery could neither read nor write and any notice of himself in a news account would exhilarate him so that he would act out anything the article might suggest he do.

Yarbery drifted into Texas at an early age and began a life of murder and other crime. He supposedly killed a freighter in a fight and fled to Dallas, Houston and Orange, Texas, then to Fort Smith,

Arkansas. where he met Dave Rudabaugh and Dave Matthews. Yarbery was said to have been a member of their gang until he murdered a drover in an attempted holdup. In Texarkana, Texas, he slew a man he believed to be a detective following him but the man later proved to be an innocent traveler. In the winter of 1876 he lived in Decatur, Texas, under the alias of Johnson and ran a combination saloon-billiard parlor with a partner named Jones. But he killed and ran again.

Dodge City, Kansas, was the next town he graced, but he got into more trouble and moved to Canon City, Colorado, and engaged in the variety theater business with Tony Preston in 1879. Soon he appeared in Las Vegas, New Mexico, but opportunities were not ripe for a man of his talents so he hit a succession of towns including Bernalillo, Albuquerque, San Marcial and back to Albuquerque.

New Town sprang up along the railroad tracks at Central and First Streets just three miles away from original Old Town. They desperately needed lawmen so somehow Yarbery got himself appointed city constable of Precinct No. 12 after its organization in 1881. He quickly gained the reputation of being a bully and handled his district with a high hand. He was unpopular with local citizens and one of his first acts was to commit murder.

Harry Brown was twenty-four years of age, the youngest son of ex-governor John C. Brown of Tennessee. Harry had been a minister to Russia and was then a solicitor for millionaire Jay Gould's railway system. He had worked as a railroad express messenger when Dave Rudabaugh attempted to rob his car. Brown shot several of the outlaws and drove the remainder off. Yarbery and Brown both fell in love with the same woman, a handsome young widow named Sadie Preston who had a four-year-old daughter. The two men quarreled over her attentions and ill feelings soon developed. New Town residents predicted the affair would end in bloodshed. It happened on the evening of March 30, 1881.

That evening Harry Brown picked up Mrs. Preston in a carriage driven by a Negro named John Clark. They went to Girard's Restaurant where Clark waited outside. After ordering dinner Brown stepped outside to speak with Clark when Yarbery came down the street with Mrs. Preston's daughter in tow. Yarbery did not look at the two men but took the little girl inside to her mother and when he returned outside Brown accosted him.

"Milt, I want to talk to you. I want you to understand I am not afraid of you and would not be even if you were marshal of the United States." Yarbery replied with a shot fired pointblank into Brown's left breast. Brown reeled backward as Yarbery fired a second shot. Clark said he saw the ball strike Brown's chest by the puff of dust that flew from his coat. As Brown lay sprawled on the wooden porch Yarbery calmly put two more shots into him. Any one of the four would have been fatal.

Yarbery surrendered to Sheriff Perfecto Armijo and was taken before Alcalde Martin in Old Town for preliminary examination. Yarbery claimed that Brown had attempted to draw a pistol on him and it was self-defense. His attorney William Childers (who later defended Pat Garrett in an Albuquerque bank lawsuit) got him released until the following term of the grand jury. At that time Yarbery produced some shady friends who testified that Brown had sworn to kill him on sight. John Clark's testimony was overlooked and a verdict of not guilty was given. He later was charged with assault upon a house and was freed on $100 bail.

A second murder occurred on Saturday night, June 18, 1881. A party of men in the R.H. Greenleaf restaurant on Front Street were engaged in a riotous party. At about 9 p.m. someone fired a pistol in celebration. Moments later Yarbery and a gambler named "Monte" Frank Boyd came down the street toward the Stover, Crary & Co. store. Two men were walking across the street away from Greenleaf's and the two bid goodbye and parted. Yarbery immediately advanced upon the man closest to him.

The man in question was Charles D. Campbell, a carpenter for the Atlantic & Pacific Railroad in Albuquerque. He was known to be a hard-drinking but harmless individual and by this time he was dead drunk. He was slightly north of Yarbery between him and Boyd. Yarbery shouted, "Throw up your hands!" and fired without waiting for a reply. Several more shots were fired while Campbell lay prostrate on the ground.

Yarbery again rode to Sheriff Perfecto Armijo's office and surrendered. Campbell's body was taken to Tom F. Phelan's office three doors north of Zeiger's saloon on Front Street. A coroner's jury was impaneled minutes later by Coroner Frank Reese in Phelan's office.

Drs. Gilkey and Howard examined the corpse and found him to be shot in three places. Two of the wounds were located in the back and one in the left side of the breast while he lay on his back. All three shots exited and any of the three would have been fatal. A search of the area was made but no pistol belonging to Campbell was located. Another search was made the following morning with similar results.

R.W. Hawley testified he was talking to Major Tom Park on the porch of the Stover, Crary and Co. store when he heard a shot on the opposite side of the street. Moments later he saw Yarbery and Boyd advancing upon Campbell who was walking away from them about twenty feet distant. Campbell turned slightly at Yarbery's order and reached toward his hip pocket without stopping. Yarbery fired immediately and Hawley heard some ten or twelve shots in all. He was only fifteen feet away from Campbell at the time. Campbell made some unintelligible reply to Yarbery's command.

Major Park verified Hawley's story except he felt Yarbery and Boyd had intended on robbing Campbell. He corroborated the fact that Campbell was unarmed and would not have had enough time to put up his hands before the shooting commenced.

Yarbery gave his version: "I was sitting in a chair in front of the Maden Hotel. While sitting there I heard a pistol shot around the corner about a block south of Maden's. I walked down the street and Frank Boyd was with me. I met two fellows close to old man Greenleaf's and Boyd, who was with me, asked one old gentleman who was sitting on the sidewalk if he knew where the shooting was. He pointed out the two men we met on the street. They had separated and one went up the street toward Stovers. I started into Greenleaf's and Boyd spoke to me saying, 'Milt, this gentleman says there goes the man who fired the shot.' I started after him and told Boyd to come ahead. I got within ten steps of the man and ordered him to hold up his hands. When I said that, he turned and said, 'You hold up yours, G__ D__ you.' Then he shot at me as soon as he got his pistol. Then he shot five or six times at me and I shot five at him. He shot two or three times after he was down. Then I went over to Maden's and shortly after surrendered myself to the sheriff." Yarbery did not mention shooting Campbell in the back as he lay on the ground and that Campbell would have had to fire seven to nine times from a pistol that held but six cartridges.

Several witnesses testified that Campbell was unarmed and made no attempt to harm Yarbery or even turn around. The coroner's jury returned a verdict of guilty and Yarbery was jailed to await the next session of the grand jury.

One of Yarbery's shady friends brought in a pistol the following morning he claimed belonged to Campbell that he had found near the spot of the incident. Yarbery took great pains to show the pistol to a reporter from the *Albuquerque Morning Journal*. Feelings ran hot and a mob appeared at the jail to lynch Yarbery but Sheriff Armijo successfully turned them away.

In the preliminary hearing Yarbery objected to Justice Sullivan for personal reasons and the prosecution objected to having Alcalde Martin preside. The prosecution later relented and the hearing was held on July 5 and Yarbery was then bound over for action of the grand jury. He was transferred to the Santa Fe jail for security reasons due to the feelings of local citizens. He was not indicted in time for his case to come up before the grand jury so he was forced to wait another month for indictment.

The trial was scheduled for the May 1882 term of the Second Judicial District of the Bernalillo County Court and began on May 15 with Judge Bell presiding. Yarbery was defended by L.S. Trimble and Colonel Frank Chavez but they were unable to stand up against the talents of prosecuting attorney William Breeden (of Billy the Kid fame) and Arnet R. Owen. The trial lasted three days and after a deliberation of only one hour the jury returned a verdict of guilty of murder in the first degree.

Yarbery brought in a procession of the flotsam and jetsam of the town composed of bunko men, killers, gamblers, and the scum of the New Town criminal element to testify in his behalf. Most of the prosecution witnesses had since left town but at the last moment Major T.W. Park arrived from Missouri and it was his testimony that placed the noose around Yarbery's neck.

Yarbery remained calm when the verdict was read and on May 23 he heard the judge pronounce the death sentence. He was unaffected by the sentence until Judge Bell said, " and may God have mercy on your soul." Yarbery's face then went ashen and his eyes flashed darts at the judge. "Judge, I have not had a fair trial. You have not treated me justly. The men in the New Town who tried to hang me have falsely sworn my life away." Judge Bell was unimpressed.

Yarbery was returned to Santa Fe and he changed attorneys to John H. Knaebel who filed a writ of *habeas corpus* to delay the exe-

cution. While waiting for a decision, on September 9, he attempted
to break out of jail in association with Billy Wilson, former companion of Billy the Kid, George Pease, and one Harris. When the
guard opened the cell door to lock a prisoner in they threw a blanket
over his head, knocked him to the floor and rushed upstairs to the
overhead guard room and leaped out the window to the ground.
Several shots were fired at them without effect.

Someone on the outside had slipped Yarbery a file and the men
had cut away their shackles in full view of the observation window
cut in the ceiling overhead. Pease was quickly captured and three
days later Chief of Police Frank Chaves captured Yarbery, Wilson
and Harris at Arroyo Galesteo. At the time they were driving a
wagon with Yarbery riding a stolen horse. They had six dollars in
their pockets.

On January 25, 1883, Justice C.J. Axtell of the Supreme Court
sustained Judge Bell's ruling while Governor Lionel A. Sheldon sat
in nodding his agreement. The shadow of the gallows now fell
across Milton Yarbery as the governor then signed and sealed the
death warrant. Yarbery was now a man legally appointed unto death.
The execution was set for February 9 between 11 a.m. and 3 p.m. At
a point in Bernalillo County to be designated by the sheriff.

Legal funds for further defense efforts were supplied by Yarbery's
friends and the *Albuquerque Morning Journal* described them as "a
desperate class of men."

When attorney Knaebel notified Yarbery of the Supreme Court's
decision he displayed no outward emotion. Knaebel again tried to
delay the execution by another writ of *habeas corpus* to have the
territorial homicide law tested in the Supreme Court, but Justice
Axtell denied this also. Knaebel then filed for a bill of exceptions on
appeal from the *habeas corpus* refusal but was again refused, so he
took steps to obtain a writ of *certiorari* from the U.S. Supreme
Court. This too failed.

Meanwhile, Chief Howe and Sheriff Armijo were looking about
Albuquerque for a suitable place for the execution. They found several locations but the Spanish owners refused them permission. The
superintendent of the local street railway company offered use of
the company corral but, as the *Albuquerque Morning Journal* pointed out, if the hanging took place there the railway company would
do a land office business. Finally it was decided to stage the execu-

tion within the jailyard which is the present day Old Town Plaza.

Various methods of scaffolds and hangings were studied and the gallows decided upon was reproduced in the *Scientific American*. Yarbery was not destined to die upon an ordinary-type gallows but his departure would, instead, come in a most unique manner. Instead of standing upon the customary platform he would stand on a small mound of earth on the ground located between two sixteen-foot posts connected across the top by a crossbeam. Pulleys were located in the center of the crossbeam and down one side to an enclosed box. Yarbery was to stand on the ground with four feet of loose rope around his neck and the rope ran through the pulleys to a roughcast piece of iron weighing 325 pounds held in place by a pin and rope.

Inside the enclosed six-foot box would be three men. One of the three would be selected to cut the rope at Sheriff Armijo's signal and none of the people present would know which man was the actual executioner. When the rope was cut the weight would fall four feet to the ground, thus, supposedly, jerking Yarbery up and breaking his neck at the same moment. The clever contraption proved to be a murderous fiasco.

Several loads of dirt were hauled into the jailyard and dumped for a firmer foundation. The actual site is about where the central band-stand is located today. A fence was built around the spot to help pro-tect Yarbery's departure from public view. The jail, which once held Billy the Kid and John B. "Squire" Wilson in 1880 (both men escaped) was a low, L-shaped adobe building. Seventy-five feet from the western wing was a high, adobe wall running north and south. This wall was to be used for the western end of the enclosure.

Local citizens bet that Yarbery would not live to hang on Friday for they figured he would be lynched before then.

At that time there were six prisoners in the west end of the jail where Yarbery would spend his final moments. There were four Mexicans, "Crazy Rube" and a man identified by the newspaper as "the notorious political nigger of the recent election contests." Four days before the hanging three of these prisoners broke out. They were not apprehended.

The gallows was completed, having been constructed under the supervision of A.H.M. Ahistrom, who told the reporters the drop would now be five feet six inches and that no finer gallows had ever been seen in the territory.

On Wednesday morning Sheriff Romulo Martinez made a routine inspection of Yarbery's cell and discovered the iron fastenings had been tampered with. Extending halfway across the outside of the door was a heavy, wooden beam fastened to the door by large, iron rivets. An iron bar fit over a staple in which the hook of the padlock was passed when the door was locked. The rivet heads were flattened on the inside of the cell and Yarbery had dug out the wood around the rivets almost through the entire beam and filled the holes with soap and soot. It was an excellent job. That night he intended on jerking the door from its fastenings and escape.

Reporters stated that Yarbery looked pale but he said he wasn't scared and he wouldn't be even if they walked him to the scaffold that very moment.

Tickets for the execution were already printed and sold. One enterprising resident of Old Town sold ringside viewing privileges on his roof at a dollar a head. Others also commercialized on Yarbery's death.

Because of the attempted escape and ill feelings of the population the governor decided to leave Yarbery in Santa Fe and deliver him by train Friday morning. Twenty-four men of the Albuquerque Guard were to protect Yarbery upon his arrival and a number of the Governor's Rifles numbered even more. He would arrive between 10 a.m. and noon. He would walk from the train to the special streetcar which would carry him to Old Town, to one block east of the Exchange Hotel, where he would walk the remaining distance. Yarbery asked for whiskey to bolster his courage.

At 6 a.m. on Friday morning the Governor's Rifles with three omnibuses arrived and Yarbery was already awake and ready. The omnibuses took him to the depot where he spoke briefly to attorney Knaebel for the final time. Though Knaebel assured him he was still filing legal writs, Yarbery had lost hope.

The special train consisted of a single coach drawn by engine No. 245 with trainmaster Charlie Dyer of Las Vegas at the controls. During the ride Yarbery kept asking for whiskey and he kept looking out the window as if to drink in as much of the world as possible. Outside of Albuquerque he asked, "Are we pretty near. there? Well, I guess they are going to hang me."

Two thousand people met the train at the depot. Guards encircled him as he walked to the waiting streetcar. They passed the spot where he had murdered Campbell and he looked at the surrounding buildings for a moment then lowered his head. At the Old Town jail he asked to see his friends and requested his relatives be notified. He displayed signs of weakening at times but managed to get hold of himself. He ate a final lunch of cranberry pie and drank a pint of whiskey and a bottle of ale.

Fathers S.J. Persone and Fede of San Felipe church in the plaza came to baptize him. As an act of purging his conscience he then professed a sudden belief in the Catholic faith and made confession. He had arrived in a seedy-looking brown suit, so friends supplied him with a new, black suit to die in. While in jail he had gone from 170 pounds to 150 pounds. The execution drop was now shortened to four feet to compensate for the weight loss.

At 1:50 p.m. a doctor examined his pulse and found it to be beating 120 times per minute. At 2:30 it was unchanged. At 2:40 p.m. the Albuquerque guards were outside and began to push back the crowd from the gallows. Sheriff Armijo then tied Yarbery's hands behind his back and prepared to lead him outside. The somber looking Yarbery was flanked by Chief Howe and Deputy Sheriff George Munroe. At 2:45 Chief Howe read the death sentence while Yarbery's feet were being bound. During the reading Yarbery did not take his eyes off Howe but afterward eyed the crowd coldly.

"You are going to hang Milt Yarbery," he shouted. "You are going to hang him not for the murder of Campbell, but for the killing of Brown. There is Colonel Bell [nodding his head toward Bell]. What did he say? Come around Bell, so I can see you. Don't hide your face. What did he say to Sheriff Whitehill when he asked him what was done to the deputy sheriff that killed Campbell? Bell said he is in the Santa Fe jail and the S__ of a B__ ought to hang."

Yarbery then went into elaborate detail to berate others who had a hand in his conviction. His farewell speech covered an entire column of the *Albuquerque Morning Journal*. He claimed the deceased Campbell had killed a Chinaman in the southern part of the state several years before. Armijo informed Yarbery that the time was growing short and Yarbery growled, "Let me finish!"

He continued talking and when he did not stop his hat was removed at precisely three minutes past three and the noose placed around his neck and adjusted. He was asked to cease speaking but he did not comply with the request. The black hood was then drawn over his face, shutting out the world, but Yarbery continued talking. Armijo made a signal and one of the men inside the wooden enclosure began cutting the rope holding the weight. Just as the signal was given Yarbery was heard to say, "Well, you are going to hang an innocent man." He had hardly uttered these words when Milton J. Yarbery suddenly shot into the air.

His body was supposed to be jerked four feet into the air but instead it flew into the crossbeam sixteen feet overhead. The breaking of his bones could be heard clearly across the entire plaza. A gasp went up from the spectators. As soon as the body dropped and began its macabre dance at the end of the taut rope, Drs. J.D. Derr and J.B. Sawyer of Albuquerque and Dr. Syminton of Santa Fe rushed forward, stilled the body with their hands and cut him down. His body was placed on the ground and his pulse reexamined. Surprisingly, Yarbery was still alive.

At the end of the first minute his pulse read 109, at the end of the second 104, third 128, fourth 108, fifth 130, sixth 140 and the seventh minute 184. Death ensued in the ninth minute. His corpse was then placed on top of a plain white casket, the hood was removed from his head and the public viewed him for the final time. His eyes were open and staring into the clear, blue sky. His jaw was slack and hanging on his breast. The corpse was placed inside the coffin and the lid nailed shut. There was no funeral. His body was taken to a nearby Catholic cemetery and buried without fanfare.

The other man involved in the shooting, "Monte" Frank Boyd. also served his time in hell. Boyd left Albuquerque two days after the Campbell murder due to the "suggestions" of the citizens. He took the Atlantic & Pacific train west to Holbrook, Arizona, and there he met his maker: On the afternoon of October 5, 1883, he was riding across the desert when he came upon two unarmed Navajo Indians near Martin's ranch. He grasped the reins of one Indian's horse while he drew his pistol with the other hand and calmly shot the Indian to death without provocation. The other Indian fled. At sundown forty armed Navajos appeared at Martin's ranch and demanded to see Boyd. Boyd did not work there but a cowboy who knew him volunteered to lead them to where Boyd was at the nearby Frank Davis Ranch.

After a short, fast ride the Navajos arrived just as Boyd was preparing to mount his horse. They surrounded him with leveled rifles. The surviving Indian identified him as the murderer of his companion and at a signal from their chief the Indians riddled Boyd's body.

Sources

1. *The Santa Fe Daily Democrat*, March 3. 1881, Tuesday, page 3. Thursday, June 23, 1881. Vol. 2. No. 51. page 2, col. 3

2. *Santa Fe New Mexican*. January 26, 1883.

3. *Albuquerque Morning Journal*, Saturday, Feb. 10. 1883. No. 8, Vol. III, col. 1-7. page 4; Sunday. Feb. 11, 1883. No. 86, Vol. III, page 4, col. 1-5; Friday. Jan. 26. 1883. Vol. III, No. 72, page 1, col. 3; Tuesday, Jan. 30, 1883, Vol. III. No. 75, page 2, col. 3; Thursday, Feb. 1, 1883, Vol. 111, No. 75, page 2, col. 2; Friday, Feb. 2, 1883. Vol. III, No. 78, page 4, col. 2; Saturday, Feb. 3, 1883, Vol. III, No. 79. page 4, col. 2; Wednesday, Feb. 7, 1883, Vol. III, No. 83, page 4. col. 2-3; Wednesday, Feb. 7, 1883, Vol. III, No. 53. page 4. col. 1-2; Thursday, Feb. 8, 1883, Vol. III, No. 84, page 4, col. 3.

4. Albuquerque Journal Library of Photos. Mary Badgley, Curator.

5. San Felipe Catholic Church Burial Records. 1883. Rev. Luis Jaramillo.

6. Bernalillo County Criminal Dricket Index Book. District Court Clerks Office.

7. State Archives & Records Center. Santa Fe. New Mexico. Dorotha Bradley, Asst. Archivist.

8. Bernalillo County Criminal Docket Records, 1879-1881; 1882-1883, page 87, May 11, 1882; page 97, May 15, 1882; page 109, May 18, 1882; May Term 1882; page 115, May 20. 1883; page 123, May 23, 1883, May 28, 1883; page 336. 1st day, 2nd day, 3rd day, 6th day. May Term 1881; page 344-345. 4th day, 6th day, 10th day.

9. Museum of New Mexico, Santa Fe, Ruth E. Rambo, Staff Librarian.

10. Museum of New Mexico, Photograph Division, Lucille Stacy, Librarian.

11. New Mexico Reports, Vol. 2. Supreme Court Decisions, pages 391-458.

12. Bernalillo County Death Records.

13. *Albuquerque Review*, May 20, 1880.

14. Fairview Cemetery Records and a search of the headstones.

15. Strong-Thorne Mortuary Records (formerly Strong Undertaking in 1883).

16. *The New Mexico Lawman*, "The Shiftless Marshall" by, Maurice

Kildare. Vol. 33. No. 2, February 1967 issue.
17. *The Scientific American* issue of 1883

Robert K. DeArment

   Born in Johnstown, Pennsylvania, in 1925, Robert K. DeArment attended public schools in Pittsburgh. Upon graduation from high school in the middle of World War II he entered the U.S. Army, went to Europe with an infantry division as a machine gunner, and saw six months of heavy combat. He was discharged as a staff sergeant after three years of service. While attending the University of Toledo he married and began working nights in a factory to augment his G.I. Bill benefits. After college graduation he continued work with the company, a large automotive parts firm, received a number of promotions, and eventually retired as Director of Distribution after thirty-eight years of service. His interest in Western history led him in the 1950s to begin research on the life of Bat Masterson, which culminated in a biography of Bat, published in 1979. In that year he also became a life member of NOLA. He has published a book on frontier gamblers and biographies of George Scarborough and Frank Canton, the latter a finalist in the 1997 Oklahoma Center for the Book awards. Soon to be published is a volume dealing with Bat Masterson's New York City years. Bob is currently completing the research on three other book projects. An active member of Western Writers of America, he has written many articles and edited several books, including the memoirs of Jim McIntire and NOLA's series of Philip J. Rasch works. He and his wife, Rose, also a NOLA member, have four grown children and seven grandchildren.

JEFF KIDDER, ARIZONA RANGER
·
By Robert K. DeArment
NOLA *Quarterly*, Winter 1982-83

Jefferson Davis Milton used to say, "The trouble with Jeff Kidder was that he wanted to be a bad man and didn't know how."[1]

Milton, who in his time had been a Texas Ranger, El Paso city marshal, Wells Fargo express messenger, Mexican border patrolman, and gunfighter with few peers, had little use for this young man who shared his first name.

But then Kidder was an Arizona Ranger and old Jeff Milton had a bias against Arizona Rangers, probably because, although he was eminently qualified, for political reasons he had not been chosen to head up the tightly knit force of hard-bitten lawmen who, in the years immediately following the turn of the century, threw fear into criminals infesting Arizona Territory.

Jeff Kidder never wanted to be a "bad man." All he ever wanted to be was a gunfighter, the greatest gunfighter of them all. Folks in Vermillion, South Dakota, where he grew up, remembered that he packed a six-shooter from the time he was old enough to hold one in his hand. When he worked in the Vermillion post office where his father was postmaster, most of his wages went toward the purchase of ammunition for his Colt's .45 and young Jeff practiced the draw-and-shoot by the hour.

The Kidders were a prominent family in Vermillion. Young Jeff was the namesake of Jefferson Parrish Kidder, his grandfather, who had served as lieutenant governor of Vermont before moving west.

In 1856 Kidder was appointed associate justice of the supreme court of Dakota Territory by President Abraham Lincoln and in later years was re-appointed to the court by Presidents Grant, Hayes and Arthur. During the 1870s he served two terms as delegate to Congress from the territory.

The elder of Judge Kidder's two sons, Lieutenant Lyman S. Kidder of the second U.S. Cavalry, died in an Indian fight on Beaver Creek in northwest Kansas in July 1867. Lieutenant Kidder's detachment of ten troopers and an Indian guide, detailed to carry dispatches to the Seventh Cavalry, were attacked and overwhelmed by a force of three hundred Sioux led by Chief Pawnee Killer. The bodies, stripped, burned and mutilated, were later found and buried on the spot by George Armstrong Custer's troops.

Silas W. Kidder, the judge's other son, settled in Vermillion in 1868 and served as clerk of his father's court. At the age of twenty-four Silas was elected to the Territorial Council and later was mayor and postmaster at Vermillion. His farm, four miles north of town, was known by all in Clay County as "Kidderminster." There was a Kidder Island in the nearby Missouri River and a Kidder Street in Vermillion, both named for the judge.

When, on November 15, 1875, a son was born at Kidderminster, he too was named for the judge and christened Jefferson Parrish.

In 1901 Silas Kidder, suffering from ill health, decided to move to southern California. His wife and daughter Lulu accompanied him, but son Jeff headed for one of the few remaining raw frontier areas of the West, the southern counties of Arizona Territory.

Perhaps not coincidentally, 1901 was the year that the Arizona legislature passed a bill authorizing the formation of a force of rangers to combat outlawry in the territory. Jeff Kidder may have chosen Arizona as his new home for this very reason. If he did aspire to be a ranger, it was two years before he was offered an appointment.

The first company of Arizona Rangers was commanded by Captain Burton C. Mossman who selected a sergeant and ten privates to aid him in the awesome task of controlling rustling and brigandry throughout the vast territory. After a year of service

Mossman resigned and was succeeded by Thomas H. Rynning. In 1903 the legislature approved a bill doubling the number of rangers. One of those chosen by Rynning to join his newly enlarged command was Jefferson P. Kidder.

At twenty-seven, Kidder was tall and slim, with sandy hair and clean-shaven, boyish features. William MacLeod Raine, the prolific Western writer who had an opportunity to meet many of the old-time gunmen in their later years, noted that most had one feature in common: "gray or blue eyes, often a faded blue, expressionless, hard as jade."[2] Jeff Kidder had such eyes—the eyes of the gunfighter.

During his two years in Arizona Kidder had worked as a cowhand on ranches in the Tombstone-Bisbee area and when he signed his enlistment papers in April 1903 he gave his occupation as "stockman." Private Kidder of the Arizona Rangers was paid one hundred dollars a month and was given commission papers and a badge of solid silver. He was expected to furnish for his own use a suitable horse, a pack animal, clothing and camping gear, and a "six shooting pistol (army size)." Rifles and ammunition were provided by the territory but the cost was deducted from the ranger's pay.

Kidder had only served a couple of months when the entire ranger company was called to the strike-bound mines at Morenci to help quell a riot. At one point during this disturbance Graham County Sheriff Jim Parks, sixty hastily commissioned deputies, and Captain Tom Rynning's twenty-four-man ranger force found themselves surrounded by twelve hundred armed and angry miners. One shot from either side would have precipitated a bloody conflict, but the officers and the mob's leaders stayed calm and the battle was averted. Soon thereafter the entire Arizona National Guard, 230 men strong, arrived to help the rangers and sheriff's deputies bring the situation under control.

On July 5, 1904, Jeff Kidder, while attempting to make an arrest in Bisbee, hauled out that "six shooting pistol" of which he was so fond, and before he was finished, three victims lay stretched out on the board sidewalk in front of Tony Downs' Turf Saloon. But, surprisingly, none of the three was shot; Kidder had cracked each one over the head with the barrel of his revolver—"buffaloed" them, in the parlance of the old-time lawmen. A large crowd of angry miners, hostile to the ranger, soon formed and there were cries of "Get a rope!" but the Bisbee constabulary took charge and placed Kidder under arrest. Arraigned in court, he was charged with two counts of assault and one of assault with a deadly weapon.

The *Bisbee Review* was scathing in its denunciation of the man it called "a thug, bully and butcher…Mr. Kidder, the big man with the big gun." It asked: "Who sent this Ranger in here with his pistol to beat up men on the streets of Bisbee? Is the reputation of a member of the Ranger force to be made and maintained by the muzzle of a .45 in the hands of a hot-headed man wearing a star? Who gave this man Kidder, wearing an Arizona Ranger badge, the extraordinary powers warranting him to cut men's heads open with the butt end of a .45?…Let the captain of the rangers come here—fair man as Captain Rynning is, and take this man Kidder out of here, strip him of his star and badge which gives him the authority to 'pack a gun' and use it like a crazy man, unfitted to be an officer by every evidence in the world."[3]

On the two charges of assault committed on men named Fagan and Graham, Kidder asked for a change of venue and the cases were moved to Tombstone where in due course he was found guilty on one count and fined fifty dollars. The other charge was dropped when prosecution witnesses did not appear. Kidder was granted a change of venue to Pima County on the third charge of assault with a deadly weapon, the judge ruling that due to "biased and prejudiced published reports of the case the defendant could not secure a fair and impartial trial" in the district. After several additional delays this charge was quietly dropped.[4]

It was during this period that Kidder's reputation as an arrogant young buck on the prod for trouble grew apace. Jeff Milton claimed in later years that he backed Kidder down one night in Nogales when he became obstreperous. The two Jeffs were having dinner in Cazabon's restaurant when Milton objected to Kidder's loud profanity with women and children present. The ranger jumped up from the table, six-gun in hand.

"I could have killed him then, dead easy," said Milton, "but I didn't want to do it there." Fixing Kidder with the icy stare that had once made John Wesley Hardin flinch, the old gunfighter muttered, "Better put that gun up. Then we'll go outside, old hoss, and if you're wantin' a fight. you're goin' to get one, certain."

Out on the street with their weapons holstered, the two stood inches apart and Milton berated the younger man in the strongest terms he could muster—and Jeff Milton had command of some rare and salty language. But Kidder took the goading and refused to draw. The ranger, said Milton, "just got up and drug it."[5]

There is other evidence to confirm Milton's contention that Jeff Kidder could be troublesome and overbearing, especially when drinking, but the inference inherent in this story that he also lacked sand in a showdown situation is not corroborated by others who saw him in action. Captain Tom Rynning adjudged him "a fearless young fellow, pleasant in his ways, and with plenty quiet good judgment..., a top hand among the Arizona Rangers."[6] Harry C. Wheeler, who served almost six years with the rangers and in March 1907 replaced Tom Rynning as captain, wrote: "Whatever criticism may be made of him is only such as might be made of many another young man, but...the indiscreetness was far excelled and overshadowed by his manly qualities...Jeff Kidder was one of the best officers who ever stepped foot in this section of the country. He did not know what fear was...."[7] W.A. "Billy" Old, a ranger lieutenant who sided Kidder in many a brush with outlaws, testified: "During our association we have been in places that try men's souls and Jeff was always found pure gold."[8] And ranger Fred Rankin affirmed: "Kidder...was one of those men who never knew fear."[9]

In later years other men who rode stirrup to stirrup with Jeff Kidder recalled vividly his quickness with a gun. Former ranger Joe Pearce told a writer fifty years later: "Jeff Kidder...was a gunman as well as a lawman and in a pinch would shoot first and ask the questions later on, if there was anybody left to answer them...Kidder was a killer."[10] And John Clarke, the last surviving Arizona ranger, in 1976 still clearly recalled Kidder's six-gun which he said was legendary in the West. "Kidder had dug the grave of many a badman," Clarke told an interviewer.[11]

The "legendary" six-shooter was Colt serial number 246844, a silverplated single-action .45 with factory engraving and pearl grips. Kidder purchased this beautiful weapon new from the Aquirre Mercantile Company in 1905 shortly after his father died at San Jacinto, California, and left him a sizable inheritance. It can be seen slung on his hip in a picture taken of him at Bisbee.

Kidder practiced constantly with this pistol as he had with other guns since he was a boy back in South Dakota. A good share of his inheritance, possibly as much as three or four thousand dollars, went to buy ammunition which he burned through the barrel of this gun. He fired off so many rounds that within two years he had to return the pistol to the Colt's factory for repair and replating.

His constant practice brought results. Said a newspaper writer in 1908: "Kidder was reputed to be the quickest man on the ranger force in drawing a gun. It was said of him that he could allow the average man to cover him with a gun, and then draw his own weapon and fire quicker than the other party. He was also one of the best shots of the rangers. At thirty paces he demonstrated repeatedly that he could hit a playing card three times out of six on the average. He could shoot equally well with either hand."[12]

Captain Rynning, who had seen many a gunslick in his time, attested: "Kidder was the fastest man with a six-shooter I ever saw; worked the hammer with the thumb of his pistol hand as fast as I could fan it with my other hand."[13]

Like all the rangers, Jeff Kidder spent a large part of his time in the field, chasing outlaws through the mountains of the sparsely settled territory. Predictably, the deprecators frequently crossed the line into old Mexico in an effort to elude their relentless pursuers.

Captain Rynning secured from General Luis E. Torres, commander of the northern military district of Mexico and governor of Sonora, special commissions for himself and selected rangers, William A. Old, John Foster, Tip Stanford, and Jeff Kidder, authorizing them to pursue their quarry beyond the border.

In Mexico the rangers worked in cooperation with the Sonora rurales under Colonel Emelio Kosterlitzky, their renowned commander, who also believed that the apprehension of desperadoes was of greater consequence than the niceties of international law.

Kidder's assignment for most of his career was patrolling that long stretch of borderland between Nogales and Douglas, ferreting out smugglers. He made his headquarters at Naco, a small town on the border where the El Paso Southwestern Railroad joined the Cananea, Yaqui River and Pacific line which ran sixty miles to the rich copper mines at Cananea, Sonora. Often he worked alone, but at times he was joined by rangers Fred Rankin, Billy Old or Bill Sparks. Rankin was with him on one occasion when they surprised a gang of gun-runners. There was a fierce fire-fight during which Kidder "shot the arm off one of the outlaws" and Rankin killed the horse of another. Numerous weapons and ten thousand rounds of ammunition were confiscated by the officers.[14]

Because of his energetic activity against the smugglers Jeff Kidder was a marked man, said Rankin. "Kidder was constantly on the trail of the smugglers who had the Mexican officers and line riders at Naco buffaloed, and carried on their smuggling as they pleased. While Kidder and I were together at Naco we were warned several times that the Mexican officers would kill us the first chance they had, and we were even told that they were openly making threats against our lives...Kidder knew his life was in danger, but he was one of those men who never knew fear."[15]

Jeff almost lost his life at Naco in 1906 during a melee which may have been staged to accomplish that very purpose. A gang of some fifteen disreputable characters began a disturbance on the railroad track west of town and when rangers Kidder and Bill Sparks arrived they were set upon by the entire bunch. The officers were knocked to the ground and pummeled and kicked. As they struggled to their feet, one of the gang pulled a knife and attempted to plunge it into Kidder's back. Ranger Sparks caught the flash of the blade. His six-gun bucked in his hand and the knife-wielder went down. "The fight went out of the others and the two rangers put them all under arrest."[16]

On the last day of the year 1906 Jeff Kidder killed a man at Douglas, Arizona. The town had become infested with hold up men and burglars. Kidder and several other rangers were called in to assist the local police in controlling the criminal element. On the afternoon of December 31 Kidder challenged a suspicious looking individual in the railroad yards. He called out to the man, who was sneaking furtively around the cars about forty yards away: "Hold on there, Jack, we are officers and want to look at you."

Instead of complying, the man drew a six-shooter, a .38 on a .45 frame, and snapped a shot in the ranger's direction. The silver-plated Colt leaped from Kidder's holster and he ripped off three rounds, one of which struck the suspect directly in the right eye. The man, identified as an unemployed bartender named Tommy Woods, lived for several hours after the shooting but died later that night.

Kidder turned himself and his gun in to the local police and a warrant charging him with murder was sworn out at his own request as he insisted on having a full investigation of the occurrence. He was cleared at a hearing ten days later, the court ruling that he acted in the proper discharge of his duty.[17]

At about this time Kidder was promoted to the rank of sergeant and his pay was increased to $110 a month. In March 1907 Tom Rynning resigned as captain of the rangers to accept appointment as superintendent of the territorial prison at Yuma. Lieutenant Harry C. Wheeler was named as the new captain and there was speculation in the Douglas newspapers that Jeff Kidder would receive another promotion to the vacated lieutenancy, making him second in command of the rangers.

"Should the lieutenancy come to Sergeant Kidder it could not be given to a more deserving officer," said the *Douglas Dispatch*. "He has been very active in the hunting down of criminals for the four years of his connection with the rangers. He has always been a careful, courageous and zealous officer and the people of Douglas would be pleased to hear of his promotion."[18] The appointment, however, went to Jeff's closest friend, William A. "Billy" Old.

Headquarters for Lieutenant Old was Flagstaff in the north-central part of the territory. Perhaps because of the threats against Kidder's life by the border smugglers and their official accomplices, he was transferred to Flagstaff for several months in 1907 to work with his pal, Billy Old. Soon after his arrival he found it necessary to prove to the local toughs that his innocent, youthful appearance belied the fact that he was a topnotch fighting man.

A hulking cowpuncher in a Flagstaff saloon made a slurring remark about "the baby-faced kid hiding behind a tin star and fancy shooting-iron." In an instant badge and gun were on the bar and the big cowboy found himself in a knock-down, no-holds-barred fight. After twenty minutes he had enough, acknowledged that Jeff Kidder was some tough hombre, and stood drinks for the house.[19]

Early in 1908 Kidder was again on duty along the Mexican border. He was at Nogales on March 29 when he received word from Captain Wheeler that his year's enlistment was almost up and that he should proceed to Naco where Wheeler, currently on a long scout through the Chiricahua Mountains in search of horse thieves, would meet him to administer the oath for another year.

Kidder knew that Wheeler could not make Naco for several days, and on April 1 he set out on a leisurely ride, allowing himself two days for the sixty-mile trip. His only companion was a tiny

JEFF KIDDER, ARIZONA RANGER

Chihuahua named "Jip" that he had found abandoned several years before. He and the dog had adopted each other. In the field Kidder carried his little pet on his saddle or inside his shirt. Jeff and Jip were inseparable.

On the afternoon of April 3 Kidder arrived in Naco, Arizona, dropped his mount at a livery stable, cleaned up a bit at a barber shop, and checked in with Sergeant Tip Stanford, on duty at the ranger headquarters. Toward evening he announced that he was going over to Naco, Sonora, "to meet a friend coming out of Cananea."

Before leaving he stripped off his heavy cartridge belt and removed the beautiful silver-plated Colt from its holster and slipped it into the waistband of his pants. As an afterthought he thumbed out a handful of .45 cartridges from the belt and dropped them in his pocket. Then he sauntered over the international line into old Mexico, his little dog, Jip, tagging at his heels.

There was speculation later that the friend Kidder expected to meet on the Mexican side was one of the spies he employed to keep him informed regarding the activities of the smugglers. Beyond speculation, there were later open charges that what transpired that night was a deliberate assassination, planned and executed by the smugglers and their confederates to eliminate their nemesis, ranger Sergeant Jeff Kidder.

It is known that Kidder visited a number of cantinas that night, that he danced with many of the dancehall girls, and that he had several drinks. Whether he became intoxicated was later argued but never clearly determined. About midnight he retired to the back room of a cantina with a girl, new to the town, who was known only as "Chia." After he and Chia spent some time "fooling around," as Kidder called it, he started to leave when he noticed a silver dollar that had been in his pocket was now missing. He accused the girl of taking the dollar and she flew into a rage, struck at him, and threw open the door, at the same time yelling for the police.

"I had not had a chance to move," Kidder told friends the next day, "when two Mexican police came through the doorway with their six-shooters drawn, and one fired, hitting me. I fell and was dazed, but knew that my only chance was to fight while I had cartridges left. I drew my own six-shooter while sitting on the floor and opened fire. I believe I wounded both of the men, and they went down helpless."[20]

The two Mexicans, Dolores Quias and Tomas Amador, were seriously, but not fatally, wounded. Quias had a bullet hole through the meat of his thigh; Amador's wound was just above the knee. Kidder had been gut-shot. A bullet from Amador's gun had entered his abdomen just to the left of his navel and ranged downward, cutting through the intestines and emerging through the lower back.

Both Mexicans lay where they had fallen, but Kidder struggled to his feet and staggered out into the night, heading for the American line, several hundred yards away. "I was very weak," Kidder said.

"Suddenly firing opened up in front of me, and I saw a number of men between me and the line armed with Winchesters. They were directing their fire directly at me..." Kidder thumbed his single-action .45 but the hammer snapped on empty cylinders. Rifle bullets cracking around him, he veered off to his left where he could see the boundary line fence.

"When I got to the fence," he continued, "I put the last six cartridges I had into my gun. During all this time these men were firing at me...I saved my fire until one of their number came within range and I shot him. I then fired until my gun was empty. When my last cartridge was gone I yelled to them that I was all in and told them to come and get me."

They came, a dozen or more, led by Victoriano Amador, chief of police of Naco, Sonora, and brother of the officer who shot Kidder. Chief Amador had been the third man winged by Kidder, receiving a minor wound in the side. "If anybody had told me that one human being could be as brutal to another as they were to me I would not have believed it," Kidder said. "I could scarcely stand, but one of this crowd...struck me over the head with his six-shooter and I fell. Between them they dragged me on the ground for about fifty yards, and then seemingly tired of their exertions stopped and beat me over the head with a six-shooter. They finally dragged me to the jail and threw me in there."[21]

Kidder lay the rest of the night in that jail cell receiving no medical assistance. In the early morning hours American officers roused a Mexican judge and persuaded him to grant permission to have the wounded ranger moved to a private residence. Doctors F.E. Shine of Bisbee and Brandon of Naco ministered to him, but gave him little hope for survival. A bullet wound through the intestines in those days was almost always fatal.

Kidder told his story of the fight to Sergeant Tip Stanford and former ranger Lieutenant John Foster, now a deputy U.S. marshal. He did not fear death, he said, but was concerned that the true facts of the affair be reported. He insisted that he had not started the fight, but was only defeated when his ammunition ran out. "I know that a great many people think I am quick-tempered," he said. "I did not precipitate this trouble, and never drew my gun until I was wounded and on the floor of that house.... If I am fatally wounded, I can die with the knowledge that I did my best in a hard situation." Later that day, as he felt life slipping away, Kidder took Foster's hand and whispered: "You know, Jack, that I would not lie to you. I know that I am done for....They got me, but if my ammunition had not given out, I might have served them the same way."[22]

Jeff Kidder died at 6:30 on the morning of April 5, 1908. At first the Mexican authorities refused to allow the removal of his body to American soil. After a day of negotiations a message was sent from General Luis Torres authorizing the removal. The body was taken to Bisbee and laid out in the Palace Undertaking Parlor.

High in the Chiricahuas, Captain Harry Wheeler learned of Kidder's death from a passing cowboy. He headed directly for Bisbee, arriving in time to serve as a pallbearer at the funeral. Kidder's remains were sent by train to his mother in San Jacinto, California, for burial.

Jip, the little Chihuahua dog, had been by Jeff's side throughout his ordeal. He had been in the cantina during the gunfight, had accompanied Jeff on his desperate attempt to reach the American border, had been with him as he was dragged, battered and bleeding, to the jail, and had snuggled against him during the day and night that the stricken ranger's life slowly ebbed away. He stood, shivering, next to the casket at the funeral in Bisbee, and, held in the arms of Ranger Sam Hayhurst, watched with the sad, protruding eyes of the Chihuahua as the train carrying his master pulled away to the west.

The rangers intended to keep little Jip as a company mascot, but it soon became apparent that the poor animal was lost without Jeff. Finally Harry Wheeler passed the hat and the collection was large enough to send the dog by train to Mrs. Kidder in California. A year later little Jip was bitten by a snake near San Jacinto and joined his master in death.

Much bitterness was felt by Americans along the border, and particularly by the Arizona Rangers, because of the circumstances of Kidder's death. The brutality of his treatment at the hands of the Mexicans they found inexcusable, and rumors that the entire affair was a deliberate plot to eliminate an enemy of the smugglers continued to circulate.

Ranger Fred Rankin was especially outspoken in his charges that Kidder had been led into a trap by the police at Naco who were in league with the smugglers. At the insistence of Captain Wheeler and others the Mexican federal authorities established a board of inquiry into the affair.

After a two-week investigation, sufficient evidence was unearthed to conclude that there was some basis for the charges, although not enough to warrant indictments against individuals. All twenty officers and line riders headquartered at Naco, Sonora, were summarily dismissed on April 24, and new officers appointed.

Billy Old was unmollified by this action. He and Jeff Kidder had been very close; Old had even named his son "William Kidder" in honor of his friend. Shortly thereafter he resigned his commission in the rangers and disappeared into old Mexico where he remained for almost two years. Many old-timers, including Tom Rynning, were convinced that Billy Old did not return until he had hunted down and killed each of the slayers of Jeff Kidder.

Notes

1 J. Evetts Haley, *Jeff Milton, A Good Man With a Gun*, p. 364.

2 William MacLeod Raine, *Famous Sheriffs and Western Outlaws*, p. 15.

3 *Bisbee Review*, July 6, 1904.

4 Joseph Miller, *The Arizona Rangers*, p. 76-77.

5 Haley, *Jeff Milton*, p. 364-65.

6 Captain Thomes H. Rynning., as told to Al Cohn and Joe Chisholm, *Gun Notches, The Life Story of a Cowboy Soldier*, p. 288.

7 "Was Victim of a Plot," undated newspaper clipping in the files of the Arizona Historical Society, Tucson.

8 Letter from W.A. Old to Mrs. Silas Kidder, quoted newspaper clipping in files of Arizona Historical Society, Tucson.

9 "Kidder Was Victim of Plot Says Rankin," undated newspaper clipping in files of Arizona Historical Society, Tucson.

10 Joe Pearce and Richard Summers, "Joe Pearce—Manhunter, Some

Adventures of an Arizona Ranger." *The Journal of Arizona History*, Autumn 1978. p. 250, 257.

11 Bill Kelly, "The Last of the Arizona Rangers." *Real West*, January 1977, p. 16.

12 *Dakota Republican*, April 23, 1908.

13 Rynning, *Gun Notches*, p. 288.

14 "Kidder Was Victim of Plot Says Rankin."

15 Ibid.

16 Miller, *Arizona Rangers*, p. 117.

17 Ibid, p. 127-131.

18 Quoted in Miller, *Arizona Rangers*, p. 139.

19 Dane Coolidge, *Fighting Men of the West*, p. 255-256.

20 Miller, *Arizona Rangers*, quoting unspecified copy of *Bisbee Review*, p. 191.

21 Ibid.

22 Ibid, p. 192.

Jack DeMattos

John Alan "Jack" DeMattos was born in Providence, Rhode Island, in 1944. After graduation from the Art Institute of Boston in 1966, he became a free-lance artist who attracted national attention for his caricatures, drawn from life, of noted show business personalities. Many of his more than four hundred caricatures appeared in publications like *Boston Magazine* and *The New Yorker*. His interest in the outlaw-lawman history of the Old West led him to research, write and publish over 100 articles on the subject. Between 1979 and 1985 he wrote and illustrated a critically-acclaimed series of fifty articles, "Gunfighters of the Real West," for *Real West* Magazine. For nine years he held the position of historical consultant for that magazine. His edited, annotated, and illustrated version of Bat Masterson's *Famous Gunfighters of the Western Frontier* was published in 1982. He has authored four other books, *Masterson and Roosevelt* (1984), *Garrett and Roosevelt* (1988), *The Earp Decision* (1989), and *Mysterious Gunfighter: The Story of Dave Mather* (1992). An early member of NOLA, Jack has served on its editorial advisory board. He is also an active member of Western Writers of America. Since 1965, he has made numerous local and national television appearances relating to both his show business and Western history pursuits. He and his wife Sandi live in North Attleboro, Massachusetts, and are the parents of two grown children.

THE DODGE CITIANS: CHARLES E. BASSETT

•

By Jack DeMattos

NOLA *Quarterly*, October-December 1995

Charles E. Bassett is best remembered today for having his photograph taken in a group portrait that contained seven other men. That photograph has become one of the most reproduced in all of outlaw/lawman history—since, in addition to Bassett, it also contains the much more glorified Luke Short, Bat Masterson, and Wyatt Earp.

The story of Charles E. Bassett began in New Bedford, Massachusetts—the same New Bedford that the fictional "Captain Ahab" set sail from to seek revenge upon the great white whale "Moby Dick." During the 1840s, whale oil lit the lamps of the world, and everyone who lived in New Bedford at that time was involved somehow in the whaling industry. Benjamin Bassett was no exception. He was employed as a "sailmaker" for the legendary whaling fleet.

On December 12, 1841, Benjamin Bassett married fifteen-year-old Julia H. Norton of Newport, Rhode Island. The marriage was a stormy one, but did result in four children. Benjamin and Julia would raise their family at a tiny house at 107 Smith Street in New Bedford. Their first child was born in 1844 and christened Sarah. Another daughter, Sophia, was born on June 6, 1846. On Saturday, October 30, 1847, Julia Norton Bassett gave birth to a son called

Charles E. Bassett. The last Bassett child was born almost two years later to the very day. That child was Benjamin F. Bassett, born on October 31, 1849. This constitutes the known list of Charles E. Bassett's siblings. Later accounts list a "Joe Bassett" as being a possible brother of Charles in Kansas City. "Joe Bassett" could have been a relative of some sort—but he certainly wasn't Charles E. Bassett's brother.

The troubled marriage of Benjamin and Julia Bassett came to an end in 1865, when Benjamin was last listed in the New Bedford city directory. It is not known if they ever actually divorced. By 1865, Benjamin Bassett and his seventeen-year-old son Charlie had both relocated to Philadelphia, Pennsylvania.

On February 14, 1865, Charles E. Bassett enlisted in the Union Army at Frankford, Pennsylvania (now a part of Philadelphia). He received a $100 bounty for signing on for one year as a private in Company 1 of the 213th Pennsylvania Infantry, a volunteer regiment. Charlie lied about his age, which he gave as eighteen. In fact, he was only three and one-half months past his seventeenth birthday. Apparently, Charlie was still growing—his enlistment papers stated that he was only 5'4". It has been recorded that during his years as a Dodge Citian, Charlie stood well over six feet tall—and his only known photo would seem to support this contention.

Charlie Bassett was mustered out of his volunteer regiment in Washington, D.C., on November 18, 1865. He served a little over nine months—not the year he had signed for. This was most likely the result of an Army cutback after Lee's surrender in April. Bassett's obituary says that he was mustered out at Fort Sill, Indian Territory. It is possible that Basset re-enlisted—but so far no documents have turned up to confirm this.

It has been alleged that Charles E. Bassett spent the period between late 1865 and early 1873 drifting around the West, serving various stints as a miner, cowboy, bartender, and buffalo hunter. He was most likely in the neighborhood of what would become Dodge City, Kansas, when his father, Benjamin Bassett died in Philadelphia on January 2, 1872.

Charlie Bassett became the real-life equivalent of Gunsmoke's "Miss Kitty" when he opened the original "Long Branch Saloon" in Dodge City in late 1872 in partnership with A.J. Peacock. Eventually, Bassett and Peacock sold the Long Branch. The saloon changed hands several times until Luke Short became one of the owners. Short's partnership in the Long Branch would cause one of the high points of Bassett's life in 1883.

On June 5, 1873, the citizens of Ford County, Kansas, chose Charles E. Bassett as their very first sheriff. His headquarters were in Dodge City. Bassett was re-elected twice, serving until 1878. Besides being the real-life "Miss Kitty," Bassett, more than any other law enforcement figure in Dodge, became the prototype of Gunsmoke's fictional "Matt Dillon." Bassett would serve as both county sheriff and later city marshal. He would perform deeds in these offices for which gunfighters such as Wyatt Earp would be given credit.

Back in New Bedford, Massachusetts, Charlie's mother, Julia Norton Bassett, married for a second time on June 26, 1874. The 48-year-old bride took as her husband John Cranston, a boat builder out of Tiverton, Rhode Island. What became of these people after this date is still not known.

On April 8, 1876, two suspected horse thieves were lynched near Dodge City by a "posse" from Sumner County, Kansas. On April 24, R.C. Callaham, the father of one of the men lynched, conferred with Kansas Governor Thomas A. Osborn and then went to Dodge City. He carried with him a letter addressed to Sheriff Bassett and the county attorney of Ford County. Governor Osborn's letter read, in part:

> There must be an end to mob violence in this state, and local officers exercising vigilance and energy in its suppression and punishment may rely on the Executive for support and assistance.[1]

On April 28, Sheriff Bassett wrote Governor Osborn reporting Callaham's findings and requesting financial aid for his investigation. Bassett's letter (with his spelling) concluded with the following:

> To be brief I am now of the opinion that the man was innocent of the crime alleged, and for which he has suffered death. Mr.Callaham wishes me to go to Sumner County and arrest the parties interested in the hanging, but without the assistance of the executive department I am totally unable to do anything, as I am in a poor fix financially to undertake so lengthy a journy [sic]. And as I have to deal with the

men who had themselfs [sic] disregarded the law, I will nessarily
[sic] have to take with me three men to assist in making those arrests.
This of course will be some slight expense to the state, without
which I am unable to operate.[2]

The governor's reply, written by his private secretary, stated that
"it is the duty of the local authorities to execute the law, and the
Governor hopes that the county board will provide the necessary
means."[3] Apparently, the murderers were never brought to justice.

On September 18, 1877, Sam Bass and his gang robbed a Union
Pacific train of $60,000 at Big Springs, Nebraska. The bandits were
reported in Kansas and Sheriff Bassett went out after them.
Bassett's posse included Bat Masterson and John Joshua Webb. The
group was unsuccessful in their pursuit of the train robbers.

On October 22, a jail break caused Sheriff Bassett some embar-
rassment. The local papers carried this "card" from the sheriff:

FIFTY DOLLARS REWARD—
BROKE JAIL.
The above reward will be paid for the apprehension of Geo. W.
Wilson, who broke jail at this place on the night of October 22d.
Wilson is 5 feet 11 inches tall, dark hair, blue eyes, good looking,
straight built, 22 years old, small mustache and goatee, has a scar
from a pistol shot in his back, wore dark clothes and a wide-rimmed
white hat.
Charles E. Bassett
Sheriff
Ford County, Kansas.[4]

By Kansas law, Charles E. Bassett could not seek a third succes-
sive term as sheriff of Ford County. On November 6, 1877, Bat
Masterson was elected as the second sheriff of Ford County. On
December 4, Bat's brother was appointed city marshal of Dodge
City. With Ed Masterson's appointment, there came an additional
law enforcement chore for Charlie Bassett, whose term as sheriff
wouldn't actually expire for another month. The local press noted
Bassett's added police chores with the following:

Sheriff Bassett has been appointed by Mayor [James H.] Kelley to
assist Marshal [Edward J.] Masterson in preserving order and deco-
rum in the city. Mr. Bassett has had thorough training and is a good
man for the place.[5]

"The Dodge City Peace Commission," June 7, 1883. This print was taken from an original copy. It has not been cropped or retouched, as have numerous other versions. Seated left to right are Charles E. Bassett, Wyatt Berry Stapp Earp, M.F. McLain (also called "Frank McLane" and "Frank McClain"), and Neil (or "Neal") Brown. Standing left to right are William H. Harris, Luke Lamar Short, William Barclay "Bat" Masterson, and William F. Petillon. *Courtesy Lee Silva.*

Bat Masterson was officially sworn in as sheriff on January 14, 1878. One of the new sheriff's first acts was to appoint Charlie Bassett as his under-sheriff. Actually, this amounted to job swapping, since Bat had been Bassett's under-sheriff. Such was politics in Dodge City during 1878.

On January 27. Dave Rudabaugh and four others attempted to hold up a train at Kinsley, Kansas. On February 1, a posse led by Sheriff Bat Masterson captured two of the robbers—Dave Rudabaugh and Edgar West. Charlie Bassett assisted his two boss-es. Sheriff Bat Masterson and Marshal Ed Masterson, in the capture of two more of the train robbers right in Dodge City. The two criminals were identified only as "Tom Gott, alias Dugan, and Green." Edgar West, Tom Gott, and "Green" were each sentenced to five years at Leavenworth. Since Dave Rudabaugh had turned state's evidence against his former cohorts, he was set free.

1878 was to be Dodge City's most colorful and tragic year. The first tragedy was the murder of Marshal Ed Masterson by two Texans named Jack Wagner and Alfred Walker on April 9. After Ed Masterson's funeral, the Dodge City Council appointed Charlie Bassett as city marshal at a salary of $100 a month. On May 12, Wyatt Earp was appointed as Bassett's assistant marshal at a salary of $75 a month.

On July 29, James "Spike" Kenedy (correct spelling), the son of the wealthy cattle baron Mifflin Kenedy (1818-1895), had an altercation with Mayor James H. "Dog" Kelley at Kelley's Alhambra Saloon. "Spike" Kenedy attempted to shoot Mayor Kelley but was stopped from doing so by Marshal Bassett. After paying his fine and court costs, "Spike" Kenedy took Marshal Bassett's advice and left town. Within three weeks, however, the young Texan would be back in Dodge and in trouble again.

According to the police docket for August 17, 1878, Kenedy was again brought into court by Marshal Bassett. This time it was on a charge of being disorderly. After paying his fine, Kenedy was told by Marshal Bassett to get out of Dodge City and stay out. But Spike Kenedy's hatred for Mayor Kelley had reached insane proportions. At four o'clock on the morning of October 4, Kenedy was back in Dodge and fired two shots through the front door of a small frame house usually occupied by Mayor Kelley. One of Kenedy's bullets killed a 34-year-old woman named Dora Hand. The *Dodge City Times* noted that;

> The pistol shot was intended for the male occupant of the bed...who had been absent for several days. The bed however was occupied by the female lodger at the time of the shooting....[6]

A nearly all-star posse left Dodge City at 2:00 on the afternoon of October 4. Its members were Marshal Charles E. Bassett, Assistant Marshal Wyatt Earp, Bill Tilghman, Sheriff Bat Masterson, and

Deputy Sheriff William Duffey. At 4:00 on the afternoon of October 5, this posse was at a ranch 35 miles from Dodge City when they spotted Kenedy approaching. The possemen turned loose a volley on Kenedy. Three shots slammed into Kenedy's horse, dropping him on the spot, while another shot, supposedly from a .50 caliber Sharp's, shattered Kenedy's left arm.

Three weeks after the killing of Dora Hand, Kenedy was released for a supposed lack of incriminating evidence. On December 15, 1878, an operation was performed that removed several inches of shattered bone from Kenedy's useless left arm. Spike Kenedy returned to Texas to manage his father's 390,000-acre LaParra Ranch. He died from typhoid fever during December 1884. The *Dodge City Times* was well-pleased with the efficiency of Ford County's police officers, reporting that:

> ...Sheriff Bat Masterson, Under Sheriff Bassett, and deputies [William] Duffey and [James P.] Masterson, have evidently earned the high praise accorded to them for their vigilance and prompt action in the arrest of offenders of the law.[7]

On April 5, 1879, Marshal Bassett witnessed one of Dodge City's most celebrated gunfights—the killing of Levi Richardson by "Cockeyed Frank" Loving. Later, Bassett gave this testimony:

> When I first heard the firing I was at Beatty & Kelley's saloon. Ran up to the Long Branch as fast as I could. Saw Frank Loving, Levi Richardson and [Deputy Sheriff William] Duffey. Richardson was dodging and running around the table. I got as far as the stove when the shooting had about ended. I caught Loving's pistol. Think there was two shots fired after I got into the room, am positive there was one. Loving fired that shot, to the best of my knowledge. Did not see Richardson fire any shot, and did not see him have a pistol. I examined the pistol which was shown me as the one Richardson had. It contained five empty shells. Richardson fell while I was there.[8]

City Marshal Bassett would again disarm the victor in another saloon altercation on September 8, 1879. Arista H. Webb murdered a certain Barney Martin by braining him with a rifle. According to the local press, Webb:

...walked to where Martin was seated, raised the rifle with both hands and brought the barrel of it down on Martin's head with terrific force. Martin fell like a log and was never conscious afterward.

Webb then jumped for his horse to make off. The murderous blow, however, had been seen by several persons, who ran to prevent the escape. Marshal Bassett seized him and took away his rifle, which was found to be loaded and cocked. He was first taken to the calaboose, but a crowd gathered quickly, among whom were some who favored lynching, the sheriff deemed it prudent to remove the prisoner to the county jail....[9]

On November 4, 1879, the Dodge City Council appointed James Masterson as city marshal, to replace Charlie Bassett, who had resigned. According to the local paper:

Ex-Sheriff Chas. E. Bassett, accompanied by Mysterious Dave [Mather] and two other prospectors, started out last week in search of "greener fields and pastures new." They went in a two-horse wagon, after the style in the days of '49.[10]

After unsuccessfully panning for gold in Colorado, Bassett and Mather drifted successively to New Mexico and Texas. Bassett and Mather were in San Antonio during the early part of 1881. Mather would remain in Texas for the next two years, but Bassett had grown homesick for Dodge City. His return to Dodge was noted by the *Ford County Globe*:

Charles E. Bassett, ex-sheriff of Ford County, and formerly city marshal of Dodge City—one of the old timers—arrived in the city last Tuesday after an absence of a year and a half. Charley looks as natural as life, wears good clothes, and says Texas is suffering from dry weather.[11]

Bassett didn't remain in Dodge for long. He moved on to Kansas City, Missouri, where he became manager of Webster & Hughes Marble Hall Saloon. The *Kansas City Journal* reported his arrival by noting:

Hon. C.E. Bassett, a well known cattle man of Kansas and Texas, returned to this city yesterday after a brief stay at Dodge City. He will remain here for some time.[12]

On April 28, 1883, the celebrated "Dodge City War" broke out between Luke Short and the authorities of Dodge City. Many fanciful tales have been woven about the cause of the trouble. The actual cause was the public's preference for the prostitutes employed in Short's Long Branch Saloon over those employed at the establishments of his rivals. Luke was run out of Dodge and headed straight for Kansas City where he looked up Charlie Bassett at the Marble Hall Saloon at 522 Main Street.

Bassett quickly proceeded to reestablish Short in Dodge City by enlisting the aid of some of the top gunfighting talent available. Quick to respond were Wyatt Earp and Bat Masterson. On May 31, 1883, Wyatt Earp arrived in Dodge City with several gunfighters. A very nervous Sheriff George Hinkle sent a telegram to the governor of Kansas, asking that the state militia be called out. The governor thought Sheriff Hinkle was over-reacting and ignored him.

Five days later, on June 5, Luke Short returned to Dodge with a heavily-armed Bat Masterson. Once again, Sheriff Hinkle sent off an urgent telegram to the governor calling for the militia. Once again, Hinkle's request was ignored. On June 7, Wyatt Earp, acting as spokesman for the Short faction, met with the authorities in Dodge City. An agreement was reached, and all was forgiven.

To maintain the shaky truce, the celebrated "Dodge City Peace Commission"[13] was formed. Its members were William H. Harris, Luke Short, William F. Petillon, M.F. McLain, Neil Brown, Wyatt Earp, Bat Masterson, and Charles E. Bassett. Before disbanding, the uninvited, self-appointed ' 'Peace Commission" gathered for a group photograph.

After the "Peace Commission" disbanded, Charlie Bassett returned to Kansas City. Bassett lived another thirteen years. How he spent those years is pretty much summed up in this obituary—much of which is inaccurate:

"SENATOR" BASSETT DEAD.
The Passing of a Frontier
Character Well Known Here.
A Quiet, Modest Man Who,

With "Bat" Masterson, Rid
Dodge City of Desperadoes
When It Was a Wild Cowboy
Town.

Charles E. Bassett, known to the sporting fraternity all over the
country, a prominent figure in the frontier days of Kansas, is dead.
News of his death at Hot Springs [Arkansas] Sunday [January 5,
1896] was received in this city today. Inflammatory rheumatism,
from which he had been a sufferer for several years, is supposed to
have been the immediate cause.

The life history of Charlie Bassett, or "Senator," as he was known
to his friends and acquaintances, is closely entwined with that of
"Bat" Masterson, Luke Short, W.H. Harris and other noted characters
who were before the public eye in the '70's. Bassett was born in New
Bedford, Mass., about 49 years ago. He came west after the war and,
after drifting about the mining camps and frontier towns for a time,
took up his abode in Dodge City, Kas.

The town was overrun with a lawless element. Desperadoes were
as numerous as flies in summer time and murders were of a nightly
occurrence. It was a wide open town with all that the name implies.
Peace loving citizens were alarmed at the condition of affairs.
Marshals who had attempted to quell the desperadoes had either been
killed or driven from town.

Finally, "Bat" Masterson was made marshal. He chose Bassett as
his right hand man and chief deputy. Bassett was of a peaceable disposition, but had nerves of steel, unquestioned courage and was a
dead shot.

Masterson and Bassett soon established a record as fearless and
desperate officials. Several of the desperadoes were killed and the
remainder were driven from the town. Afterward, in recognition of
his services, Bassett was made sheriff of the county.

About fifteen years ago, Bassett came to Kansas City as manager
of Webster & Hughes "Marble Hall" saloon on Main Street, between
Fifth street and Missouri avenue. Subsequently he opened the
"Senate" saloon on West Ninth street and there he obtained the sobri-
quet of "Senator." The venture was a failure and Bassett went to
work as bartender for Frank Jones and Hannon & Dixon.

A year ago he went to Europe with Emil Werk, the millionaire,
now of Cincinnati, but formerly of this city. On his return from
Europe, Bassett went to Hot Springs, Ark., in the hope that the water
would benefit his health.

It is said that like "Bat" Masterson, Bassett had several notches
on his revolver, each of whom stood for a human life. Concerning

this he never spoke, even to his most intimate friends, and he rarely referred to the exciting times when he was sheriff and deputy marshal in Dodge City.

While living in this city, he was a member of the gun clubs and took a prominent part in all sporting matters. When a mere boy, Bassett enlisted in the Union Army in Philadelphia. He served through the War of the Rebellion and was mustered out at Fort Sill, I.T.[14]

Today, Charles E. Bassett is all but forgotten. The fact is that he probably wouldn't interest us at all if he hadn't wandered into the studio of a Dodge City photographer, during June 1883, to have his photograph taken with two former deputies named Wyatt Earp and Bat Masterson.

Notes

1 "Governors' Correspondence," Archives Division, Kansas State Historical Society, Topeka.

2 Ibid.

3 Ibid.

4 *Dodge City Times*, October 27, 1877.

5 Ibid., December 15, 1877.

6 Ibid., October 8 1878.

7 Ibid., January 11, 1879.

8 Dodge City *Ford County Globe*, April 8, 1879.

9 Ibid., September 9, 1879.

10 Ibid., April 27, 1880.

11 Ibid., September 13, 1881.

12 *Kansas City Journal*, as reprinted in the *Dodge City Times*, September 22, 1881.

13 In recent years, historians have questioned whether that group of eight men was actually known as the "Dodge City Peace Commission" in 1883. Some have gone as far as to suggest that the term wasn't coined until more than a half century later. In fact the group was known by that designation in 1883. On July 21, 1882, *The National Police Gazette* contained a lengthy account of the "Dodge City War" which stated that "after some trouble the peace commissioners' as they have been termed, accomplished the object of their mission...."

This same account from *The National Police Gazette* described each of the eight "Peace commissioners." The editors gave this description of Bassett:

"Charles Bassett was the first sheriff of Ford County, with his headquarters at Dodge City, being twice elected to that office, and succeeded by Bat Masterson. In those days men always went armed, but he astonished the natives by taking post at the court house door when the district court was in session and disarming all persons desiring to enter. Of the small party that attended court he gathered no less than forty-two six-shooters and only killed one man."

Here is the earliest known reference to Charles E. Bassett having killed a man. The newspaper files and court documents during Bassett's terms as sheriff of Ford County are far from complete. If Bassett did indeed kill someone, the extant documentation does not disclose that person's identity.

14 *Kansas City Star*, January 7, 1896. Typical of so many involved in the history of the wild west, Bassett's obituary is an annotator's delight. The obvious errors here are that Bat Masterson never served as "marshal" of Dodge City with Bassett as his "chief deputy." Certainly Bassett was not made sheriff of Ford County "in recognition of his services" as Bat's "chief deputy." Bassett started out as sheriff of Ford County—long before Bat appeared on the scene. The article goes on to claim that Bassett had "several notches on his revolver." As stated in note 13, there is no documentation showing that Charles E. Bassett killed even one victim—let alone "several" as his obituary implies. This doesn't mean he didn't. It just means that, at this time, we simply don't know.

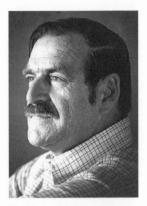

Richard H. Dillon

Born in Sausalito, California, in 1924, Richard H. Dillon began his advanced education at the University of California at Berkeley, but World War II intervened. Wounded by a German mortar shell, he spent three months in a French hospital before being sent home. Returning to college, he earned degrees with honors in history and library science. He headed the Sutro Library at San Francisco from 1953 until his retirement in 1979. He has taught history during summer sessions at UCLA and the Universities of San Francisco and Hawaii. The author of dozens of books, he has received many awards, including a second place Phelan award for his first book, *Embarcadero*, published in 1959; a Gold Medal from the Commonwealth Club of California for *Meriwether Lewis* (1965); a Silver Medal from the same organization for *Fool's Gold* (1967); and the Spur Award from the Western Writers of America for *Burnt Out Fires* (1973). He has received awards of merit from the California Historical Society, the American Association for State and Local History, and the San Francisco Historical Society for his notable research and writing, and has been honored with the Laura Bride Powers award for distinguished service to San Francisco and the Oscar Lewis Book Club Award. A member of the Western History Association, the Book Club of California, the Society of California Pioneers, and Phi Beta Kappa, he is listed in Who's Who in America. He is currently working on two new books.

THE HANGTOWN APPRENTICESHIP OF A WELLS FARGO DETECTIVE: JAMES B. "JIM" HUME

By Richard H. Dillon
NOLA *Quarterly*, Autumn 1978

W hatever claims are made to the contrary, the gent who was really responsible for putting Black Bart where he belonged—in San Quentin Prison—was James B. Hume. Not Sheriff Ben Thorn of Calaveras County, California, Tom Cunningham of San Joaquin County, or Hume's assistant, ex-Sheriff Harry Morse of Alameda County. Wells Fargo's Hume was also the first lawman on the Pacific Coast to depend more on his head, his brains, than on his gun in order to solve crimes. It was with his career, indeed, that scientific detection finally became part of law enforcement in the Far West.

What was Jim Hume's background? How did he prepare himself for such a brilliant, but demanding, career as that which he enjoyed as Wells Fargo's Chief of Detectives?

As a matter of fact, Hume literally drifted into the field of law and order simply because the mines of the Sierra Nevada did not pan out for him. And he joined Wells Fargo because he was "fired" (actually, not re-elected) as sheriff of El Dorado County, California. But these bare facts hardly suggest the whole story of Hume's apprenticeship.

Men and women, in NOLA or not, who are seriously examining the subject of western crime have more than the absurd High Noon

quick-draw hobbyists to worry about. They must deal with both academicians and popular historians at whose careless hands the topic
has long suffered. The former, perhaps hoping to exploit America's
faddish guilt complexes, blame half the world's ills on a supposed
Yankee preference for violence in resolving problems. This, they
claim, came to full flower in the nineteenth century West. (Actually,
of course, violence was more typical of Irish and other ghettoes of
New York during the period.)

Popularizers who write about lawmen and evil doers often encrust
their history with dramatic bunk, and make their characters into
larger-than life super-badmen and knights in shiny buckskin. They
join the professors in a wary, uneasy alliance in order to insist
together that it is hard to tell the good guys from the bad guys on
the old frontier. This, of course, is sometimes true. Henry Plummer
of Montana leaps to mind like a gazelle. But the sheriff of
Beaverhead County was the exception, not the rule, as was the case
of the little-known Californian, Under-Sheriff Thomas Bell Poole,
whose path crossed Hume's. Certainly, "It takes a thief..." is no scientific maxim. Hume, though he was no paragon, and although he
indulged in what today would be called "dirty tricks" in order to
snare his suspects, does not fit the false generalization of the breast-
beating academicians and their curious allies, the Greenwich Village
idiots who write and direct the unconsciously semi-spaghetti westerns of TV and movies.

It is not necessary to harp upon the classic Black Bart case, nor to
fake Jim Hume's career in any way. It would be dishonest to make
his apprenticeship more interesting by making it more violent,
bloody and exciting than it was. Actually, the details of his early
career were rarely dramatic, but they were essential to his ultimate
success as a peace officer. They were a kind of unmilitary basic
training for his role in western life.

It is unlikely that Hume ever killed a man. He wounded only a few
of his opponents. He himself was wounded but once. Killings, even
shootings in general, were not all that common even in such rough
Mother Lode mining camps as Placerville, or Hangtown, where
Hume served his apprenticeship.

Where to start? James B. Hume was born in 1827 on a farm in
Delaware County, New York, southwest of Albany. He came to
California from Indiana in 1850. At that date, he did not dream of a

career in law enforcement. Black Bart declared war on the Establishment, from a boulder near Copperopolis, on July 26, 1875. That is much too late a date to choose as the beginning of the gradual process which took place. Perhaps New Year's Day, 1855, is as good a date as any.

As the new year began, Hume was a frustrated gold miner at Grizzly Flat, a beautiful area where the Mother Lode's Northern Mines touch the pines of the Sierra proper, some thirty miles east of Placerville. With the winter weather too fine, even by California standards, and thus unproductive of water to wash the gravel, Hume was beginning to have second thoughts about his career as a miner. A dry spring and summer followed. Then came a cold and dry winter, with the freeze-up further inhibiting placer mining. So it was that Jim Hume began to have contact with the county seat, Placerville, where his brother was an attorney involved in local politics.

Unfortunately, Jim was drawn to the American Party in local, state and national politics during the heyday of Nativism in California. It was a bigoted outfit, called the Know Nothing Party because of the secrecy of its xenophobic members. It was anti-everything, but chiefly anti-Catholic and, thus, anti-Irish. But the Whigs were decadent, the Republicans just a'borning, and the pro-slavery Southerners ran a corrupt Democratic Party. As gamblers used to say, when explaining why they would sit in at a crooked poker table, the American Party was "the only game in town." Hume's brief contact with the small city, as a delegate to the nominating convention of a (thank heavens) short-lived party, may have been a major turning point in his career. By 1855, the Gold Rush was over, though it would not be pronounced dead until the panic of 1857.

Hume really began some soul-searching at this time. He considered himself, at the ripe old age of 30, to be a perennial prospector and a confirmed bachelor. He only *dreamed* of change, though he spoke of going to Sonora, Mexico, for gold. Later, he talked of following the crowds (1859) to the Comstock when Nevada silver was discovered. He even thought of abandoning California, which he loved, to go home to Indiana, which he did not like. But it was all talk. Hume sunk in a rut of his own making. His will was paralyzed. He continued his unsuccessful career as a gold miner for years after his comrades gave it up as a bad deal. Jim might well be called "The

Last of the Argonauts." For him, hope seemed to spring eternal, though he wrote a friend, "The Prince of Ill Luck seems to have followed me unceasingly....In my operations this summer, I have not made a dollar."

Late in 1859 or early in 1860, gold miner Hume began to "moonlight" to keep himself in beans, bacon and coffee. He served as a deputy under Sheriff E.B. Carson of El Dorado County. Far from tracking down horse thieves or shooting it out with murderers, the ex-Indianan found himself to be quasi-tax collector, covering the eastern and southern parts of the county. But he liked the job, probably because it promised him three "squares" a day.

On March 4, 1860, after almost ten years of hopeful but fruitless prospecting, Jim Hume abandoned gold mining, forever. He figuratively threw away his pick and pan, though he did not, as yet, pin on a star and buckle up a Colt pistol. He was appointed deputy tax collector. His chores were not all pleasant—collecting taxes from the poor, chasing tax dodgers for their delinquent payments. But none was worse than the badgering of the county's aliens, particularly the Chinese, for the hated and unfair Foreign Miner's License Tax.

Like the growth of the Know Nothing Party itself, the anti-foreigners' law is a part of the underside of California history, of which native sons are not proud. But it was symptomatic of hard times looming on the horizon. It was also an early example of an American weakness, an unfortunate character trait. This was a willingness to blame personal misfortunes on scapegoats—and the more exotic the better. The Sonorans or Mexicans, the *Chilenos* (Chileans), the Chinese, and even the few French miners were natural targets.

Certainly, collecting the odious Foreign Miner's License fee was no way in which to start a great career as a lawman. The original punitive law of 1850 had been repealed and the tax dropped from twenty dollars a month to just four dollars by the time Hume had to collect it. But it was still discriminatory, though the State Supreme Court said no, it was just a fee, not a tax.

It would be pleasant to think that Hume privately protested the law as a disgrace. But he did not. This is expecting too much of him. He was a man of his times. He was required to carry out laws, not to interpret them, or to seek their removal. And, of course, like all the other lawmen, he got a 15 percent commission on all taxes collected. And he had to eat.

Hume kept his tax collecting job in 1862 when he received an appointment which was more to his liking, that of city marshal and chief of police of Placerville.

How in the world would Hollywood handle Jim's first role as lawman? Along with the preservation of law and order went other duties. He was street commissioner. He was, yes, dog catcher. Worse, he was in charge of ridding the streets of the carcasses of dead animals.

The *Daily News* liked to josh him, poking fun at his canine funeral processions up Center Street. And the editor warned readers who owned live animals to beware of Hume: "You had better tag your dog!"

However, the paper was genuinely fond of Jim Hume, and applauded the city council for appointing such a conscientious man to a position of so many and so varied duties. "Order begins to reign in Warsaw," cried the editor, poetically. "The streets are being thoroughly cleaned, nuisances are slinking out of sight, and crime is lowering its flag." The reference to clean streets was literal as well as figurative or metaphorical. James B. Hume, as street commissioner, had all the a gutters in town cleaned, that summer of 1862. He then repaired all broken sections of the board sidewalks on Main and Sacramento Streets, and he graveled the length of Main Street from the Plaza to Stony Point.

Small wonder that the local papers cheered Hume. "The streets and sidewalks are beginning to look 'niff (i.e., nifty). Our city, under the administration of our able, efficient, and energetic Marshal, James B. Hume, presents a fine appearance. Order and cleanliness is manifest everywhere. Main Street, with its new coat of gravel laid down with care and precision, will soon be the finest street in the county."

Jim was easily reelected city marshal in April of 1863, with 466 votes to his opponent's 185. He seemed settled down again, safely in a new rut, this time that of a low-level municipal administrator. The county sheriff handled the big cases—robbery and homicide, leaving Jim cases of drunkenness, indecent exposure, the illegal blocking of Hangtown Creek, or a minor Chinese riot. Hume was saved from boredom by an occasional interesting case: a horse rustling, a tunneling robbery, a Mexican *bandido* waving a wicked knife. Nevertheless, he must have eagerly accepted the appointment

of under-sheriff of El Dorado County which was offered him on
March 4, 1864. But was the *Mountain Democrat* prescient when it
cheered him as a clever gentleman who would make a good officer, or
was it just being polite to a diligent, but rather plodding, city official?

Hume's first real case was no triumph in his own mind, though the
newspapers praised him for faithful and fearless discharge of duty.
In May of 1864, he led the pursuit of the three-man McCollum
Gang of robbers which had escaped from the Marysville jail. The
trio fled to El Dorado County, where Hume found Scotch Tom,
abandoned by his pals at the head of Irish Creek because he was
sick. Hume arrested him and then overtook the other bandits near
Fiddletown. So far, so good.

But in the shooting which followed, Hume's little posse got the
worst of it. Forty rounds were fired; he thought that he had hit Ike
McCollum, but it was impossible to see the outlaws. They were only
sixty yards away, but were in thick manzanita brush—and night was
falling. Hume had only two men with him and when Constable John
Van Eaton was shot in the side, and Deputy Joseph Staples' horse
was wounded, Hume could not stop the outlaws from escaping in
the darkness. He tried to pick up their trail in the morning, but was
unsuccessful. The best that he could do was to put Van Eaton in a
settler's cabin, then return to town with his one prisoner and ask
Sheriff William H. Rogers to send a doctor to treat the wounded
officer. And while the *Mountain Democrat* and *Sacramento Union*
praised him, the under-sheriff swore to do better next time.

By the end of June 1864, he had a crack at one of the most bizarre
cases of robbery in the history of the West. Still, his streak of bad
luck continued. He was out of town, in Stockton on sheriff's office
business, when the Bullion Bend robbery took place. He also
missed the subsequent gun battle and sadly learned that Deputy Joe
Staples, who had fought beside him against the McCollum Gang,
had been shot dead.

As Hume reconstructed the story, two Placerville-bound stages
from Lake Tahoe had been stopped on a narrow curve high above
the South Fork of the American River, near today's Pollock Pines.
The leader of the masked road agents, who was addressed as
"Captain" by the others, assured the frightened travelers, "We are
not robbers, but a company of Confederate soldiers. We don't want
anything of the passengers. All we want is Wells Fargo's treasure, to

assist us to recruit for the Confederate Army." And when he was done, the self-styled Confederate officer gave one of the drivers a receipt for the bullion, signed "Captain R. Henry Ingrim, Confederate States Army."

Sheriff Rogers led a posse in pursuit of the bandits. He split his party and, unluckily, it was the smaller unit of three men that picked up the trail. Van Eaton, still hurting from his wound, was sent back for reinforcements while Deputy Sheriff Joseph Staples and Constable George Ranney overtook the badmen at Somerset House, a roadhouse at a junction on the route to Hume's old stomping ground of Grizzly Flat.

Ranney was willing to wait for help, but Staples wanted to take on the whole gang, alone. He was foolhardy. But his pride had been stung when his courage was questioned by saloon bums in Hangtown after his horse was shot by McCollum. The deputy had publicly declared, "Next time I go, I'll be brought back dead, or I'll bring back my man!"

So it was that Staples pushed his way into a roomful of outlaws, brandishing his shotgun and shouting, "You are my prisoners! Surrender!" Instead, the six or seven men inside fired. The deputy's buckshot charge caught one badman in the face, but Staples was soon down, and dying. Ranney made a run for the cover of the chaparral, but he did not make it to safety. He was shot in the back and, hemorrhaging, he surrendered. Only the intercession of the lady innkeeper saved him from murder, execution style, by the angry Rebels.

When Hume finally arrived on the scene, the trail was cold. But he began an exhausting pursuit. He finally gave up, seven days later, when the outlaws abandoned their horses and split up, on foot. Once again the under-sheriff was hailed for his zeal and tenacity. Once more, he cursed himself for failing to overtake his quarry. But the *California Police Gazette* called Hume's chase through El Dorado, Amador, Calaveras, and San Joaquin Counties' roughest terrain, with little food or rest, the most untiring pursuit in California history.

Hume was skillful at grilling prisoners and he soon had all the real names of the bandits from the wounded fellow. The "Captain," he learned, was no Ingrim but was Thomas Bell Poole, ex-undersheriff of Monterey County! Taking great pains, Hume tracked the robbers to Fresno and Tulare County secret way stations on a sort of Copperhead or Confederate underground railroad. Finally, on August 1, with loyal Van Eaton by his side and a handful of bench warrants, he raided a hideout in San Jose and nabbed ten Confederate sympathizers, including most of the Bullion Bend gang. But not the "Captain"; the under-sheriff-turned-Rebel had vanished, and he never surfaced again.

There was enough variety in Jim's job to keep it from becoming humdrum even without a Bullion Bend case. He continued to patrol and protect the vital Carson Road, with its rich shipments of silver bullion from Nevada's Comstock Lode. He became a notary public. He served on the board which chose a fire chief and assistants for Placerville. And he helped Rogers conduct sheriff's sale of property. More interesting was the 1865 case which had its denouement at Railroad House in Clarksville, where two cattle rustlers were holed up. Hume shot one and bagged them both.

Jim Hume ran for sheriff in 1865 but lost. Surprisingly, he won the race at the polls for chief engineer of the fire department. But, to everyone's surprise, his victorious opponent, Sheriff Maurice G. Griffith, appointed him under-sheriff, rival or not, because he was so efficient and zealous in his duties.

In 1867, Hume added to his growing reputation by putting an end to a rash of robberies on the Carson Road. Learning that the three men responsible for the crimes were on their leisurely way east, he galloped ahead of them via a shortcut and, with a few men, set up an ambush. His choice of site was perfect, for Echo Creek Bridge, just south of Lake Tahoe, was the one bottleneck of their escape route.

As the three horsemen approached at twilight of August 2, 1867, Hume hollered for them to halt and surrender. Halt they did, but not to surrender; just to take aim with their rifles. The leader, Hugh De Tell, shot Hume in one arm. The under-sheriff and his men returned the fire. When the smoke of the black powder drifted off into the pine trees, one bandit, Faust, lay dead. Another, Sinclair, surrendered to Hume. But De Tell made his escape in the gathering darkness. Hume bandaged up his arm and began the chase. It was his luck not to be in on the gang leader's actual capture. He had to split his party at a fork in the road and it was his men who got the drop on De Tell and took him prisoner.

The *Mountain Democrat* of Placerville, and other papers, sang Hume's praises anew. (Doubtless, Wells Fargo officers in 'Frisco were not deaf.) "The masterly manner in which the affair was conducted throughout reflects the greatest credit upon our under-sheriff, and we mean it as no empty praise when we say that in this, as in his official acts in general, he has exhibited in high degree those qualities that are requisite in a first-rate executive officer of the department to which be belongs. We congratulate him and his fellow-citizens of El Dorado at the good fortune that spared his life."

Hume's next major case involved his arrest of some Indians for the murder of a miner. He was then reappointed under-sheriff when Griffith again took office in March of 1868. The next year saw him crushing a cowardly gang which was pillaging Chinese in the Sierra foothills with impunity, because the courts refused to accept Chinese testimony. Since he could not use the Chinese victims as witnesses, Jim decided to let the gang members convict themselves. He studied them, picked up several, and let the weakling of the lot cool off for quite a spell, in solitary confinement. He was pleased to hear him "sing," shortly, like a meadowlark. This technique might be *tabu* today, as also his trick of planting a false story in the press in order to trap another crook. But it worked. And for the first time in years the Mother Lode Orientals could breathe easily. (Ironically, Hume's next big arrest was that of some Chinese who killed a storekeeper during a burglary.)

Jim Hume was finally elected sheriff of El Dorado County, apparently in a special election. But he did not spend all of his time presiding over the jail—which he called The Gridiron Hotel—as his predecessors in office had been tempted to do. For lack of an insane asylum in the county, he had to lodge a madman there— raving and violent until he died. Perhaps because of the madman's presence there Hume was happiest when in the field, usually on arson or murder cases. His record was becoming very impressive, so he confidently expected to be reelected in the fall vote of 1871. To his surprise, for he never understood the shifting wind of politics, he was crushed in the Republican landslide victory. The local editor also blamed the Democrats, whom Hume had joined after the war when they lost their Rebel taint: "Personal spite and soreheaded disaffection in our own ranks have defeated one of the best and most, deserving officers this, or any other, county has ever had in its service."

The lameduck lawman did not sulk. Instead he set out after the robber of a Wells Fargo strongbox on the Georgetown-Auburn stage. Again, he used his brains—yes, trickery—to trap the culprit. Hume spread the word that there were no clues; that he was giving up the case as hopeless. Secretly, he sent descriptions of the stolen treasure to thirty Wells Fargo agents. Sure enough, three months later, a gold buyer in Michigan Bluff alerted him and he got his man, E.G. "Kentucky" Watkins.

The papers again praised him to the skies, though his last day as a sheriff was coming up, March 4, 1872. But Hume was not in mourning. Already, Wells Fargo had offered him its post of Chief of Detectives. This he accepted, after being given leave to clean up the Nevada State Penitentiary in Carson City.

The *Mountain Democrat*, in bidding him goodbye, cited the Kentucky Watkins case as typical of his thoroughness and skill: "From the Sheriff's Office we lose one of the best officers that the Coast has produced....If any further proof was needed of Hume's detective ability, which is statewide, the working up of this case would furnish it. Had he listened to the urgent appeal of others and arrested parties on suspicion, the chances are that neither the gold dust nor the man who committed the robbery would ever be discovered. The whole credit of ferreting out this affair belongs to Hume."

Jim Hume's seeming bad luck, his defeat for reelection, actually proved to be a lucky break for him. And for Wells Fargo. Increased opportunity nurtured his native ability and he became a brilliant detective, ranging over many states of the West. But part of his expertise came out of that decade-long apprenticeship in the sheriff's office of El Dorado County, riding herd on murderers, stray dogs, and madmen.

Harold L. Edwards

Harold Edwards was born in 1927 in Hanford, California, and attended public schools in Visalia. Immediately upon graduation from high school in 1945 he enlisted in the U.S. Navy. After two years of service he began his academic career, first at the College of the Sequoias in Visalia, and then at Fresno State College, where he received a BA degree. After college he took employment as a deputy probation officer for Tulare County and later as a parole officer for the state of California. After ten years as the district chief of paroles in Bakersfield, he ended his career as a staff officer to the chief of paroles in Sacramento. Always interested in Old West history, he joined NOLA in 1984 on the recommendation of the late Philip J. Rasch, and began research and writing. Since then he has published two books, *The Killing of Jim McKinney*, and *Goodbye Billy the Kid*, and more than 135 articles, including two dozen in the NOLA Quarterly. In 1997 he was the recipient of NOLA's literary award for his contribution to our knowledge of Western outlaw and lawman history. He has served on NOLA's board of directors and as president. Married to his wife Eula for more than fifty years, he has a son and daughter and one granddaughter.

TRIBUTE TO FRANK S. WHEELER: ARIZONA RANGER
•
By Harold L. Edwards

NOLA *Quarterly*, January-March 1995

During June of 1903, the Arizona Rangers were dispatched to Morenci in Graham County to quell a labor disturbance, which was caused by disputes between striking miners and officials of the mining syndicates. While there, twenty-five rangers, including Captain Thomas Rynning, proudly posed for two group pictures, which, today, are familiar to western history enthusiasts, famous to the public and often published. Ranger Frank Subat Wheeler is in both pictures, which visually cements him into Arizona's law enforcement history and, into the traditions of the Arizona Rangers, that post-frontier body of exceptional lawmen.

The Arizona Rangers was a select company of mounted constabulary created in 1901 by the territorial legislature to cope with the mounting crime problems in Arizona, particularly in Graham, Cochise, and Pima Counties in the southeastern corner of the territory. They were territorial troops, organized along military lines although not uniformed. They had broad peace officer powers, which extended beyond county lines. They operated much like the famed Texas Rangers, and, indeed, many of the Arizona Rangers were former Texas Rangers. Frank S. Wheeler enlisted in the Arizona Rangers on September 10, 1902, and he served continuously from that date until the rangers were disbanded on February 15,

1909. Only one ranger served longer than Wheeler, James T. Holmes, and his service exceeded Wheeler's by only eight days. Early in his ranger career, Wheeler was promoted to sergeant, but on his next enlistment he reverted to private. Since he was an outstanding officer, it appeared that he was more comfortable doing the day-to-day work rather than being in charge. Most of his ranger service was in and about Yuma, where he was regarded as a "fine officer and a first-rate man."

It was common on the frontier and even in the later transition period for law enforcement agencies to hire professional gunmen to police unruly elements. However, Frank Wheeler was not a "professional gun hand," but he wouldn't hesitate to shoot when he felt it necessary. This was the case on June 30, 1907, when he was in a gunfight with horse thieves at a lonely water hole in Arizona's southwestern desert.

On June 26, 1907, Wheeler received a command from Captain Harry Wheeler (no relative) to locate and apprehend two horse thieves who were operating west of Ajo. Their names were James Kerrick and Lee Bentley, and some weeks before, they had advised acquaintances in Tucson and Gila Bend that they were going prospecting in the region between Gila Bend and the Mexican border. They rented several horses from Indians in Maricopa County for the trip. However, within a short time after they left Gila Bend, ranchers in the proposed prospecting area began complaining of losing horses, and they claimed that Lee Bentley and James Kerrick were the thieves.

Wheeler met John Cameron at or near Wellton, a stop on the Southern Pacific railroad line northeast of Yuma. Cameron had two Papago Indian guides, mounts and provisions. Cameron was a rancher local to the search area, and he was also a Pima County deputy sheriff, even though the contemporary press variously listed him as a Gila Bend constable, Maricopa County deputy sheriff, Yuma County deputy sheriff and Arizona Ranger. Cameron advised Wheeler that he was surprised to learn that they were looking for Bentley and Kerrick. Cameron knew both men, Kerrick for ten years. In fact, both men had stopped by his ranch earlier with the horses, but at that moment Cameron had no reason to suspect that they were wanted for theft. Wheeler and Cameron rode into the desert with their Indian trackers.

Frank Subat Wheeler, 1905. *Harold
L. Edwards Collection.*

The posse crossed and recrossed the region south of Gila Bend to
the Mexican border, riding an estimated 140 miles in five days. The
trip was exceptionally grueling on horses and men; the June heat
was so severe in the daytime that the men couldn't drink the water
in their canteens because it was so hot. The posse finally located the
outlaws about midnight on June 30, 1907, west of Ajo at a water
seep known as Sheep Dung Tanks.

By the light of a pale moon, and from embers of the campfire, the
officers, after creeping up to the camp in their stocking feet so as
not to alert the outlaws to their presence, observed one man, later
identified as Lee Bentley, sleeping by the fire. The other man was
sleeping about one hundred yards up a draw. The Indian guides
watched from higher ground, and when it became light enough for
good vision, Wheeler shouted for the sleeping men to surrender to
the law. While Wheeler called on the men once more to surrender,
Bentley and Kerrick reached for their rifles.

As Bentley, by now kneeling on one knee, raised his rifle to shoot at the officers, Wheeler snapped a quick shot at him with his rifle. Wheeler missed his shot, and Bentley fired at him. Bentley also missed, and by this time both officers were shooting at Bentley. Although hit several times, Bentley remained upright and still tried to shoot Wheeler. Wheeler's fifth shot struck Bentley in the head, killing him instantly. In the meantime, Kerrick entered the fight by shooting at Cameron. Cameron killed Kerrick with one well-placed shot through the body.

The dead outlaws were lashed across their saddles and their horses were led, along with the recovered stolen stock, to Tom Childs' ranch at Ten Miles Wells, some 22 miles from where Bentley and Kerrick were killed. Childs dispatched a man on horseback to Ajo, where the Ajo Copper Mining Company transported him by automobile to Gila Bend. From that town, the messenger telephoned Pima County Sheriff Nabor Pacheco of the events and waited. Sheriff Pacheco entrained for Gila Bend, and from there the Ajo Copper Mining Company's automobile transported him to the Childs' ranch, where Wheeler, Cameron, and the dead outlaws awaited him.

There would be no immediate coroner's inquest as Sheriff Pacheco could not interest the coroners of Yuma, Maricopa and Pima Counties in the killings. They happened in an area that appeared vague, and the officials each felt that they had no jurisdiction in the matter, even though Sheriff Pacheco, Wheeler and Cameron all felt that the shootings occurred in Pima County. Sheriff Pacheco brought ice with him in hopes of preserving the remains until an inquest could be held, but on his arrival it was apparent that the desert heat had taken its toll, and he ordered the bodies buried immediately. Wheeler built two boxes from rough lumber, and Bentley and Kerrick were buried in them. Since there was no coroner's inquest, Wheeler surrendered himself to Sheriff Pacheco to stand trial in the matter, but Sheriff Pacheco felt that arrests for the shootings were not in order. Wheeler returned to his home in Yuma with another assignment completed for the Territory of Arizona.

The shootings of Bentley and Kerrick made headline news in southern Arizona. The press stated that Bentley was about 26 years of age and "in the prime of his life" when he was killed. Bentley, although suspected for some time of stock-stealing, seems to have had no prior criminal history. It was reported that James Kerrick was long-suspected of cattle and horse theft, and that he once served a two-year term in the Arizona Territorial Prison at Yuma for stock theft. If this report was true, Kerrick served the sentence under another name as "Kerrick" doesn't appear on the inmate register. The press also reported that Kerrick was an ex-convict from California, having served a term in San Quentin prison for murder. In this case, the press was correct.

In 1876 or 1877, Kerrick shot and killed sheepman Michael Maher in his camp, which was located in an obscure canyon between the middle and south forks of the Tule River in the Sierra Nevadas east of Porterville in Tulare County. At the same time, he probably shot and killed Michael Maher's brother and partner in the sheep business, James Maher. James disappeared, and his body was never found. However, Kerrick appeared with the Maher sheep and a bill of sale from the Maher brothers to him for the sheep. It was a forgery, and Kerrick was arrested, stood trial, and was convicted of the charge. He was sentenced to San Quentin prison for ten years.

In 1878, a man stumbled onto the Maher camp and found the skeletal remains of one man. There were some spent cartridges in camp, and a newspaper on the body had a bullet hole through it. The remains were identified as those of Michael Maher, and Kerrick was the suspected murderer. Kerrick was brought back to Visalia to stand trial for murder in the Tulare County Superior Court. He was convicted of the charge and sentenced to life in San Quentin prison. He arrived there on October 8, 1878, and entered the prison as inmate #8474. On May 8,1884, he was transferred to Folsom prison and entered the institution as prisoner #819. At the time Kerrick entered San Quentin, he was 27 years of age and was noted to have been born in Arkansas. His parents were born in Tennessee. Kerrick was a model prisoner, and on February 17, 1888, his sentence was commuted to twenty-five years, and he was released from prison to later reappear in Arizona.

The press also speculated about the outlaws' true intentions in the desert. Bentley and Kerrick had a number of excellent saddle horses with them when they were killed, and they seemed to be in no hurry to get out of Arizona with them. It was thought that they intended to rob the bullion stagecoach that plied between the King of Arizona Mine near Ajo to the town of Sentinal on the Southern Pacific railroad between Yuma and Phoenix. Contributing to this view was that the outlaws were well-armed and had no prospecting tools with them when they died.

W.L. Bentley, a brother to the dead outlaw, questioned the shootings and said that the officers shot his brother and Kerrick without provocation and without giving them a chance to surrender. He also claimed that Bentley and Kerrick were not horse thieves; that they had rented their horses from the Indians at the rate of $1.00 per day for their prospecting trip into the desert. W.L. Bentley pressed Pima County District Attorney Benton Dick for a coroner's inquest or at least an investigation into the matter. When asked by the press for his views, Bentley responded: "I am not stating as a positive fact that the killing was not justified, but there is reasonable doubt, and it would be the most satisfactory thing to all parties concerned if an investigation or coroner's inquest be held."

District Attorney Dick agreed with Bentley, and he prevailed on Silver Bell Justice of the Peace John Doan to hold an inquest. Finally, on August 18, 1907, the inquest was held.

Wheeler, Cameron, Sheriff Pacheco, and the Indian trackers testified. It was determined by the coroner's jury that Lee Bentley and James Kerrick were justifiably wanted by the law for horse theft. They had rented the horses from the Indians, but they had not returned the mounts on the contract date as promised, and they had not paid the Indians for the service. The jury further found that the officers were justified in the killings, that they were in pursuance of their duties when the killings occurred, and, further, they were shooting to preserve their own lives. The matter was settled, and Wheeler returned to Yuma to continue his official duties and his personal life.

The Arizona Rangers prohibited its members from holding multiple law enforcement commissions because of the possibilities of conflicting interests. However, it was a common practice in those days for one officer to hold several commissions in order to give him the right to make arrests under several jurisdictions or serve processes from several levels of courts. Usually, he was salaried for his main job, but he was paid fees for the other work.

This was expeditious in the sparsely populated areas of the West. In Wheeler's case, an exception could have been made as the 1905-1906 and 1907-1908 Arizona Business Directories for Yuma list him as a deputy sheriff and a deputy U.S. marshal in addition to being an Arizona Ranger.

After the Arizona Rangers disbanded in 1909, Wheeler became a full-time Yuma County deputy sheriff. He also worked as a guard at the territorial prison, and he was a night watchman for the Bureau of Reclamation's Laguna Dam project headquarters near Yuma. Wheeler's law enforcement career looked bright, and his family's future appeared secure; however, on December 18, 1909, an unfortunate incident occurred which ended his career as a lawman.

Wheeler and his wife allowed two girls named Phillips to reside in a tent in their yard while they attended school. The girls also kept a piano in the Wheeler home. It is presumed this arrangement was made to allow the girls to attend school in town as their parents resided out of town. In any event, the arrangement became unsatisfactory, and Wheeler asked the Phillips family to move the girls. The girls' father, M.T. Phillips, arrived at the Wheeler home with his brother-in-law, Frank Butts, to remove the piano from Wheeler's home. Butts was a large man and had a reputation as a hard drinker and a "roisterer." Harsh words passed between Wheeler and Phillips and Butts. Suddenly, blows were struck between Wheeler and Phillips. It isn't known who struck first, but Phillips took the drubbing. Butts jumped into the fray to assist his brother-in-law, and this time Wheeler was trounced. Phillips and Butts filed an assault charge against Wheeler, who was arrested.

After his arrest, Wheeler posted bail and was immediately released. Upon leaving the courthouse, he said to friends that Butts called Mrs. Wheeler a "liar." No man of Wheeler's background and vintage could accept that without calling for an accounting. Apparently, the matter was still unsettled, and to keep officialdom out of it, Wheeler immediately resigned his commission as a deputy sheriff.

That evening, Wheeler went into the Barrelhouse Saloon. The place was busy and crowded as a construction contractor was paying his employees in the saloon's backroom. Unobtrusively, Wheeler walked along behind the men drinking at the bar. One witness said that Wheeler kicked Butts; another stated that Butts kicked Wheeler as he passed. In any event, witnesses were clear that Wheeler, facing Butts, said: "You can't talk to me that way." Butts struck or lunged at Wheeler.

During the ensuing scuffle, Wheeler drew his revolver and shot Butts in the body. After the shooting, Wheeler immediately walked to the office of the local justice of the peace and surrendered for trial. Butts was given first aid by a physician and placed on the next train for Phoenix, where he underwent surgery for his wound. Butts recovered from the shooting, and, interestingly, Wheeler was not arrested nor charged with a law violation although he was placed under a peace bond. Perhaps no one pressed for a charge. Was Butts armed at the time of the shooting? The reports at the time do not say. Had Butts previously threatened Wheeler's life? Members of Wheeler's family believe that he did and that Wheeler confronted him on the matter. In the end, Wheeler pleaded guilty to the original charge of assault, paid a fine, and was released.

After the Butts shooting, Wheeler continued residing in Yuma as a respected citizen but no longer an officer of the law. By 1910 he was employed by the federal government as a "fireman" at the Laguna Dam project. He also farmed cotton, and, in general, did well. However, by 1914, he suffered severely from bronchial asthma, and his doctor suggested that he move to a coastal climate in California. Wheeler and his family moved by horse-drawn wagon to Lomita, southwest of Los Angeles where his father-in-law and his family owned property and resided. While living in Lomita, Wheeler was employed as a teamster and helped construct streets in Los Angeles. However, his health failed to improve, and his physician directed him to move to the San Joaquin Valley in central California.

Following his doctor's advice, the Wheeler family moved to Selma in Fresno County. While there, Wheeler worked on the near-by farms. Within a short time, Wheeler moved his family some fifty miles southeast to the farming village of Poplar near Porterville in Tulare County. Again, Wheeler was employed on the nearby farms while his children attended the district schools. Finally, in 1929 or 1930, his encroaching disease forced him into retirement and he moved to a home near downtown Porterville.

Today, we tend to think of those old-time peace officers and out-laws almost totally in the context of their activities, and we equally tend to overlook or even discount their personal lives and accom-plishments. Frank Wheeler was born of traditional southern stock in Hazelhurst, Mississippi. His father, Erastus B. Wheeler, was born in Alabama in 1840, and his mother, Elizabeth, in Mississippi in 1842. After leaving Alabama, Erastus Wheeler settled in Copiah County, Mississippi, where he was caught by the arrival of the Civil War.

During that epic conflict, Erastus Wheeler saw Confederate service as a private soldier in Company K, 3rd Mississippi Infantry Regiment. Returning from the war, Erastus Wheeler married and established a farm. By 1870, he and his wife had children, Cora A. and Robert. Frank was born later that year or in 1871. By 1880, the Wheeler family had migrated to Texas and settled in Vernon in Wilbarger County, where Frank learned the ways of the cattle range. Sometime around 1900 he moved to Arizona, where he joined the Arizona Rangers.

In 1905, Frank Wheeler married Lenora Rieff in Yuma. In time, ten children were born to the union: Winifred, Luanna Elizabeth, Ethelene Belle, John Cameron, Lenora Adrin, Connie Ray, Frankie Josephine, Lincoln Albert, James and Irma Lee. John Cameron was obviously named for Wheeler's fellow peace officer and companion in the shooting scrape at Sheep Dung Tanks years before.

Mrs. Ethelene Belle Overcash, of Porterville, California, recalls her father as a large and imposing man, about 6'3" in height, physically active when his health permitted, and an expert horseman. She stated that he was a quiet man who didn't talk much and was serious minded. He didn't laugh easily, but would laugh outright when his humor was touched. A reserved man, he was meticulously honest and respectful of others. Mrs. Overcash stated that in temperament her mother was the opposite. She enjoyed laughter and fun, and she wanted others to have a good time, too. The Wheeler home was a happy one, and Mrs. Overcash emphasized that she is proud to be Frank Wheeler's daughter.

In the end, Frank Wheeler's asthma worsened, and he developed a heart condition. He died of heart failure on December 20, 1932, in Porterville, and he was interred in the Plano, now Vandalia, cemetery.

His plain but dignified granite grave marker simply states: "FRANK WHEELER 1871-1932." It doesn't tell us that Frank Wheeler was a product of the old south and of the southwestern frontier; that he was a great peace officer who survived those turbulent days to live and die a respectable citizen in a modern and peaceable time. Frank Wheeler was challenged, and he met the test.

He deserves his place in Arizona history.

Sources

Mrs. Ethelene Belle Overcash, Frank Wheeler's daughter; interviewed by author at her home in Porterville, California, on August 25, 1994.

Mr. George Overcash, Frank Wheeler's son-in-law; interviewed in Porterville, California, by the author on April 9, 1994, and August 25, 1994.

Letter dated April 9, 1994, from Frank Wheeler's son, Lincoln A. Wheeler, to his sister with family information.

Porterville Cemetery District; Porterville, California. Grave records: Vandalia Cemetery; Wheeler, Frank S. Lot 96, Block 5, Grave 8-east.

Death Records: Wheeler, Frank S. Book-1932, page 742. Tulare County Recorder's Office: Visalia, California.

Porterville *Evening Record*: December 20, 1932, Death notice for Frank S. Wheeler.

National Archives, Washington, D.C. Civil War Confederate Records. Service of soldiers: Wheeler, Erastus B., Private and Sergeant, Company K, 3rd Mississippi Infantry Regiment.

U.S. Census Reports: 1870, Copiah County, Mississippi. Post Office, Hazelhurst; Townships 9 & 10 east of the railroad. Dwelling #567; Family #534: Erastus Wheeler family.

U.S. Census Reports: 1910, Yuma County, Territory of Arizona. Yuma City; Sheet #2. Dwelling #28; Family #47. Wheeler, Frank S. family.

Yuma Public Library, Yuma, Arizona. Betsy Gottsponer, Reference Librarian. Letters to author in May and September of 1994, with ranger and family information on Frank S. Wheeler.

Yuma Public Library, Yuma, Arizona, Alice D. Holmes: Independent researcher. Included: Yuma Great Register, 1910: Yuma *Daily Sun*, Yuma, Arizona; September 18, 1909, December 24, 1909, and April 7, 1910.

The Arizona *Sentinal*, Yuma, Arizona, December 23, 1 909.

Yuma *Daily Examiner*, Yuma, Arizona, April 4, 1910.

Arizona Business Directory, Yuma, Arizona.1905-1908.

The Arizona Rangers. Edited by Joseph Miller, Hastings House Publishers, New York, New York, 1972.

The Weekly Delta, Visalia, California, September 24, October 4, 11, 1878: Maher murders.

California State Archives, Sacramento, California. Prison Records: San Quentin and Folsom; Kerrick, James; Prisoner, San Quentin #8474, Folsom #819.

U.S. Census Reports, 1880 Marin County, California. San Quentin Prison; Page 52, Kerrick, J. J. Laborer, born in Arkansas, parents born in Tennessee, age 27 years.

Ball, Larry: *Desert Lawmen: Sheriffs of Arizona and New Mexico.* University of New Mexico Press, Albuquerque, New Mexico. 1992.

O'Neal, Bill: *The Arizona Rangers.* Eakin Press, Austin, Texas. 1987.

Donna Ernst

A native of Massachusetts, Donna Ernst was born in 1946 and attended two colleges in Boston. In 1967 she married Paul Ernst and in the course of researching the family genealogy discovered that her husband was the great-nephew of Harry Longabaugh, the Sundance Kid, and that the famous outlaw had been born not far from the Ernst home in Pennsylvania. This led to an extensive study, beginning in 1976, of outlawry in the Wild West in general and the Sundance Kid and the Wild Bunch in particular, which in turn took the Ernsts on an odyssey to the Western haunts of the notorious turn-of-the-century outlaw gang. Donna has published her findings in over thirty articles and two books, *Sundance, My Uncle* (1993), and *From Cowboy to Outlaw, The True Story of Will Carver* (1996). Two more books are in the process of publication. A member of several local historical societies, Western Writers of America, and NOLA, she also currently serves on the board and edits the Newsletter for the Western Outlaw and Lawman History Association. She continues her research and is a frequent speaker at local engagements and historical conventions, while remaining active as a realtor and bookkeeper for her husband's real estate company. Donna and Paul Ernst are the parents of three grown daughters and currently reside in Ocean City, New Jersey.

BLACKENED GOLD
&
THE WILD BUNCH
•
By Donna B. Ernst
NOLA *Quarterly*, January-March 1994

M ost outlaw history buffs know the story of the Wild Bunch bank robbery in Winnemucca, Nevada, on September 19, 1900. Harry Alonzo Longabaugh, alias the Sundance Kid, Bill Carver, and Harvey Logan, alias Kid Curry, made camp on the George D. Bliss C S Ranch, fourteen miles east of Winnemucca, on September 9, 1900.[1]

Using this campsite as a base, Sundance, Carver, and Logan checked the area for escape routes, watched the bank activity, and became familiar with the town in general. Each day they talked with youngsters in town and on the ranch, gaining much useful information for their planned robbery.

Because they had not made any efforts to hide their presence at the ranch, the local posse members had no trouble finding the campsite after the robbery. In a search of the area for clues, three letters were found, torn into small pieces. These were pieced together and glued, and copies of all three letters were sent to law officials and agencies tracking the Wild Bunch.

The first letter was written on August 24, 1900, to "My dear Sir." It carried the name and address of Douglas A. Preston, a Wyoming attorney who had befriended Butch Cassidy. The only sentence read, "Several influential parties are becoming interested and the chances of a sale are getting favorable." The second letter had no heading, but the handwriting matched that of the first letter and was signed "P." It said, "Send me at once a map of the country and describe as near as you can the place where you found that black stuff so I can go to it. Tell me how you want it handled—you don't know its value. If I can get hold of it first, I can fix a good many things favorable. Say nothing to any one about it."

The final letter was dated September 1, 1900, and was written to C.E. Rowe of Golconda, Nevada. It read, "Dear Friend: Yours at hand this evening. We are glad to know you are getting along well. In regard to sale enclosed letters will explain everything. I am so glad that everything is favorable. We have left Baggs so write us at Encampment, Wyo. Hoping to hear from you soon I am as ever, Your Friend, Mike." These letters were interpreted by some as evidence of an inside embezzling job at the bank with the robbery as a very useful cover-up.[2] Head Cashier George S. Nixon of the Winnemucca bank bore the brunt of these accusations, but nothing was ever proven.

A recent search, however, through Sheriff Frank P. Hadsell's private papers casts a different light on the meaning of the letters. Hadsell was a respected sheriff and United States marshal, working out of Wyoming. In fact, he was one of the posse leaders who had chased some of the Wild Bunch after the Tipton train robbery. Much of his correspondence is between fellow law officers and is currently held in the Wyoming State Archives in Cheyenne, Wyoming.[3]

On November 26, 1900, attorney Homer Merrill of Rawlins, Wyoming, wrote to Hadsell about an informant's story. Jim Rankin, the informant, reportedly told Merrill, "The Winnemucca outfit were in a few days ago with powder-burned currency, which they attempted or did exchange for gold."[4] Since no dynamite was used at Winnemucca, this powder-burned currency must have been from another of the Wild Bunch holdups.

Then on December 3, 1900, Frank Murray of the Pinkerton's Denver office wrote Hadsell, giving him agency information about the Winnemucca robbery. Murray said the letter signed "Mike" had been identified as being written by a woman, further identified as Mrs. Mike Dunbar. He also said Dunbar was a contact person for Butch Cassidy and the Wild Bunch, and was being watched by the Pinkertons.[5]

Union Pacific posse, Tipton, Wyoming, August 1900. *Wyoming State Archives.*

Murray further claimed that the robber known as Alonzo was a man also known around Rawlins as "Swede."[6] He stated, "About six weeks ago Swede came into Rawlins with a lot of gold coin that seemed to be blackened or burned considerably. He knew Ryan and tried to have Ryan exchange the gold for him."[7] According to Murray, Ryan had said that over $1500 worth of the blackened gold had been exchanged by local gamblers and a rancher from the Dixon, Wyoming, area. Sundance had previously worked for two ranchers from that area, the Frank Kelsey Ranch and freight business and the Beeler Ranch.[8] Butch was also known to have frequented the area often.

Jack Ryan was a known contact of Sundance's, which therefore made his statements that much more believable to the authorities. After the Tipton train robbery, Pinkerton interviews found that Ryan had told Bob Cruzan that "Harry Alonzo says he cannot be at that place."[9] This had given the Pinkertons cause to suggest that Ryan "should be arrested as accessory before and after the fact" based upon his statement.[10] Ryan's statement had also cleared Sundance of blame in the Tipton robbery.

In a letter to Sheriff Hadsell and dated December 29, 1900,

Pinkerton Agent Murray said, "Jack Ryan told me that the man who had the money at Rawlins was Swede...and he might also be the third man in the Winnemucca robbery."[11] An unsigned, handwritten note in Hadsell's files reads, "Chas. Crouse is at the head...and handled the bad money." Was the bad money more blackened gold?

Considering the letters from Winnemucca in light of the information found in Hadsell's papers, an embezzlement at Winnemucca seems to be unlikely. A better interpretation of the letters might be connected to the Wilcox train robbery on June 2, 1899. Because the first letter from Preston was dated on August 24, 1900, the Tipton robbery would have been eliminated since it had not yet occurred. The next previous robbery was Wilcox, when a great deal of dynamite was used. The force of the explosion was so strong that the express car was blown to pieces and even the safe was shattered.[13] A dynamite explosion of this proportion would easily have blackened both the currency and the gold. And Sundance had participated in both the Wilcox and Winnemucca robberies. Thus, he would have had access to the blackened gold.

Sundance, Alonzo, and Swede all seem to be the same person. Was he also the C.E. Rowe who received the letters? He at least had them at the campsite outside Winnemucca. A quick "sale" of some previously hidden "black stuff" would have given Sundance and Butch more money to finance their planned trip to Argentina. Finally, both Rawlins and Dixon, where Swede exchanged the blackened gold, were very near Baggs and Encampment—the area where Mrs. Mike Dunbar wrote one of the letters, and where Sundance was known to have once worked.

It would make another interesting story if we could ever discover what had happened to the blackened gold after it was laundered. If someone has access to lawyer Douglas A. Preston's private papers, maybe more light can be shed on this mystery since he had written two of the letters. And certainly after all these years, it would appear that we owe George S. Nixon, head cashier at the Winnemucca bank, an apology for the many embezzlement accusations suggested over the years.

Notes

1 Ernst, Donna B. *Sundance, My Uncle*, The Early West, 1992, p. 130.

2 Pinkerton Detective Agency Files, undated; Hadsell, Frank P. Papers,

#H70-18/107-125.

3 Hadsell, Frank F. Private Papers, in Wyoming State Archives, Cheyenne, Wyoming.

4 Hadsell, Frank P. Private Papers, #H70- 18/107- 125, letter dated November 26, 1900.

5 Hadsell, Frank P. Private Papers, #H70-18/107-125, letter dated December 3, 1900.

6 Hadsell, Frank P. Private ID; Papers, #H70- 18/107- 125, letters dated December 3, 1900, and December 29, 1900.

7 Hadsell, Frank P. Private Papers, #H70- 18/107- 125, letter dated December 3, 1900.

8 Ernst, Donna B. *WOLA Journal*, Vol. I, No. 3, Spring, 1992, p. 17.

9 Ernst, Donna B. *Sundance, My Uncle*, op. cit., 126-127.

10 Ibid.

11 Hadsell, Frank P. Private Papers, #H70-18/107-125, letter dated December 29, 1900.

12 Hadsell, Frank P. Private Papers, #H83-62/28, undated and unsigned notes.

13 Ernst, Donna B. *Sundance, My Uncle*, op. cit., 110.

Gary Fitterer

Gary Fitterer was born in Dickenson, North Dakota, in 1946. At the age of four he moved with his parents to the state of Washington, where he lived, first in Yakima, and later in Kirkland, near Seattle. After graduation from high school in 1964 he was drafted and served two years in the United States Army, one of them in Vietnam. Following his military service he attended the Burnley School of Professional Art in Seattle for a year and a half, but left school in 1977 to take work with a circuit board manufacturing firm. He spent fifteen years on his family genealogy, experience which was of great help when he began researching the events and characters of the frontier West, a subject which had fascinated him since he was a boy. He has written a number of articles on Western gunfighters for the NOLA *Quarterly* and popular non-fiction Western magazines. He co-authored *Captain C.B. McKinney, The Law in South Texas*, with Chuck Parsons. For many years Gary has delved deeply into the life and times of Texas gunfighter Alfred Y. Allee, a study which has resulted in a lengthy biography nearing completion. He has also done extensive research for a planned double biography of the Thompson brothers, Ben and Billy. Other interests include hiking and backpacking in the Cascade Mountains of Washington, writing science fiction, and, as he says, "watching good action movies in a theatre on a big, wide screen." He is the father of two sons, Jesse, 20, and Noah, 16.

LET JUSTICE BE DONE
OUR WESTERN CITIZENS
•
By Gary P. Fitterer
NOLA *Quarterly*, July-September 1992

O n the last day of May, 1876, the *San Antonio Daily Express* ran the following front-page story: "Fight on Comanche Creek. Cattle Thieves Pursue, Attack, and Play Havoc with Peaceable Men. Special to the Express."

> Eagle Pass, May 30, 1876.
> A bloody fight occurred on Comanche Creek, about twenty-five miles below here yesterday morning at ten o'clock. Alejo Gonzales, of Rio Grande City, with three others, were killed, and five persons wounded. Gonzales was pursued by cattle thieves, who made the attack upon his party. The authorities of Maverick [County] will visit the scene, and care for the dead and wounded.

Another San Antonio paper, the *Herald*, told the story a bit differently, stating that Gonzales and "eight hands followed about thirty cattle thieves and found them to be white men." The gun battle that took place, it said, lasted from about nine o'clock in the morning until four o'clock that afternoon, resulting in the killing of Gonzales and four of his men. Also, "five white men...were seen to fall from their horses during the fight."[1] Similar accounts appeared in the dailies of other large cities of Texas. The *Galveston News*, for instance, reported the death of Gonzales and half of his men and claimed victory for the thieves, even though an equal number of

113

them, five, had also been killed.[2] Clearly, each report distorted the tale a little bit more.

What these and other reports failed to mention, however, was the fact that the central figure involved in this incident, which became known as the "Comanche Cattle Fight," was the notorious John King Fisher. As it turned out, he and a number of fellow ranchers were the alleged "cattle thieves," and they were the ones who pursued and attacked the "peaceable men" led by Alejo Gonzales, supposedly killing and wounding several of them. However, these were not the facts.

As in many other frontier incidents, the truth of the matter was not contemporarily reported and remained unknown at the time. Later recitals only succeeded in distorting the truth and confusing it with other incidents. A good example of this is an account of the fight that was told eight years later by Major Trevanion T. Teel, one of King Fisher's attorneys. He recalled that Gonzales had followed a trail of stolen cattle, tracking them to Fisher's pasture. King had ninety head of cattle on hand, for which he had bills of sale, but he had reportedly purchased them from Mexican cattle thieves. Gonzales and his men rounded up these animals and a number of King's as well and headed them back to Mexico. Teel related how King, with several men, immediately went in pursuit and quickly overtook Gonzales. During the ensuing gun battle, King single-handedly killed three men and wounded several others.[3]

Teel's account appeared at the time of King Fisher's death. It is a version that has been repeated many times since and is essentially accurate, but Teel exaggerated King's role in the fight. The embellishment tended to fit the image the public of that time had of King Fisher, one that pictured him as a fearless and relentless mankiller. King had become a legend during his own lifetime, through tales of his exploits spread by word of mouth and by stories published by the contemporary press. Not surprisingly, upon his death, the legend continued to grow.

The dispatch to the *San Antonio Express* reporting the fight on Comanche Creek contained several errors, some of which were corrected by the paper a few days later. It informed its readers that Alejo Gonzales had not been killed as reported, but was still alive after having been shot three times. Furthermore, only one of his men had actually been killed, although three others had been

John King Fisher (left) and John H. Culp. from an old tintype, circa 1873. *Western History Collections, University of Oklahoma.*

wounded.[4] Still missing, however, was any mention of King Fisher's involvement. That would not be until more than a year later.

Unlike some other incidents of that time, the Comanche Cattle Fight received little newspaper coverage. Violence was an all too frequent occurrence along the Texas-Mexico border and the news of the fight, lacking King's name, became just another episode that was quickly forgotten. In fact, it was almost immediately eclipsed by the sensational news of the capture of the chief of the border outlaws.

The arrest of King Fisher occurred less than a week after the fight and was carried out by Captain Leander H. McNelly and his company of Texas Rangers. A detailed account of the capture, which will not be repeated here, was later written by Napoleon A. Jennings, one of McNelly's men.[5] Recalling events over a span of twenty years, Jennings also related an incident which took place just before the arrest and which may have prompted McNelly to make the sudden raid on King's headquarters.

According to Jennings, King and a man known as Frank Porter, "by themselves, stole a herd of cattle from eight Mexican vaqueros who were driving the herd for its owner, near Eagle Pass. Fisher and Porter rode around the herd and killed every one of the eight Mexicans." Jennings further claimed that the dead men were all buried together at a place afterwards known as "Frank Porter's Graveyard."[6]

This story is clearly another exaggerated version of the Comanche Cattle Fight. Jennings places this incident "a few weeks before" the arrest of King Fisher. In truth, the actual fight took place on May 29 and King's arrest came five days later on June 3.[7] On that date, Captain McNelly and about twenty-five rangers swooped down on Fisher's headquarters ranch on Pendencia Creek in Dimmit County, catching King and nine other fugitives by surprise, and arresting them without a struggle.

Eagle Pass was King Fisher's favorite hangout. It was also the seat of Maverick County. Since Dimmit County was not yet organized, it was attached to Maverick for judicial purposes. For this reason McNelly carried his prisoners to the jail at Eagle Pass. From there, on June 4, 1876, he sent the following telegram to Adjutant General William Steele at Austin:

> Have arrested King Fisher and nine of his gang and turned them over to sheriff[.] Will camp at Fort Ewell and scout country between here and Oakville until otherwise instructed[.] Country in a most deplorable condition[.] All civil officers helpless[.]
> L H McNelly[8]

McNelly's telegram refers to ten men being arrested. However, both Jennings and a fellow McNelly ranger, George Durham, who were there, give only nine names in their respective published memoirs: King Fisher, Frank Porter, Bill Bruton, Wes Bruton, Al Roberts, Warren Allen, Bill Templeton, Will Wainwright, and Jim Honeycutt.[9]

Leaving his prisoners in the care of the county officials, McNelly and his men departed Eagle Pass to round up witnesses against them. But they had not gone far when the captain was outraged to learn that King Fisher had been set free almost immediately upon their departure. According to reports at the time, an armed body of men had ridden into town and demanded swift trials for all the prisoners. The local justice of the peace, being understandably intimidated, opened court and, because of the lack of witnesses, dismissed the charges against all of the prisoners except King. He too, however, was quickly freed after readily obtaining sureties for bonds totaling $5,500. McNelly, to say the least, was very angered over the whole proceeding. He considered the bonds given by King to be "not worth five dollars."[10]

The release of Fisher and his men created quite a furor. Subsequent news reports of the affair painted a dismal picture of the conditions in the country about Eagle Pass. One said: "It is supposed that Fisher and his men constitute part of a large band of desperate men who have infested the country west of San Antonio for some months." This same report stated that a number of citizens had telegraphed the governor, informing him that witnesses feared for their lives and were unwilling to testify against the outlaws.[11] Another report alleged that citizens were saying that "they have not suffered half the anguish from Indian and Mexican forays that Fisher has caused them." And furthermore: "The reign of lawlessness and terror is not confined to one county. It is spreading [and] Fisher's band is reinforced by cutthroats almost daily."[12]

As far as the contemporary press was concerned, there was nothing redeemable about the character of King Fisher. He was considered to be a total scoundrel, badly in need of eradication. These journals concerned themselves mainly with the notoriety of the man by recording his shooting scrapes, his alleged rustling and smuggling operations, his court battles, and so forth. But these stories provided only one aspect of this complex man's character. Are they really a fair appraisal? Maybe not.

At the time of the Comanche Cattle Fight, King Fisher was barely out of his teens, being only twenty-two years old. He had also just recently been married. According to one description of him, he stood an inch over six feet and weighed 185 pounds.[13] His wife, Sarah Vivian Fisher, has also left us a description. To her, with his black hair and dark eyes (she said he had one black and one brown), King was an unusually handsome man. He was fond of wearing the best white shirts and black broadcloth suits that money could buy. For his crown, he preferred the big white sombreros from south of the border, and for his feet, expensive black patent leather boots with fancy trimmings. His clothes buying was done on a regular basis at Piedras Negras, Mexico, located just across the Rio Grande from Eagle Pass.[14]

A native-born Texan, King was easily the most colorful character of his time inhabiting the border country. He became a leader of men while still in his teens when the opportunity to assert his independence and demonstrate his natural leadership abilities presented itself about 1871, at age seventeen. Four years earlier, in 1867, while he was still a youngster growing up at Goliad, Texas, a wagon train of Goliad County residents had gone west to Dimmit County. There they had stopped and settled in the wild and unpopulated area of the Pendencia Creek. Among these hardy pioneers were various members of the Vivian clan, including King's future wife. Their life on the Pendencia proved to be hard and dangerous, with frequent raids upon their lives and property by marauding Indians, Mexican bandits, and renegade whites. Since organized law enforcement was nonexistent then, the settlers were forced to rely upon themselves and their own resources; they had to enforce their own laws by whatever means was available to them.

One of their resources was the youth, John King Fisher. In 1867 he had been too young to accompany the settlers, but as he grew older, he became determined to leave Goliad to seek adventure on the far frontier. So, in 1871, when he received word from the Pendencia settlement that he would have a job waiting for him if he came out, King quickly headed west. When he arrived, the ranchers hired him to patrol their rangeland and protect their livestock from the frequent raids of bandits. King quickly proved to be a relentless and dangerous adversary of the raiders. His daring exploits of pursuing bandits into Mexico to recover stolen stock for his employers won for him the gratitude and praise of the early stockmen of Dimmit County. During this time, he matured into an expert horseman, an excellent pistol-shot, and an adept range detective. As he fine-tuned these talents, he often assumed leadership over men many years his senior during the performance of his duties.

Patrolling the range proved to be a good opportunity to round up stray, unbranded cattle and horses from the chaparral. At first, King sold these animals to stockmen who were putting together herds to be driven to market. However, being an ambitious young man who was looking forward to starting a place of his own and raising a family, he soon registered a brand (or brands) and located a ranch on the Pendencia.

This ranch subsequently became the headquarters for many men of questionable character. King was said to have been indifferent to who or what these men were, taking in all comers, feeding and sheltering them, and then putting them to work. Most of them were of a transitory nature, but out of their number gathered a core of friends who considered King their leader, and who became known as "King Fisher's gang." And the border country in which they lived and fought became known as "King Fisher's Territory." This territory reportedly comprised an area of more than five thousand square miles along the Rio Grande. Here, for several years during the 1870s, King Fisher ruled and his word was law.

While the newspaper and the authorities may have had a low opinion of him, King was generally well-known and liked by the small Anglo population inhabiting the border country, especially by those who knew him personally. Those who did not like him usually had reason to fear him.[15]

Numerous tales have been told, of King's shooting prowess and the number of his victims varies from one account to the next. After his capture by McNelly, the *Galveston News* commented that he "has killed nine men within less than a year."[16] The *San Antonio Express*, ten years after his death, observed retrospectively that "King Fisher was noted for having in one way or another killed twenty-three men, but his reputation was not so bad for the reason that most of his victims were Mexican outlaws."[17] In a similar vein, newspaperman Frank H. Bushick, in his book *Glamorous Days*, recalled that King and his men were credited with numerous killings, but added that they were "mostly of Mexicans."[18]

Mrs. Albert Maverick, Sr. had the experience of meeting King Fisher when he was twenty-seven years old. She had a very pleasant conversation with him about his family, not realizing at the time who he was or what kind of reputation he had. "To my inexperienced eye," she later wrote, "he was a very innocent looking cow boy, tall and thin and dark." Afterwards, however, she was shocked to learn that he was a notorious mankiller who claimed to have killed twenty-seven men, one for each year of his life.[19]

Another statement made about King was that he kept an accurate count of the men he killed. What is more, it was also said that he had a list of victims whom he planned to kill in the future.[20]

Just how many men King may have actually killed remains an open question, one that cannot now be answered with any certainty. Major Teel, following his client's demise, claimed that he had successfully defended King for seven killings.[21] However, it is very doubtful that the noted shootist was ever indicted for all of his homicides. King himself alluded to more than seven victims in a conversation with Judge A.W. Bonnet, whom he befriended when the latter was a boy growing up at Eagle Pass. During their chat, Bonnet asked King how many men he had killed.

"Seven," King answered.

"I thought it was more than that."

"Oh, I don't count Mexicans."[22]

King was often accused of stealing cattle in Mexico for disposal in the Texas cattle market. Frank Bushick, onetime editor of the *San Antonio Express* and a contemporary, excused King of this practice by pointing out that Mexican bandits had been driving off Texas cattle for years and Fisher and other stockmen "thought it was all right to play for even."[23]

Judge Bonnet also wrote defensively of King. In recalling some of the infamous exploits of the shootist that occurred in and around Eagle Pass, he said: "Please do not think from what I have said that King Fisher was a bad man, as men were here then. There were many like him, only worse...it took men like this to make the frontier fit for us to live in today."[24]

In 1884, Major Teel expressed his opinion that his late client was often misrepresented by the press. He maintained that King was a far cry from being the "dangerous and unscrupulous desperado he is represented [to be]." He said that, although Fisher's ranch had become the headquarters for all kinds of outlaws and renegades, King himself had not participated in their lawlessness. He pointed out that King was credited with being their leader only because of his association with them.[25]

Another friend of King's was the famous Texan, John R. Baylor.

He related to his son, George, that whenever anything happened in that country with no witnesses, people had the tendency to remark, "King Fisher must have done it."[26]

A case could be made against King Fisher for having little or no regard for his Hispanic neighbors, especially in light of statements made to the effect that most of his killings did not matter, or count, because the victims were Mexicans. While it is true that he had many enemies among these people, it is also evident that King had many good Hispanic friends on both sides of the border. One was Trinidad San Miguel, a highly respected citizen of Eagle Pass who held, among other prestigious jobs, the position of tax collector of Maverick County. An admirer of King, he was always quick to defend the Anglo gunman's name against any criticism. As far as he was concerned, King was a "*muy bueno hombre*" who always "meant well"[27]

General Porfirio Diaz, who was elected president of Mexico in 1877, was also a good friend of King's. For a time he lived in Piedras Negras, and on several occasions he invited King and his wife across the border to be guests at balls and receptions. King's enemies in Mexico had threatened to kill him if they ever caught him there, so, as a precaution, Diaz always sent a bodyguard to escort the Fishers to and from these social gatherings. The Hispanic leader showed his high regard to the Anglo gunman on one occasion by presenting King with a beautifully crafted pistol.[28]

King also carried Mexican vaqueros on his payroll. One of them, remembered only by the name of Pancho, was his most trusted and faithful employee. Pancho was often out with his boss for long, extended periods of time and, as a result, it was said that he knew King better than any other man who had occasion to ride the range with him.

Many of the different stories told of King Fisher shooting it out with Mexican bandits or vaqueros seem to be based upon a handful of actual incidents. His devoted vaquero, Pancho, was a witness to one of these unfortunate affrays. According to his story, as related to John Leakey many years later, King was forced to kill four vaqueros who were working for him branding some cattle that were to be sold off. The four men became dissatisfied over how the cattle were being divided up and, although King assured them that they would receive their full share out of the next bunch brought in, they made

plans to kill him. King, however, grew suspicious and as he helped
with the branding, kept a close watch on them. When they made
their move on him, he brained one with a branding iron and shot
and killed the other three. Pancho helped his boss dig graves and
bury the slain men. It was later said that King had killed eight men
that day, but Pancho, who had witnessed the fight, stated that the
rumor was false.[29]

The reports of King Fisher being involved in the killing of eight
Mexicans persist, as in the account of the ranger, N.A. Jennings,
which has been given. George Durham also recalled a similar tale,
stating that King may have killed eight Mexicans near Espantosa
Lake in Dimmit County after quarreling with them over the price of
a herd of "wet horses" they had just delivered to him.[30]

One incident, which also has a familiar ring to it, was reported
soon after its alleged occurrence in the *San Antonio Express* of
January 14, 1876:

> We had a short conversation yesterday with a stockman, just
> arrived from the vicinity of Brownsville. He says that we do not hear
> half the troubles Texans have on the river. He was near where King
> Fisher had his recent fight, and says that it was a terrible affair.
>
> King was riding a horse, which some Mexicans, who stopped
> him, claimed, and insisted that he should give up. After some words,
> one of the Mexicans rode up beside King, cut the girt of his saddle
> and pushed him off the horse, when the other two (there were three
> Mexicans in the party) drew their revolvers and dared King to budge.
> But his ire was aroused, and no threats from the bandits would avail
> anything; so he pulled his pistol and fired, shooting the man who cut
> the girt through the head, killing him instantly. He was then fired
> upon by the other two, and slightly wounded, but two further dis-
> charges from King's pistol sent these, too, to their "happy hunting
> grounds." He then re-saddled his horse and started home, having
> slain all his opposers, but was chased by another gang of six
> Mexicans for some distance, who shot at him with Winchesters, but
> without effect.

The trouble between King Fisher and Alejo Gonzales dates back
to a year earlier than the Comanche Cattle Fight, which occurred
soon, after the fight related above. On July 8, 1875, the *San Antonio
Herald* reported:

A man who calls himself King Fisher has been arrested on the
Salado, and placed in the [Bexar] County Jail, on the affidavit of
Alejo Gonzales, the arrest being made yesterday by Deputy Sheriff
[Tom] Dashiell for stealing cattle. The accused claimed a herd of cattle as his own which is made up of a great many different brands, and
has other indications that create the impression the owners of the cattle have not been consulted in the matter.

King got out of jail on a bond which he forfeited by not appearing
for his trial. This episode probably had a direct bearing upon the
events leading up to the fight on Comanche Creek eleven months
later. Since Gonzales had failed to find satisfaction in the courts of
Texas, he probably decided to take matters into his own hands,
should there be a next time.

Alejo Gonzales was an energetic young man who was well known
in San Antonio, where he had grown up. He was described by the
Herald as "a bold, fearless man [who has] plenty of the old Spanish
grit in him." At the time of his troubles with King Fisher, he was
operating a thriving mercantile business in Piedras Negras, as well
as running cattle.[31]

The details of the Comanche Cattle Fight were revealed on August
28, 1877, more than a year after its occurrence, when the *San
Antonio Daily Express* printed a lengthy article entitled, "Let Justice
Be Done Our Western Citizens." The subtitle declared that, "The
Mexicans, and not King Fisher, [were] the robbers in the
'Comanche Cattle Fight.'" Presented in the article was the testimony
of several of the participants in the fight, elicited at a habeas corpus
hearing that King had attended at Castroville. The following
account of the fight and the circumstances leading up to it, is reconstructed from this testimony.

In late May 1876, Frank Porter arrived at the ranch of Charley
Bruton with about 150 head of cattle to sell. How he had come into
possession of the cattle was not asked, but of significance was the
fact that a large number of the animals bore four or five different
Spanish brands (the remainder had American brands). He wanted to
sell them to Bruton, but the rancher put him off, saying he might
buy them the next day. When Porter returned the following day, he
found King Fisher at the ranch. Bruton witnessed the "trade" and

the cattle were then moved to a pen several miles from his house, where King proceeded to apply the "KP" brand, "right fresh peeling," over the old brands.

There was some mystery over who or what Frank Porter was, and whether or not he was a partner with King Fisher in the cattle business. Charles B. Bruton, who was well acquainted with both men, claimed he had no knowledge of where Porter lived, nor was he even sure that the man was a genuine stockman. And, although he was adamant that the two men were not partners, he maintained, nevertheless, that Porter "was with King right smart." Some of the other ranchers in the area were not of the same opinion. Charles H.F. Vivian, for one, believed that the two men were partners and that, together, they owned the "KP" brand. Or so he had heard. Bruton, on the other hand, claimed that only King owned that brand (and the "K" brand as well).

There was also some question over Porter's real name. Rangers Jennings and Durham both stated that he was actually one Burd Obenchain, from Kansas, who, under the name of Porter, had become the lieutenant of King Fisher's band of desperadoes. Before coming to Texas he had, according to Durham, fought with Quantrill's guerrillas and had ridden with the James boys.[32]

Bruton's ranch was located on Comanche Creek, about fifteen miles from the Rio Grande and some thirty-five miles east of Eagle Pass. It was also not far distant from King Fisher's ranch on the Pendencia, which stream flowed less than ten miles east of Comanche Creek. It was somewhere in the vicinity of the latter stream that King penned the cattle he had acquired from Porter.

About two days later, between three and four o'clock in the afternoon, a party of fourteen horsemen came riding up to Bruton's place from the south. The three men present, Charley Bruton, Franklin Claunch, and his son, George, saw that the riders were Mexican vaqueros, heavily armed with pistols and Winchesters.

The spokesman and apparent leader of the group was Alejo Gonzales. He informed Bruton that he and his companions were looking for about eighty head of cattle belonging to them, and asked the rancher if he knew of any cattle in the vicinity of his ranch. Bruton answered truthfully, telling him that King Fisher had a herd in a pen several miles away. Gonzales then grew indignant and snarled that he meant to have those cattle or he would "follow them to hell," whereupon he and his men wheeled their mounts and rode off in the direction of the cattle pen.

Bruton interpreted Gonzales' declaration as a threat against Fisher and immediately sent George Claunch on a ride to King's camp to warn him that an armed and dangerous party of Mexicans was on its way to take his cattle. Soon afterwards, King rode up to the house and Bruton joined him in pursuit of the invaders. The vaqueros, upon discovering that they were being followed, dismounted and drew their Winchesters, but King wisely chose to avoid such an uneven confrontation and circled around them. Bruton chose not to accompany him any further and must have returned home.

King was determined to stop Gonzales from running off his cattle. He rode on and managed quickly to gather a handful of men to help him. These men probably were Frank Porter, Nick Reynolds, and William C. Bruton. Since they were too few to make a fight against fourteen heavily-armed men, King told his men that they were going to scatter the cattle into the dense brush in an attempt to keep them from the vaqueros. With no time to spare, they rode directly to the cattle pen, arriving there before Gonzales had time to locate the spot. The cattle were then quickly driven from the pen and scattered through the chaparral. King realized, however, that this was merely a delaying tactic and would do little more than slow his adversaries down a bit, but he hoped that it would gain him some time.

King returned to the Bruton place at about nine o'clock that evening. From there, he sent word out to neighboring ranchers, calling for a general assemblage. The response was quick. Throughout the night, men arrived by twos and threes until a force equaling that of Gonzales' was present. A discussion was held about what should be done about cattle raiding in Texas by Mexicans, and, more specifically, what they should do about the armed party presently invading their rangeland. According to Ed Cavin, one of those present, King expressed his intention of riding out in the morning to hunt down his cattle and the thieves, kill the thieves, and recover any stolen cattle. After some discussion, this course of action was then agreed upon by all present.

In the meantime, Gonzales and his men had succeeded in rounding up a large number of cattle in the vicinity of the cattle pen. Fisher had turned out into the brush some 250-300 head, double the number he had acquired from Frank Porter. Of these animals, the

vaqueros managed to gather over 200 head into their possession—
quite a number more than the eighty stolen head mentioned by
Gonzales to Bruton.

By daybreak, May 29, 1876, about a dozen men were gathered at
the Bruton ranch. They included King Fisher, Frank Porter, Nick
Reynolds, William C. Bruton, John H. Culp, John Hudgins, J.E.
(Ed) Cavin, Bob Lewis, Dick Horn, and a man named Gildea. The
story in the *San Antonio Express* did not give Gildea's first name,
but almost certainly he must have been Augustine M. (Gus) Gildea,
who was well known in the area and had his photograph taken at
Eagle Pass that same year.[33]

Charley Bruton, on whose ranch they were assembled, was not a
member of the hunting party. King had tried to talk him into accompanying them, but Bruton had ridden out earlier that morning to go
out to his cattle camp, and was not present when the party left his
place.

It was a seven or eight mile ride from Bruton's house to the pen
where King had kept his cattle. The Texans caught up with
Gonzales and his companions only another five miles beyond that,
at about ten o'clock that morning They found the vaqueros scattered
around the cattle that had been seized, slowly driving them along
Comanche Creek towards the border. The vaqueros, however, as
soon as they saw the Texans coming, began to fall behind the herd
to meet the approaching threat.

At the same moment that the Texans first spotted the vaqueros,
their group happened to be split up. Several of them were falling
behind to catch a stray horse, while the remainder of them were
continuing to ride on. One of the latter, though, immediately called
out to the men behind, "Here they are, boys, come ahead."

Those in front then raced ahead and, when within a hundred yards
of the vaqueros, dismounted and drew their rifles. William C.
Bruton, who was the first to hit the ground, fired the opening shot.
Then, as the vaqueros were in the act of dismounting to draw their
weapons, the stockmen opened up on them with a thunderous fusil-
lade. Alejo Gonzales was hit three times and fell seriously wounded.
One of his companions fell dead, shot through the head by Nick
Reynolds. Three others, maybe more, were also hit, but in all the
excitement the Texans could not tell for sure.

Gonzales and his men never had much of a chance for an effective resistance. The immediate attack upon them by the Texans was devastating. It thoroughly demoralized them, and, as a result, their return fire was meager and ineffectual. Not one of their attackers was hit. With one companion killed outright, their leader and several others shot up, and with bullets whining all about them, the nerve of the vaqueros broke. They fled the scene in much confusion, some afoot, some on horseback, leaving behind the cattle and the body of their slain comrade. And King Fisher—having regained possession of his cattle—let them go.

By coincidence, the fight took place about fifty yards from Charley Bruton's cattle camp. Bruton was in his camp and he heard, but did not see, the battle take place. He later estimated that upwards of one hundred shots were fired during the brief encounter. About two hours later, he rode over to inspect the battlefield. He saw a hat lying in the dirt and recognized it as the one that Alejo Gonzales had worn. He also examined the body of the dead man, who, he noted, had been shot "through the head from ear to ear." And he observed King Fisher and Gildea nearby —"they were holding the cattle there rounding them up."

The foregoing narrative is based upon the court testimony of Charles B. Bruton, J.E. Cavin, Charles H. Vivian, and Franklin Claunch. As can be seen by it, King Fisher did not kill eight Mexicans single-handedly or otherwise. He did not even kill one man during the fight. This is a good example of how an actual incident can be blown way out of proportion and almost immediately colored to fit the alleged reputation of a legendary figure like Fisher. This reputation, however, was something that King did not want. and maybe, one that he did not deserve.

"Let Justice Be Done Our Western Citizens" was published in defense of the action taken by Fisher and his friends against the Gonzales party. It was submitted by a correspondent calling himself "Western Texas." He considered the stockmen justified in killing one man and wounding several others while recovering what they deemed to be stolen property, and quoted several articles from the Criminal Code of Texas to back up his reasoning. Article 2226, for one, declared that: "If homicide takes place in preventing a robbery it shall be justifiable if done while the robber is in the presence of the person robbed, or is flying with the money or other article taken by him." Western Texas went on to criticize the way in which Texas

law was being meted out, and concluded his correspondence by saying: "The facts in this case and the law arising upon them are published that the citizens of Western Texas may do justice to their own
people, and at the same time learn that the law, as administered, will
prohibit their preventing Mexicans from crossing to this country and
robbing them of their property; that they must either submit to being
robbed or be arrested. incarcerated and refused bail for asserting
their legal rights."

In fairness to Alejo Gonzales and his companions, there is no indication that they were actual thieves or in any way connected with
thieves. They seem to have been nothing more than ordinary citizens of Mexico, who, being angered and frustrated over the loss of
their cattle, had decided to cross into Texas and "play for even" by
taking them back by force of arms. They probably felt very justified
in running off any extra cattle that fell into their hands—as payment
for their troubles if for no other reason. And by this action, they did
nothing more, nor less, than what King Fisher himself was accustomed to doing

For the killing of the unnamed vaquero who had ridden with
Gonzales, King Fisher was indicted and tried for murder. This was
only one of a number of murder cases involving King. However, he
was never convicted on any of the murder indictments returned
against him, nor for any of the numerous other charges made against
him. He was always either acquitted or his cases were dismissed for
reasons of insufficient evidence. His final murder trial occurred in
April, 1881, when he was tried at Uvalde for the murders of two
Mexican employees of Alexander Zimmerman. He was found not
guilty in both cases, and in July he made his last appearances in
court to answer six charges against him for horse theft. In three of
these cases, he won acquittals, and the remaining three were dismissed.[34]

With a clean slate at last, King Fisher was determined to remain a
respectable citizen. In November, 1882, J.B. Boatright was elected
sheriff of Uvalde County, and King was sworn in as his chief
deputy. The following year, after Boatright was indicted for some
personal trouble, King was appointed acting sheriff on October 1,
1883. Subsequently, in early 1884, he announced his candidacy for
sheriff of that county for the fall election.[35] However, before he
could fully realize his dreams of respectability, King accompanied

Ben Thompson to San Antonio on March 11, 1884, where they both were cut down by the bullets of assassins in the Vaudeville Variety Theater. King was only thirty years old.

Notes

1 The *San Antonio Daily Herald*, May 30, 1876. Although it did not know that King Fisher was involved, this issue speculated that "it is probably at the hands of [Fisher's] thieves and murderers that Gonzales met his death."

2 The *Galveston Daily News*, May 31, 1876.

3 The *San Antonio Daily Express*, March 13, 1884.

4 Ibid., June 9, 1876.

5 Jennings, N.A., *A Texas Ranger*, 1960 facsimile reproduction of the first edition, The Frontier Book Company, Ruidoso, New Mexico, pp. 222-225.

6 Ibid, pp. 226-227.

7 The *San Antonio Daily Express*, June 6, 1876.

8 Capt. L.N. McNelly to Gen. William Steele, June 4, 1876, General Correspondence, Adjutant General's Record Group (RG 401), Archives Division, Texas State Library and Archives Commission, Austin Texas.

9 Jennings, p. 225; Durham, George, as told to Clyde Wantland, *Taming The Nueces Strip*, University of Texas Press, Austin, 1962, p. 141.

10 The *San Antonio Daily Express*, June 10 and 17, 1876.

11 Ibid., June 10, 1876.

12 Ibid., June 23, 1876.

13 Roberts, Bruce, *Springs From the Parched Ground*, self-published, 1950, p. 73.

14 Fisher, O.C., with J.C. Dykes, *King Fisher, His Life and Times*, University of Oklahoma Press, Norman, 1966, pp. 45-46.

15 Ibid., chapters III-VII.

16 Reprinted in the *San Antonio Daily Express*, June 25, 1876.

17 Ibid., May 28, 1894.

18 Bushick, Frank H., *Glamorous Days*, The Naylor Company, San Antonio, 1934, p. 174.

19 Maverick, Sr., Mrs. Albert, "Ranch Life in Bandera County in 1878," in *Frontier Times*, Dec. 1940, Vol. 18, No. 3, p. 144.

20 Raymond, Dora Neill, *Captain Lee Hall of Texas*, University of Oklahoma Press, Norman, 1940, p. 88, note 13.

21 The *San Antonio Daily Express*, March 13, 1884.

22. Bonnet, Judge W.A., "King Fisher, A Noted Character," in *Frontier Times*, July 1926, Vol. 3, No. 10, pp. 36-37.

23 Bushick, op. cit., p. 174.

24 Bonnet was writing after the turn of the century.

25 The *San Antonio Daily Express*, March 13, 1884.

26 Fisher, op. cit., p. 58.

27 Ibid., pp. 43-45.

28 Ibid., p. 46.

29 Ibid., pp. 54-55, 57.

30 Ibid., p. 55. Actually, George Durham, in an article, "On The Trail of 5,100 Outlaws-Beyond the Nueces" (printed in *The Valley Morning Star* of Harlingen, Texas, November 8, 1959), repeated a tale that told of Frank Porter killing nine men over a herd of "wet horses," which was later changed to King Fisher killing eight men over a herd of "wet cattle."

31 The *San Antonio Daily Herald*, May 30 and June 1, 1876.

32 Jennings, p. 225; Durham, *Taming the Nueces Strip*, p. 140.

33 Two years later, Gildea, who had a varied career, was allegedly a member of John H. Selman's so-called "Scouts," when that lawless group rampaged through Lincoln County, New Mexico, in 1878.

34 Fisher, op. cit., pp. 108-109.

35 Ibid., pp. 1 14-1 16; Tise, Sammy, *Texas County Sheriffs*, self-published, 1989, p. 503.

Marcus Huff

Born in Albuquerque, New Mexico, in 1968, Marcus Huff earned degrees in Journalism from Northern Oklahoma College and Journalism/Editing from Oklahoma State University, after a tour of duty in the U.S. Navy. His life-long fascination with the Old West in general and the Lincoln County War, Oklahoma territorial history, and the history of the Ozark region of Missouri and Arkansas in particular, led him to membership in the Lincoln County (New Mexico) Historical Society, the Chickasaw Historical Society, the Western History Association, Westerners International, Western Writers of America (WWA), Western Association of Outlaw and Lawman History, Oklahombres, and the National Association for Outlaw and Lawman History (NOLA). He has been a judge for WWA's prestigious Spur award and has been interviewed on the subject of the West for National Public Radio and numerous regional papers and magazines around the country. In 1995 he became editor of *True West* and *Old West* magazines, and nonfiction history titles under the Barbed Wire Press imprint. At the age of 27, he became the youngest editor in the 46-year history of *True West*. To date, he has edited over 100 issues and half a dozen books. He and his wife, Betty, and their children, Morgan, Elias, and Hawkeye, reside in Cave Creek, Arizona.

OLD HABITS DIE HARD:
A NOTE ON FREDERICK T. WAITE
•

By Marcus J. Huff

NOLA *Quarterly*, October 1998

In the fall of 1878, following the turbulent Lincoln County War, former Regulators William H. Bonney, Tom O'Folliard, John Middleton, Henry Brown, and Fred Waite found themselves in the rough-and-tumble Texas panhandle town of Tascosa. Having given up the warrior trade after the death of Alexander McSween and the crumbling support of John Chisum, Bonney and his brigands had chosen Tascosa as a stage to unload a herd of stolen horses, and to enjoy the liberty afforded the new found wealth.

After a few weeks of attending local dances, horse races, and shooting matches, the small group departed their separate ways. Upon the better judgment and advice of their friends, Bonney and O'Folliard returned to New Mexico, and eventually, the waiting arms of Pat Garrett and a grave in Fort Sumner. Middleton traveled on to Kansas and relative obscurity. Brown took up the trade of lawman and practiced in Tascosa and Caldwell, Kansas, until he resorted to bank robbery to supplement his income and was gunned-down by a mob. Frederick Waite, the closest thing to a "blue blood" in the group, returned to his comfortable, and respected, family in Indian Territory.

Born September 23, 1853, at Fort Arbuckle, Indian Territory, Frederick Tecumseh Waite was the eldest of ten children born to Thomas Fletcher Waite and Catherine McClure Waite.[1] Around

1858, the Waite family moved to the north, along with Catherine's mother, Ellen, and father-in-law, Smith Paul, to the fertile farmland along the Washita River. The land was good to the Waites, and they soon became one of the most respected families in the Chickasaw Nation. Fred's grandfather, Smith Paul, opened a successful mercantile and thereby established "Smith Paul's Valley," present-day Pauls Valley, Oklahoma. Young Fred was afforded only the best in education and upbringing. Sent away to private school in Arkansas, Waite ultimately attended college at the Illinois Industrial University, Champaign, receiving his final degree from Mound City Commercial College in St. Louis, Missouri, in 1874.[2] After his period of education, Fred came home, became an active Mason (Waite would later serve three terms as treasurer for his lodge), and worked in the family mercantile in Pauls Valley. After the April 28, 1874, death of Thomas Waite, Fred's mother and his youngest sister, Irene, departed the Territory for Ohio.[3] With the establishment of railheads, and a strong economy based on farming and ranching, the area around the Waite home in Pickens County was beginning to show signs of prosperity. Despite the prospect of local success, Fred bid his brother Amos goodbye, and around 1876, went west in search of adventure. It wasn't long before he found it.

While traveling across the Texas panhandle, Fred was approached by a group of riders intent on finding a horse thief who had been plaguing the area. Coming upon Fred, the men made overtures toward hanging the young man; his being a stranger was as good an admission of guilt as any. Frantic at the thought of being lynched, Waite started giving the Mason distress signal, which was quickly recognized by a fellow Mason in the group. The startled and relieved Fred was sent on his way, no doubt happy when Texas was well behind him.[4]

After knocking around Colorado for some time, Fred surfaced in Lincoln County, New Mexico Territory, in 1877, where his eventual employment under John Tunstall ensured him a footnote in one of the oft-told chapters in American western history. When Fred departed company with his compadres in Tascosa, his name was still on New Mexico Governor Lew Wallace's list of "wanted men" for the April 1, 1878, murder of Lincoln County Sheriff William Brady and Deputy George Hindman.[5] Students of the Lincoln County War know that Waite also had a hand in the March 9, 1878, deaths of

Frederick Waite around the time of the Pauls Valley killing.
Courtesy Jim and Janelle Shepherd.

William Morton and Frank Baker, although he was never formally charged with their murders. His hands were well bloody by the time he returned to the comfort of his childhood home.

The home Fred returned to in 1878 had changed drastically from his youth. Referred to as the "Free State of Pickens," the area around "Pauls Valley" had become a haven for thousands of whites who could steal, rustle, and murder at will. Organized law enforcement was considered a joke; jurisdiction of the Chickasaw Nation fell into the gray area between tribal courts and those of the United States in western Arkansas. The result was a free-for-all of murder, drunkenness, and mayhem; just the type of place Fred Waite had grown accustomed to.[6] While Billy the Kid was answering charges for the murder of Sheriff William Brady back in New Mexico (the warrant for Fred was returned "unable to find" in 1879), Waite was starting a new life in the Nations.

Settling into his old stomping grounds, Fred wasted no time in sticking his nose into trouble. Although no documentary evidence of the fact exists, Fred was rumored to have had a wife, or at least paramour, back in San Patricio, New Mexico.[7] Apparently, this didn't keep him from dalliances with the wife of another man. In 1880, Fred fathered a son with Patsy Hawkins, the wife of one James Hawkins. The child, ironically, was named "Billy" and was sent to live with George Walthall, a caretaker, when he was three years old.[8]

But illegitimate children were to become the least of Waite's worries.

In June 1881 a stranger, a white man identified only as "Smith," rode into Pauls Valley leading a horse that was identified as having been recently stolen from a local named John Covey. Accompanying a three-wagon train driven by one "Old Man" Ross, his son Sam Ross, and two unidentified men, Smith was seen about town, going from business to business, apparently preparing for a trip across country. A local cowboy named Frank Welch, who had discovered the horse missing from his employer's corn crib, relayed the information to Constable Sam Paul, Waite's uncle. Constable Paul immediately deputized Welch, Waite, and Tecumseh McClure (Catherine McClure's brother and Fred's uncle), to help search for the man. Later that morning, the four-man posse visited Miller & Green's store, armed with revolvers, and announced that they intended to capture Smith and Sam Ross at the same time. They were afraid if they only got one, the other would still get away with the stolen horse.[9]

Later that afternoon, Welch, riding alone, passed Smith and the Ross wagons on the road toward Rush Creek. Welch followed for some time, but "took to the timber" when Sam Ross noticed him and moved his hands toward his pistol, menacingly.[10] Welch doubled back to the store. Within the hour, Smith himself stopped at Miller & Green's. Smith climbed off his horse, took his Winchester in hand, and entered the store. Once inside, the man nervously walked the aisles, keeping his rifle at the ready. The store's clerk,

John Wantland, noticed that Smith paid close attention to the various exits, as if planning a robbery. After buying a few small items Smith remounted his horse, laid his Winchester across his lap, and rode away.[11]

Unfortunately for Smith, Wantland wasn't the only one taking notice of the stranger; Constable Paul and deputies McClure, Waite, and Welch were in the back room, watching Smith's every move. Paul sent a boy named Mitchell to follow the suspected thieves and report their location. When it was learned that the wagons had stopped, and camp had been made on Rush Creek, the posse decided that dawn would be the best time to attempt an arrest, and the group split up to get some sleep.

The next morning, the posse, now numbering ten or twelve, approached the camp and split up into groups of two, pairing McClure and Welch, and Waite with Paul. As deputies Welch and McClure approached from the side, gunfire erupted in the camp. After three or four shots, all was quiet. Oddly, Deputy Welch opted to go eat lunch before determining what had happened.[12] After a meal at Rainey's store, in town, Welch traveled to the camp site. He met Sam Paul on the road, armed with a shotgun and leading the stolen horse. Paul remained silent about the actions at the camp, and passed Welch without a word. Once at the camp, Welch found a crowd numbering around 150 people, and the dead body of Smith laying on the ground. The man had been shot three times in the side, and was still in his sleeping clothes. From the way he was bleeding, Welch assumed he had been laying down, possibly still asleep when killed.[13] No weapons were found around his body, and nothing in his clothes other than a small piece of tobacco. No one made mention of who fired the fatal shots, but it was apparent from the wounds that the weapon used was a pistol, which ruled out Sam Paul, who had by now returned to the camp with his shotgun.

As the men were inspecting the scene Welch found out from "Old Man" Ross that the horse in question had been legally purchased from Welch's employer for $86. As word spread that an innocent man may have been killed, blame was placed squarely on the shoulders of Fred Waite and Sam Paul. Smith was buried, the horse was returned to Ross, and the wagon train was allowed to leave, which they did, promptly.

Waite and Paul made an appearance that day at Miller & Green's store, and told clerk Wantland precious little about the murder, only that Smith was indeed dead. Wantland noted that Constable Paul was still carrying a shotgun, but no pistol. Fred Waite, with revolver strapped to his hip, was beginning to look more and more guilty.

For some time, the murder of Smith was seemingly forgotten, despite evidence that he may have indeed been innocent of horse theft. On December 1, 1881, Fred Waite married Mary Thompson, a cousin.[14] Life, at last, had turned normal for Waite, who returned to the tried-and-true family practice of merchant with his brother, Amos. But one more obstacle stood between Frederick Waite and the life of a family man and respected citizen. In June 1882, exactly a year after the fact, Commissioner Stephen Wheeler of the Western District Court in Fort Smith, Arkansas, issued formal murder charges against Waite, McClure, Paul, and Welch, for the murder of Smith.[15]

On July 5, 1882, Waite, Welch, and McClure became guests of the United States Jail at Fort Smith, pending a hearing for the murder of "one Smith, a white man whose full name is unknown." Witnesses and defendants testified before Commissioner James Brizzolara on June 7, and on June 10 Welch, Smith, and McClure were discharged. Fred Waite became the sole defendant for the murder of Smith. Commissioner Brizzolara found "probable cause to believe him guilty" of murder on June 12. On July 14, Waite was released on $2,000 bond, and ordered to return to Fort Smith to answer the charges against him on August 7, 1882.[16]

With White-Chickasaw relations reaching a boiling point, many in Pauls Valley felt that another dead white man was nothing to make a federal case of. Apparently, the federal courts agreed. On August 12, 1882, the case of the *United States v. Fred T. Waite* was dismissed.[17] Thus ended the last recorded violent episode in the life of Fred Waite.

Life for Waite, finally, reached a level of normalcy. He and Mary Waite produced a daughter, Kate, in 1883. Waite dabbled in journalism and politics, fighting fiercely to keep the Nations closed to white settlement. *Leaders and Leading Men of the Indian Territory*, published in 1891, heralded the careers of Waite and his uncles, Sam Paul and Tecumseh McClure. Waite is noted as riding with the Indian Police Force in 1887, serving as Chickasaw Nation speaker of the house in 1889, and running for the Senate as a progressive in

1890. He is described as being "a good speaker and an excellent writer" and one of "the handsomest and most intelligent of his race."[18] No mention is made to the fact that Fred was also skilled with firearms, or his past adventures in New Mexico, although both probably had a lot to do with his becoming a leader in the movement to keep whites out of the Nations. In the same volume, readers are enlightened to the fact that Sam Paul became the leader of the Progressive party, and ran, without success, for governor in 1890. The author notes that Paul "has committed some errors which set the wagging tongue of scandal in motion more than once."[19] Tecumseh McClure is noted as having served as president of the Chickasaw Nation Senate in 1886, and refusing the nomination for governor in 1890. He is also, interestingly, described as "respected by all—his record is without a blur or blemish."[20] One might think that poor, dead Smith would have disagreed.

In 1890 Mary Waite took Katie and moved to St. Paul, Minnesota. There is no record of why Fred and Mary split, although it appears the marriage ended in divorce.[21] In 1893 Waite again stuck one foot outside the law. Around the same time Chickasaw Governor Jonas Wolfe appointed Fred Attorney General for the Chickasaw Nation, the federal government started cracking down on the sale of illegal liquor in the Nations. Attorney General Waite had apparently been selling beer from the back of a local drugstore, and barely escaped conviction when a friend smuggled his brew kegs to a hiding place along a creek bed.[22]

On August 30, 1894, Waite fell victim to debilitating rheumatism and was confined to bed at a family home in Pauls Valley. Governor Palmer S. Moseley appointed Fred National Secretary of the Chickasaw Nation in September 1894.[23] On September 24, 1894, Frederick Waite died at his home in Ardmore, Indian Territory. He was buried in the family plot in Pauls Valley.

Acknowledgments

The author is indebted to Jim and Janelle Shepherd; Lois Tesky; Robert Torrez, Historian, New Mexico Archives; Frederick Nolan; Nora Henn; Julie Golanska, Historian, Fort Smith Historical Site; Drew Gomber, Historian, Lincoln Heritage Trust Museum; and Glenn Shirley, for explaining the intricacies of the Western District Court.

Notes

[1] Shepherd, Jim and Janelle, *Isaac Waite & Connections*. Privately Printed, 1992, p. 63.

[2] O'Beirne, H.F., *Leaders and Leading Men of the Indian Territory*. Chicago: American Publisher's Association, 1891, p. 218.

[3] Nora Henn to M.J. Huff, personal conversation, April 15, 1998.

[4] Shepherd, *Isaac Waite & Connections*, p. 163. Although a fanciful story that has been repeated in various sources on Waite's travels, the tale of the "distressed traveler" is common in Masonic lore, even playing a small role in the initiation rites. More than likely, Fred embellished an otherwise boring ride across the Llano Estacado for the sake of entertaining family and friends back home.

[5] Rasch, Philip J., "Wanted Men of Lincoln County." Los Angeles Westerner's *Branding Iron*, No. 15, 1951. Reprinted in *Warriors of Lincoln County*. Stillwater: Barbed Wire Press, 1998, pp. 3-4. The author notes in his article that original documents, in Wallace's own handwriting, can be found in the Lew Wallace Papers in the William Henry Smith Memorial Library of the Indiana Historical Society.

[6] Baird, W. David, *The Chickasaw People*. Phoenix: Indian Tribal Series, 1974, pp. 60-67.

[7] Henn to Huff, April 15, 1998. Robert J. Torrez, State Historian, New Mexico State Records Center and Archives, informs the author (personal correspondence, August 19, 1998) that Civil marriage records for Lincoln County begin in May 1882. Catholic marriage records for Lincoln County for 1874-1881 are available on microfilm, but have not been checked by Torrez. References for Waite are also absent in the Lincoln County voter registration records, poll books, or brand books.

[8] Lois Teskey, granddaughter of William Hawkins, to M.J. Huff, personal correspondence, July 5, 1998. Like his father before him, William Hawkins would eventually end up in New Mexico, adding his own resume of murder and lawlessness to the family legacy. Hawkins gained employment with the Cananea Cattle Company, committed a number of murders in New Mexico and Arizona, ran illegal liquor operations during Prohibition, and married into the Clanton family of Arizona. The life of William Hawkins will be the subject of a future article.

[9] National Archives, Fort Worth. United States v. Sam Paul, Frank Welch, Fred T. Waite, Tecumseh McClure. Western District of Arkansas July 8, 1882. Deposition of John Wantland, Witness.

[10] Ibid. Deposition of Frank Welch, Defendant.

11 Ibid. Deposition of John Wantland, Witness.

12 Ibid. Deposition of Frank Welch, Defendant.

13 Ibid.

14 Shepherd, *Isaac Waite & Connections*, p. 63.

15 National Archives, Fort Worth. Subpoena, United States v. Sam Paul, Frank Welch, Fred T. Waite, John Cortney, Tecumseh McClure for the Crime of Murder. Western District of Arkansas June 27, 1882. Subpoena served by U.S. Marshal Thomas Boles.

16 National Archives, Fort Worth. United States v. Sam Paul, Frank Welch, Fred T. Waite, Tecumseh McClure. Western District of Arkansas July 8, 1882.

17 Fort Smith Historical Site. Common Law Book entry, United States v. Fred T. Waite. August 12, 1882.

18 O'Beirne, *Leaders and Leading Men of the Indian Territory*. pp. 218-219.

19 Ibid, pp. 282-283.

20 Ibid, pp. 308-309.

21 Shepherd, *Isaac Waite & Connections*, p. 76. According to the authors, a letter written in 1968 indicates that Mary and Fred divorced, with Mary later marrying a man named Jones.

22 Ibid.

23 Ibid, p. 77.

Dave Johnson

A long-time member of NOLA, Dave Johnson was born in Pennsylvania on February 23, 1950. After graduation from Pennsylvania State University, he moved to Indiana in 1973 and enrolled at Purdue University, where he earned an advanced degree. Although he has maintained an interest in all facets of Western outlaw and lawman history, his main focus has been on the events and individuals of the Texas Hill Country, especially the history of the Mason County War. *John Ringo*, his biography of the celebrated gunfighter, published by the Barbed Wire Press of Cave Creek, Arizona, was a finalist for the prestigious Spur Award of Western Writers of America in 1998. Dave has also edited a new edition of The Life of Thomas W. Gamel, a rare and little-known volume that ads greatly to our knowledge of the turbulent times in Mason County. Currently he is working on a history of the war that ravaged that county in the last century. He currently lives on a small farm in central Indiana with his wife, Ieva, daughter, Kristina, and three dogs and a cat.

G.W. Gladden: Hard Luck Warrior
•
By Dave Johnson
NOLA *Quarterly*, July-September 1991

It is given to few men that their names are immortalized by history while others, equally famous (or infamous) at the same time, are relegated to history's footnotes. Such a man was George Gladden, a tough feudist who rode with John Ringo and Scott Cooley during the Mason County War. Unlike Ringo, who was transformed into a gun fighter par excellence by such writers as Burns and Lake, or Cooley, whose violent encounters in Mason earned him a place in feud history, Gladden, whose life was both longer and, to a degree, more dramatic, remains an obscure and shadowy figure.

George W. Gladden appears to have been born in Missouri in 1851.[1] The 1850 Missouri Census indicates five Gladden families living in the state during this time from which Green Gladden emerges as the only possible candidate for being George's father.[2] The 1850 census indicates that Green and Elizabeth Gladden, aged 26 and 22, were living in Platte County, Missouri. With them was one Arthur Neill, age 26. Both Gladden and Neill gave their occupation as farmers.[3] There is no entry for a son named George however, and by 1860 the Gladdens had moved from the state. Lacking a later census entry, the present Gladden's parents remain a matter of speculation.

The earliest mention of George Gladden located to date is by J.M.

Franks. Franks recalled that in 1870 he met Gladden at Junction
City, Kansas, while on a trail drive. Gladden, who Franks asserted
lived in Travis County, Texas, joined the herders and returned as far
as Waco where he was paid off.[4] Family records indicate that he
married Susan Amanda McFarland on October 18,1872, in
Mississippi, although the exact locale has not been determined with
certainty.[5] What is certain is that Gladden was in central Texas during the summer of 1872 where, on June 4, he was arrested by L.J.
Parker and N.J. Miller of the State Police in Llano County on a
charge of theft of a horse.[6] Nothing further is known of this incident. The 1873 tax records for Mason County indicate that he was
living in Loyal Valley where he owned 2-1/2 town lots valued at
$1,000. A small rancher, Gladden also had 300 cattle, 8 horses, and
2 mules valued at $1,750.[7] The same year W.L. Hayes noted in his
trail log that he drove several head of cattle north for Gladden (and
others). Gladden's brand was noted as FL.[8] From other documents
it appears that Gladden had purchased his town lots from Joseph
Slack (the name is unclear) for $1,200 "to be paid in good steers
from 2 years old up to Mr. Charlie Lehmberg." The cattle were to be
delivered between March 1 and March 10, 1874. The document further notes that Gladden's brands were P and FL.[9]

Cattle were one of the root causes of the Mason County War,
whose embers, still smoldering from the bitterness of the Civil War
and Reconstruction, began to flare again early in 1874. In the previous year there had been an upsurge of stock theft. In May of 1873
the *Brenham Banner*, quoting the *Burnet Exponent* of May 17,
reported that a gang of horse thieves had been captured in Llano
County who had disguised themselves as Indians.[10] Again, in
October, the *Banner* quoted the *Lampasas Dispatch* concerning a
raid in that section which netted the thieves nearly 100 horses. The
Dispatch cautioned: "Our citizens cannot be too cautious in guarding their property, both from Indian depredations and from the
hands of the many thieves infesting the frontier."[11]

In the spring of 1874, stockman Joe Olney became engaged in a
cattle dispute which ended with Olney shooting his adversary and
seizing the cattle.[12] Olney was indicted, but in the summer a second,
and more serious, raid (or cattle drive depending on who one
believes) occurred in the Llano-Mason area resulting in the arrest of
a number of men by Mason authorities. A letter from Mason, dated

George W. Gladden. *Author's collection.*

August 14, stated the "...great excitement exists at Quihi, on account of the Sheriff of Mason County arresting 11 of the Llano cowboys. Some 40 of their friends came in and attempted a rescue but failed in the attempt...This disturbance like many others is attributable to the confusion caused by the stock law."[13]

This "raid" appears to have triggered the violence that enveloped Mason County during 1875. It appears that M.B. Thomas, a cattleman from Burnet County, had ridden with ten other men from Burnet and Llano Counties into Mason to gather their stock. The men stated later that "knowing the animosity that some of the people of that county have toward non-resident stock men, and wishing to have no misunderstanding or trouble, Thomas hired two men of Mason County to stay continually with the herd that he was collecting and cut out every animal that might get into the herd belonging to anyone in that county."[14] Sheriff John Clark and posse rode into Llano County and arrested Thomas and the other ten nonresidents. Then, contrary to law, the posse scattered the herd. The two men from Mason County were not held. Following their release, Thomas and his men filed charges against Clark and his posse for robbery and false imprisonment.[15]

Who the two men from Mason were is uncertain, but it may be reasonably theorized that George Gladden was one of them based on his ensuing actions. The other may well have been Timothy P. Williamson, a recent arrival at Loyal Valley from Burnet County. Williamson had known Thomas from Burnet during the time he lived there and would have been a natural choice. It is possible that Williamson had recommended Gladden to Thomas.

In February 1875, four men were killed in Mason County by a mob generally believed to be under the control of Sheriff Clark. Then, in May, Tim P. Williamson was killed by a band headed by Pete Bader while being taken to Mason by Deputy John Worley. When the mob appeared, Worley shot Williamson's mount to prevent his escape. No one was ever charged for any of the killings.

Williamson's murder proved to be the incident which led directly to bloody revenge. Scott Cooley, a former Texas Ranger and friend of Williamson, rode to Mason and observed. The failure of Clark to make arrests, coupled with his own investigations, led him to conclude not only who Williamson's killers were, but also that Clark was a leader of the mob. Cooley bided his time. Then, on August 10, he killed and scalped Worley in Mason.[16] Nine days later he killed Carl Bader, Pete Bader's brother, at his home.[17]

The killings stunned Mason, and tempers flared as accusations were made by both sides. One confrontation took place between Gladden and Daniel Hoerster, the county brand inspector, resulting in a fist fight in Ben Stewart's store.[18] The exact cause in unknown, but if Gladden had been one of the two locals employed by Thomas, it may well have been due to Gladden's involvement and possible testimony in the robbery charges filed in Llano. Fists quickly gave way to guns.

On September 7, Clark struck the next blow in the feud. Jim

Cheyney, a local gambler, had been hired by Clark to ride to Loyal Valley and summon both Gladden and Moses Baird, one of Thomas' men on the "raid," to come to Mason. Clark then set up an ambush consisting of forty to fifty men at Hedwig's Hill, a small town which lay on the natural route between Loyal Valley and Mason. Dan Roberts, who later hunted Gladden, recalled that "...when they got pretty close to the store, Sheriff Clark saw that they were Mose Beard [sic] and George Gladden...the Sheriff stepped out on the porch, with his rifle in hand, and the firing commenced..."[19] Shot in the face and body, Gladden managed to stay on his feet. Baird was less fortunate. Unable to mount by himself, Gladden helped Baird onto his own mount, then swung up behind him. The men managed to ride to Beaver Creek before Gladden, weakened by loss of blood, fell from his horse. Baird managed to cling to the saddle for some time before falling off. Pete Bader rode him down and finished the luckless man off. Then, noting a ring on Baird's finger, Bader cut off the finger to get his prize. Gladden was more fortunate. One of the posse, Charlie Keller, drew on his companions and prevented Gladden's killing.

This brutal shooting was quickly justified by Clark, who claimed that the men had attacked him and his posse—all fifty of them! "The men shot were alone and were killed by a large number of Germans with Mr. Jns. Clark, Sheriff of the county at their head. The Germans claim that Beard [sic, Baird] and Gladden began the fight firing about fifty shots at ten or twelve paces from Mr. Clark."[20]

The shooting stunned central Texas. "A letter from Fredericksburg, dated Sept. 8th, has been received in this city, and conveys the following startling news: 'H-ll has broke loose up here. Mose Beard [sic] was killed yesterday; Geo. Gladden is badly wounded, but there is some hope of his getting well. He is shot through the arm, and in the face. All this happened at Keller's store on the Llano.' We fear this is but the beginning of a bloody solution of the difficulties about stock, that have become so serious of late."[21]

The writer was correct in his assessment. Enraged by his brother's murder, John Baird swore vengeance. He led forces to Loyal Valley where he was joined by Scott Cooley. Determined to carry the fight to Clark, the men struck two weeks later. On September 25, Cooley brazenly led seven or eight men into Mason. While most of the men ate breakfast, John Ringo and a man named Williams rode on to Cheyney's place and gunned him down.[22]

Gladden, heavily wounded, was expected to die. Roberts recalled that he had been shot nine times, while others put the number of wounds all over his body,[23] while a granddaughter informed the author that "They shot him to rag dolls."[24] Despite this, Gladden was back on his feet and primed for revenge by month's end. On September 28, Mrs. Lucia Holmes noted his presence in Mason. On the morning of the 29th, John Baird apparently joined them. As Daniel Hoerster and two other men, Peter Jordan and Henry Pluenneke, rode down Mason's main street, Baird suddenly killed Hoerster with a blast from his shotgun while Cooley and Gladden opened fire on the others. Jordan and Pluenneke managed to reach cover and returned the gunfire. "Peter Jordan and Pluenneke jumped off their horses and ran around the back of the Southern Hotel and went in...Peter Jordan walked out on the porch of the hotel and used one of the posts as a rest for his gun. There was a lot of shooting."[25]

As gunfire blazed back and forth across the street, Jordan saw one of the men make a dash between two buildings carrying a rifle in one hand and a box of cartridges in the other. Jordan fired and saw the cartridges fly everywhere as the bullet hit the man in the hand. He was always convinced that the bullet had severed the man's thumb.[26] The man was George Gladden.

The Texas Rangers arrived in Mason the next day under the command of Dan Roberts. Baird, Gladden, and Cooley, elated over their success, then retired to Burnet County where friends and family of Baird provided refuge. It was not to last, for in December of 1875, both Cooley and Ringo were arrested in Burnet for threatening the lives of local lawmen. Following attempts to either rescue the men or give bond for them, Baird, Gladden, and a third man, tentatively identified as Ed Cavin, returned to the Llano-Mason area intent on killing Peter Bader (Clark had already fled from the county). They caught him on January 13, 1876, as he left his sanctuary. Thomas W. Gamel recorded that on that day Pete Bader, one Miller, and two others were confronted by John Baird who opened fire. Bader's horse wheeled and ran about fifty yards when its rider fell, dead.[27]

Gladden later provided additional evidence concerning Bader's death when he appealed his case in court. The Texas Court of

Appeals noted in part: "The evidence shows that the appellant had previously threatened to take the life of Bader, and that on the day of the homicide he and his co-defendant, Baird, and another party, who was not identified by any of the witnesses, way laid [sic] the deceased upon the highway, and fired upon him with shot-guns and pistols as he passed by—three shots being fired by Baird and two by Gladden..."[28]

With Bader dead and Clark in hiding, the Baird faction now turned their attention to freeing both Cooley and Ringo. On April 30 four men made an attempt on the Lampasas jail where the pair had been transferred by way of Austin. The *Fayette County New Era* of May 12 reported their actions. "Between midnight and daylight on Sunday last, four disguised men suddenly sprang upon the jail guard at Lampasas, seized and tied him to a picket fence, his face towards the foe and his back towards the fence. They with pistols presented towards him, commanded him to be silent or die. He didn't die. Two of the four proceeded to the jail, and after handing Scott Cooley a file, they began boring and chiseling to make a hole where by the prisoners [Cooley and John Ringo] might escape. But they were compelled to raise the siege without obtaining their object. The near approach of daylight is supposed to have caused them to abandon their enterprise..."[29] The raiders, however, were undaunted. On May 5 some 13 or 15 men rode into Lampasas and liberated the pair.

His friends free, Gladden then fled the country. On August 1, 1876, Sheriff J.J. Strickland learned that three men wanted in Burnet had been seen in Medina County. Strickland set out to capture the trio, and while en route learned that Gladden was there. "On the way I was advised not to attempt such an undertaking, as there was a band of some forty men commanded by George Gladden (of Mason notoriety) ready to pounce upon any officer who might venture into their place of concealment."[30]

Strickland captured two of the men he was hunting, plus a third fugitive, but the other man eluded him. At that point Strickland returned home.[31]

Perhaps Gladden could have remained safely in Medina County, but the need to be with his wife, now pregnant with their first child, apparently lured him home. It proved to be a mistake. In October, both he and John Ringo were surprised by a combined force of

Texas Rangers from Company "C" and local lawmen led by Sheriff
J.J. Bozarth of Llano County. Captain Sparks later reported, in part:
"On the following Monday, the sixteenth, I detailed Sergeant
Robinson to proceed to Loyal Valley in Mason County and ascer-
tain, if possible, the whereabouts of Messrs. Gladden, Ringo, [Billy]
Thompson and others for whom I had warrants, and also to learn the
direction taken by a herd of cattle in charge of Eb. Stewart, which I
had been informed had passed down the west side of the Colorado
River towards Austin."[32, 33]

Sparks' information was correct, and with nine others he started in
pursuit. Sparks overtook the herd some thirteen miles northeast of
Austin and captured both Stewart and Thompson. In the mean time,
Sergeant A.W. Robinson had received word that Ringo and Gladden
were at Loyal Valley. "Soon after my departure information was
received that George Gladden and John Ringo were at Mosely's
ranche in Loyal Valley. Sheriff Bozart[h] with his men and Sergeant
A.W. Robinson with six men proceeded to the aforesaid point, and
arrested both Ringo and Gladden..."[34]

Gladden and Ringo were taken under heavy guard to the Travis
County jail in Austin. By December Gladden was back in Llano
charged with the murder of Pete Bader. On December 8 he was
tried, the testimony lasting some five hours. The jury took fifteen
minutes to deliberate. Gladden was convicted and sentenced to life
in prison. The case was appealed.[35] The *Burnet Bulletin* commented
thusly: "The people here express themselves that his conviction will
do a great deal towards restoring law and order in this portion of the
country. Court adjourned on Saturday sine die. It is said to be one of
the most important and interesting terms ever held in Llano. Now
that since the civil authorities are determined to enforce the law,
despite the threats that have been made against the State witnesses,
we presume we will have more prosperous times. And that immi-
grants will feel more secure in selecting homes in our sparsely settled county."[36] Jailed in Austin, Gladden missed the birth of his first
child. On March 29, 1877, a daughter was born in Mason County.
Her mother named her O'Beria Ann Gladden.[37]

Gladden's appeal was heard during 1877, and the court reaffirmed
the sentence. George served eight years in the penitentiary. Then, on
December 30, 1884, he was pardoned by the governor on "the recommendation of the District Judge, District Atty., County Judge and

most of the other County officials and many citizens."[38] Gladden apparently returned home for a brief time to Mason, but by July his name appeared in New Mexico. The *El Paso Lone Star* reprinted this item from Las Cruces: "Max Goldenberg is out in Arizona on the track of a trusted employ[e] who recently absconded with about $2,500 of Max's money. The man, whose name is George W. Gladden, was sent to Texas to buy cattle for Goldenberg's ranch in the San Andres. The next thing that was heard from him was that he was moving west with a bunch of horses. It is to be hoped that his capture will be effected and the stolen money recovered."[39]

This may not have been the George Gladden of Mason, however. A second George Gladden was reported killed in New Mexico two years later: "We are credibly informed that George Gladden, alias Geo. Lee, alias Hardy was killed a few days since in Hell's Canon, New Mexico, for resisting arrest as a trainwrecker."[40]

Gladden resettled his family in Apache County, Arizona, during 1886.[41] With them on this journey may well have been the Blevins family from Llano County. Martin Blevins and his wife, Mary Atkinson, left Texas to join their son Andy. With them came four more of their sons.

Tension was high in Apache County when the families arrived. Overgrazing and the threat of bringing sheep into traditional cattle country had men threatening one another. Gladden sided with the cattlemen. In the fall of 1886 George led a band of drovers into Payson and boasted that "I have killed two men, I had to do it."[42] He then offered to treat the crowd in the local saloon. As drinks were poured, he noted Ed Tewksbury, a very dark complected man, standing at the bar.[43] Gladden's southern background showed itself, and he swore that he would not drink with a black man. Tewksbury, enraged at the insult, slapped Gladden's face and told him to draw. Instead Gladden fled.[44]

Gladden remained in Arizona into the spring of 1887, but as the situation deteriorated in Apache County, he resolved not to be drawn into the feud. A second daughter, Grace Eleanor, had been born on April 1, 1887, and this may have contributed to his decision.[45] Susan, however, claimed that she had moved for the last time. Whatever the underlying reasons for her decision, the two separated. George headed back to Texas.[46] He was quickly arrested. The details have not come to light but Uvalde County Sheriff Baylor arrested Gladden and lodged him in Uvalde jail on June 22. He was arrested on the basis of a notice from Kimble County to arrest Gladden for having in his possession stolen horses.[47]

The outcome of George's problems has not been determined and his whereabouts remain obscure. The *1889 Fugitives From Justice* notes that a George Gladden was wanted in Williamson County on unspecified charges, and Gamel recalled that he had heard Gladden had been arrested and sentenced to the penitentiary for 25 years.[48] This may be so, but in 1895 Gladden was free and in El Paso. Once again he was destined for a confrontation with violence.

The cause in this case was Charles C. Perry, sheriff of Chaves County, New Mexico. Born around 1855 in Texas, Perry had gone to New Mexico in the 1870s. Perry proved himself an able man catcher, and in November of 1894 he was elected sheriff. Yet Perry also had his darker side. He enjoyed gambling and fraternized freely with hoodlums. He was also given to heavy drinking at times.[49]

In May of 1895 Perry invited his friend Dee Harkey, sheriff of Eddy County, to accompany him to El Paso. On his way he informed Harkey that he planned on killing John Wesley Hardin.[50] Perry encountered Hardin in the Wigwam Saloon. With Hardin was George Gladden, whom Hardin had first met in the Travis County jail. "In that jail I met some noted men. Bill Taylor, George Gladden, John Ringo, Manning Clements, Pipes and Herndon of the Bass gang, John Collins, Jeff Ake, and Brown Bowen."[51]

Hardin refused to fight, and Perry turned his attention to Gladden. City Prosecutor D. Storms recorded: "[Gladden] said he was unarmed and thereupon the defendant pulled out two pistols and offered the man one and the man would not take it. Thereupon def. threw down both pistols on the bar and told the man to take his choice. The man would not do it and def. slap[p]ed him and told him to go out and arm himself and he would meet him there next morning at 9 a.m."[52]

Gladden had no intention of meeting Perry, with whom he had no quarrel. He filed charges through Hardin, who was then practicing law. Perry was arrested by Old John Selman, the man who would later kill Hardin.[53] On May 24, 1895, Perry was hauled into court and charged with both assault and battery and unduly displaying a pistol. He was fined $5.00 and released.[54]

From El Paso, Gladden disappears. Family sources indicate the

belief that he was in Antelope, Oregon, around 1939, but no trace of
him there has yet been located. So, for the present, the fate of
George Gladden, hard luck warrior, remains a mystery.

Notes

1 The 1880 Walker County, Texas, census, taken while Gladden was in
the Huntsville Penitentiary, lists his age as 29 and his birthplace as
Missouri.

2 This assumption presupposes that no Gladden family moved to Missouri
during 1851.

3 Census of 1850 Platte County, Missouri. The family was enumerated on
October 9,1850, by William F. Barton.

4 Franks, J.M., *Seventy Years in Texas*. Publisher, not listed, Gatesville,
Texas, 1924. pp. 111-112.

5 Francis Blake to the author, April 29, 1989. Gladden has not been located in the 1870 census for Mississippi nor Texas.

6 Police Arrests Ledger, P. 78. Courtesy Texas State Archives, Austin.

7 1873 Tax Records, Mason County, Texas.

8 Trail Log of W.L. Hayes. Courtesy Jane Hoerster, Mason County
Historical Commission.

9 Civil Case 14, Amanda Gladden vs. August Jones. Mason County Civil
Records, Mason, Texas.

10 *Brenham Banner*, Brenham, Texas, May 24, 1873.

11 Ibid., October 4, 1873.

12 *1878 Fugitives From Justice*. Courtesy Texas State Archives.

13 *San Antonio Daily Herald*, August 24, 1874.

14 *Burnet Bulletin*, September 4, 1874.

15 Ibid. Only two of the men, Thomas and A.G. Roberts, were ever
brought to trial. Both men were cleared.

16 *San Antonio Daily Herald*, August 18, 1875.

17 De Vos, Julius, Editor. *One Hundred Years of the Hilda (Bethel)
Methodist Church and Parent Organizations 1856-1955*. Hilda
Methodist Church, 1973. P. 47.

18 Gamel, Thomas W. *The Life of Thomas W. Ganel*. Privately published,
no date nor place. p. 26.

19 Roberts, Dan. W. *Rangers and Sovereignty*. State House Press, Austin,
Texas. 1987. pp. 97-98.

20 Henry M. Holmes to Governor Richard Coke, September 8,1875.
Texas Ranger Files, Courtesy Texas State Archives.

[21] *San Antonio Daily Herald*, September 14, 1875.

[22] Williams has been identified as Bill Williams. A James W. Williams was killed by mob members during 1876 in Llano County, but his connection, if any, to Bill Williams has not been determined.

[23] Author's interview with Francis Blake, March 31, 1989.

[24] Author's interview with Sarah Lockwood, March 27, 1989.

[25] Gamel. p. 28.

[26] Author's interview with Walker Jordan, July 7, 1989.

[27] Gamel. p. 31.

[28] *Cases Argued and Adjudged in the Court of Appeals of the State of Texas. Vol. II*. The Gilbert Book Co., St. Louis, Missouri, 1878. p. 510.

[29] Fayette County *New Era*, May 12, 1876.

[30] *Burnet Bulletin*, August 11, 1876.

[31] Ibid.

[32] Billy Thompson was the younger brother of Ben Thompson, the notorious gunfighter-gambler. Thompson was wanted at the time for two murders: one in Texas and one in Kansas.

[33] *Austin Daily Statesman*, December 1, 1876.

[34] Ibid.

[35] *Burnet Bulletin*, December 15, 1876.

[36] Ibid.

[37] Correspondence, Francis Blake to the author, April 24, 1989.

[38] Clemency Records, Texas State Archives

[39] *El Paso Lone Star*, August 1, 1885.

[40] *St. John's Herald*, February 3, 1887.

[41] The newspaper *Hoof and Horn* for October 14, 1886, noted Gladden's brands and marks. His range was given as Canyon Creek, Arizona.

[42] Dedera, Don. *A Little War Of Our Own*. Northland Press, Flagstaff, Arizona, 1988. p.110. Dedera was quoting L.J. Horton's unpublished manuscript on the feud.

[43] Ed Tewksbury was one of the main fighters in the Pleasant Valley War. Born to James Dunning Tewksbury and a Shoshone woman whose name is unknown, Tewksbury proved to be a fierce fighter. He died of tuberculosis on April 4, 1904.

[44] Dedera. p. 110.

[45] Correspondence, Francis Blake to the author, April 24, 1989.

[46] Author's interview with Francis Blake, March 31, 1989. Blake also stated that George returned for her once, but she refused to move again.

[47] *San Antonio Daily Express*, June 23, 1887.

[48] Gamel. p. 32.

[49] Ball, Larry D. "Lawmen in Disgrace: Sheriff Charles C. Perry of Chaves County, New Mexico." *New Mexico Historical Review*, Vol. 61, No. 2, April 1986. p. 129.

[50] John Wesley Hardin was without a doubt Texas' premier gunfighter. Born May 26, 1853, in Texas, Hardin killed a number of men during both Reconstruction and its aftermath. He was finally apprehended in Florida and sent to prison. Here he studied law. He was killed by John Selman on August 19, 1895.

[51] Hardin, John Wesley. *The Life of John Wesley Hardin*. University of Oklahoma Press, Norman. 1961. p. 126.

[52] Memoranda of Court Cases, D. Storms, County Attorney, El Paso County. Vol. 2. pp. 17-18. Courtesy El Paso Public Library, El Paso, Texas.

[53] John Selman had been a notorious outlaw during the Lincoln County War. While he killed a number of men during his lifetime, he is primarily noted for the killing of Hardin. He was later killed by George Scarborough.

[54] El Paso County Court Records. Causes 1548 and 1549.

Edward Kirby

A charter and lifetime member of NOLA, Ed Kirby was born in Sharon, Connecticut, in 1927. His interest in the West was encouraged by his father, an avid reader of Zane Grey and Max Brand novels, and was later strengthened by his first trip west, courtesy of the U.S. Army. A 1946 graduate of the Engineer School at Fort Belvoir, Virginia, Ed served in the army as a topographic surveyor in Japan, Okinawa and other Ryukyus Islands. He holds a BA in education from Central Connecticut State University and a masters in administration from the University of Hartford. He has taken advanced studies in geology, administration, staff development and educational law at the University of Connecticut, Vassar College, the University of Hartford and Seattle Pacific University. Between 1951 and 1990 he was a classroom teacher, coach of baseball, football and basketball, athletic director, high school principal and assistant superintendent of schools. During his coaching years he also worked as a baseball scout. Among his published work are biographies of Butch Cassidy and the Sundance Kid, and articles on Western characters ranging from members of the Wild Bunch to Bill Miner and Theodore Roosevelt. First elected to the NOLA board of directors in 1976, he has served four terms as president of the organization. Ed was inducted into the Connecticut High School Coaches Hall of Fame in 1983 and the NOLA Hall of Fame in 1988. He currently works as a consultant and writer in geology, history, and industrial archeology.

TEDDY ROOSEVELT: COWBOY, DEPUTY SHERIFF
·
By Edward M. Kirby
NOLA *Quarterly*, Autumn 1984

Theodore Roosevelt, twenty-fifth U.S. President, has been recognized as an outstanding patriot and politician, a naturalist,
big game hunter, author, Rough Rider, ranchman, and statesman. He was a New York State politician with a Harvard education.
At age twenty-three he was elected to the New York State Assembly
as representative from the Twenty-first District in New York City,
serving three terms.

But from 1883 through 1887 he was one of the most tenacious
characters that the Dakota Territory ever knew. He was a ranchman,
a working cowboy, president of the Stockmen's Association, and a
deputy sheriff of Billings County.

Roosevelt was born in the family home on East 20th Street in
New York City on October 27, 1858. As a child he had weak eyes
and was asthmatic. But despite his frailness as a youth it was soon
obvious he was precocious and had an intense persistence seldom
seen. His mind was keen and perceptive though his body was weak.
His father told him, "You must make your body." And build his
body he did, but not without a long and sometime heartbreaking
struggle.

From a well-to-do family, he had many advantages that other
growing boys of the period never had: a strong and wealthy father
and family that provided gymnasium equipment, encouragement,

trips abroad, time in the woods of Maine and the opportunity to learn to ride and shoot.

Roosevelt was well prepared for his entrance to Harvard in the fall of 1876. In his junior year he developed a lasting friendship with freshman Owen Wister of Philadelphia who was to graduate summa cum laude in music in 1882. While at Harvard Wister wrote of Roosevelt's experiences as a boxer. When in 1902 Owen Wister published *The Virginian*, set against the background of Wyoming's Johnson County War, he dedicated the book to Roosevelt. In 1932 Owen Wister was to publish a complete book about Roosevelt: *Roosevelt—The Story of a Friendship, 1880-1919*.

At Chestnut Hill, Massachusetts, on, October 18, 1878, young Roosevelt met Alice Lee Hathaway at the home of Richard Saltonstall. He married her two years later on his twenty-second birthday. The next fall, 1881, he was elected to the New York State Assembly.

On May 28, 1883, following the completion of his second term in the legislature, "T.R." was honored at a party at Clark's Tavern in New York City. Politics soon faded from the conversation as the gathering became more social. As the wine flowed Roosevelt became engaged in conversation with H.H. Gorringe. The talk drifted to buffalo hunting. By the end of the party Roosevelt had agreed to accompany Gorringe to the Dakota Territory Bad Lands in September to hunt buffalo. Gorringe suggested traveling to the banks of the Little Missouri River where he knew western game of many species was abundant. Roosevelt's excitement was great as he counted the days to September.

On September 3, 1883, Roosevelt bade a pregnant Alice farewell and boarded the train west. A week earlier he had learned that Gorringe would not be able to go west. But Roosevelt decided to go alone to the land of Indians, wild animals and even wilder men.

After a series of travels on several railroads he finally boarded a train on the Great Northern Railroad, crossing the Dakota Territory, and arrived at the dubious town of Little Missouri on September 7, 1883, at 2 a.m. Through thick glasses he searched the dark and dusty street for his destination. Finally, he located the Pyramid Park Hotel and after considerable pounding on the door he was admitted. Upon mentioning Gorringe's name he was given lodging and slept through what little was left of the night.

Theodore Roosevelt in buckskins, 1884. *Theodore Roosevelt Collection, Harvard University.*

Roosevelt awoke early and, following breakfast at the Pyramid, toured what there was of this outpost of the west known as Little Missouri. The town was on the west bank of the meandering river that gave it the name. A decrepit saloon stood near the Pyramid, specializing, as the sign stated, in "Forty Mile Red Eye." The general store, bordered by questionable buildings, sat just across the tracks of the Great Northern.

Several dwellings dotted the town, but aside from some railroad structures there was little else to suggest that upward of fifty citizens resided in that forsaken area. But it was a true western town of the period and location, with no law except for the six-gun.

In the spring of 1883 a young French nobleman, Antoine-Amedee-Marie-Vincent-Amat Manca de Valombrosa, arrived in America with three million dollars. He purchased forty-five thousand acres in the Dakota Territory at a cost of less than one dollar per acre. He became known as the Marquis de Mores in the territory where he arrived about three months before Roosevelt.

The Marquis came to Little Missouri with dreams of building a great cattle industry. Spurned by the citizens of Little Missouri he set out to build his own town across the river, naming it "Medora" after his wife. The large building under construction was a twenty-eight-room mansion where the Marquis and his wife would live. On the main street nearing completion was the de Mores Hotel, flanked by a saloon and theater.

In the morning when young Roosevelt asked where he might find a guide to take him to shoot a buffalo, he was directed without enthusiasm a few hundred yards north of Little Missouri to an old army base no longer in use. Finding a guide could be as difficult as finding a buffalo.

Much to his surprise he learned that the Sioux Indians had killed thousands that summer and the great beast was now scarce.

At the old army post he found a young Canadian named Joe Ferris who at first had no interest in guiding the bespectacled dude from the East. But the persistence of this dude with the toothy grin and obvious financial rewards soon changed his mind. T.R. had a guide.

Late in the day, with horses and a buckboard full of provisions, Roosevelt and Ferris were ready to cross the Little Missouri to go up river to the south. But Roosevelt discovered that the hammer on his Sharp's .45 caliber rifle was broken off. Even with other rifles the Sharp's was needed for buffalo.

The pair stopped at a shack and borrowed a Sharp's and secured a hammer for the damaged weapon as well. The lender was the Marquis' friend, a tall, two-gun character, Eldridge G. Paddock, one of the first white settlers in the region.-

Roosevelt and Ferris drove the buckboard south on the east side of the meandering river. This entire region was part of the Missouri Plateau, a territory with a formation of substantial lignite which was often spontaneously ignited, giving an eerie smoky appearance to part of the Bad Lands.

In an hour Roosevelt and his guide passed the Custer Trail

Ranch. They crossed the river, fording the stream on several occasions before arriving at the Maltese Cross Ranch eight miles south of town.

There Roosevelt met ranchers Sylvane Ferris and Bill Merrifield. Sylvane, brother of Joe, and Merrifield were anything but cordial to young T.R. But through the incidents of the evening they warmed up to the easterner and they parted on friendly terms the following morning. Such was the charm of Roosevelt, as many would learn in the years to come.

The next two weeks were absolute hell. And Joe Ferris was to learn that this was indeed an extraordinary character that he was guiding. The rugged stark topography was enough to defeat the most physical of men.

Yet, Roosevelt thrived on the conditions; rain, mud, burning sun, enough to deter Ferris himself. T.R. never wavered in his quest for the great buffalo. He was inspired by the country when he started the hunt, but his desire to be part of it now became insatiable.

Despite the reluctance and protests of Ferris, Roosevelt went on day after day and finally on September 20, he killed a bison bull. His goal was accomplished. He also soon purchased enough cattle to start a ranch, putting down $14,000 and enlisting the services of Ferris and Merrifield as ranchers.

Roosevelt returned to New York in time to campaign again for the twenty-first district assembly post. His campaign successful, the young politician served once more. But a cloud was to come over his life with the death of Alice, weakened by Bright's Disease, two days after the birth of a daughter. Several hours earlier his mother had died of typhoid fever. It was February 14, 1884.

Despite the shock to the young man he was back in the legislature by February 20, finishing the session. Next Roosevelt was on his way to the Republican National Convention in Chicago. Then he returned to the West. It was June of 1884 and his greatest adventure to date was to begin.

Arriving at the Maltese Cross Ranch on June 22, Roosevelt began the life of a cowboy. Medora was now the growing cow town and Little Missouri was rapidly sliding to the ghost level.

As he rode about on his horse Manitou it was obvious that his beef cattle enterprise was growing.

Roosevelt shortly met with the Marquis de Mores and later headed north, downstream along the Little Missouri River. He found the ranch country to his liking, purchased it, and then with the Marquis headed north to Montana.

By July 1 he was traveling back east to find his old friends William Sewall and Wilmont Dow of Maine, in hopes of bringing them west to run his Elkhorn Ranch, some thirty miles north of Medora.

After visiting his new daughter Lee he shortly contacted Sewall and Dow, asking them to come to New York. With time allowed for politics, by late July Roosevelt, Sewall and Dow were on the train west, spending the night of August 1 in the Bad Lands.

Sending his Maine friends north to the Elkhorn Ranch with a herd and a cattle herder, Roosevelt spent time at the Maltese Cross with Merrifield and Ferris who were somewhat disgruntled at the intro- duction of two Maine lumbermen into their territory.

In the days south of Medora he spent hours in the saddle, usually in search of lost horses. Each day he became stronger. One evening in Mingusville, thirty-five miles west of Medora, he headed for Nolan's Hotel, tired and hungry. As he approached he heard gunshots.

He strode into the barroom where there were a number of rough looking men. He noticed first a man with two pistols who had just shot holes through the face of the saloon clock. The sight of Roosevelt, his garb and thick glasses were too much for the hombre, who shouted "Four eyes is going to treat!"

Roosevelt seated himself, trying to attract no notice. The pistol- carrying man, using extreme profanity, repeated his order. Roosevelt, apparently resigned to his fate, rising slowly muttered, "If I've got to, I've got to." But as he rose he lashed out quickly and drove his right fist to the jaw of the gunman. Then a left and another right as both guns went off and the bully fell, striking his head against the bar. Roosevelt quickly grabbed the guns. Other patrons hurried the dazed bad man out of the bar to the street. The next day the gunman left town.

A month later Roosevelt went hunting again. The arsenal he car- ried was impressive even during that wild period. In addition to the customary Colt .45 he carried a shotgun, a .40-90 Sharp's rifle, a .45-75 Winchester, and a .50-150 double barreled Webley. T.R. was well armed with over fifteen hundred rounds of ammunition to load into his weapons.

The hunt lasted from mid-August to mid-September and his kill included all sizes of game. His total increased as he rode back to Elkhorn from the Big Horns. The game he took ranged from a variety of birds to a huge grizzly that he shot dead between the eyes.

The trip back to Elkhorn was long and arduous. Roosevelt, becoming impatient, rode the last seventy-five miles non-stop with Bill Merrifield. The two were in the saddle for twenty-four hours on the final run to the ranch. Roosevelt left for New York to vote in the fall election. The hunt had purged his mind and enabled him now to finally accept the loss of Alice.

In the Dakotas the winter of 1894-1895 started even earlier than usual. Roosevelt was back in the area by mid-November. He returned to the ranch at Maltese Cross to write after further outdoor escapades. He was frostbitten on his face, hands, and feet in the sub-zero temperatures. He returned from this western ice box in January where in the east he wrote prolifically of his adventures. By April 15 he was on his way west once more.

Visiting his friend de Mores, he found the Frenchman prospering and now in addition to his other ventures owning the Medora-to-Deadwood stagecoach line. This line boasted four stagecoaches, the "Kitty," "Deadwood," "Medora," and "Dakota." The line operated on a regular schedule, covering the two hundred-mile trip between the two terminal points, and was supervised by A.T. Packard, a former college baseball star and editor of the weekly newspaper, *The Bad Lands Cowboy*.

His cattle having survived the winter, Roosevelt purchased fifteen hundred additional head for $39,000, bringing his total investment in the Dakota Territory to $85,000. The additional herd arrived in Medora from Minnesota on May 5 with most of the cattle going north to the Elkhorn Ranch, where T.R. was living at a new ranch house.

On the first night the herd at Elkhorn stampeded, with only Roosevelt and one other cowhand guarding them. Only after an hour of punishing riding were the two successful in quieting the herd.

Two weeks later Roosevelt joined the spring roundup north of Elkhorn. He wrangled calves, roped steers and generally proved his mettle with the local cowhands. He rode more miles each day than any of the others. Up at three o'clock in the morning, in the saddle all day, going through several horses, turning in late at night, he soon earned the respect of all.

He was tanned and tough and finally the man he wanted to be as he returned to New York. Roosevelt was now twenty-six and for the next year would continue to divide his time between New York and Dakota Territory.

In the late summer Roosevelt was at the Elkhorn ranch with the families of Sewall and Dow. He settled in and before long was back at work. A letter to Roosevelt from the Marquis de Mores posed some threat, but T.R.'s firm stance and letter in return settled matters short of a duel and maintained friendship between the two.

A confrontation between Roosevelt and five Indians also occurred during this western tour. T.R. faced them down in the back country with strong words, his rifle, and a firm approach.

On the morning of March 24, 1886, Roosevelt went out expecting to find the boat that he had tied on the bank of the Little Missouri, but found instead that the craft had been stolen. The boat was vital in this part of the country and Roosevelt decided to go after the thieves.

As part of his position as president of the Stockmen's Association, Roosevelt was a deputy sheriff of Billings County. As deputy sheriff he knew he had a responsibility to pursue any outlaws in the country.

Roosevelt was convinced that the thieves must be the only other men in the area, Red Head Finnegan, a known gunman and horse thief, and his companions Burnsted and Pfaffenbach.

A new boat was quickly built by Sewall and Dow, who, along with Roosevelt, headed north, downriver, to capture the culprits. The river was icy but nevertheless they moved through the freezing late winter under difficult conditions. The sides of the scow were covered with ice as were the oars, but the trio pursued.

In three days they came upon their boat. Stealthily they moved upon the sandbar and Roosevelt, using his rifle, captured Pfaffenbach. Then waiting quietly, they captured Burnsted and Finnegan on their return to camp. They disarmed the thieves.

For the next five days they boated downriver, then traveled overland to the C-Diamond Ranch. Roosevelt hired a wagon and two horses with a driver and put the outlaws in the wagon. Leaving Sewall and Dow, Roosevelt walked south for thirty-six hours behind the driver and outlaws, carrying his rifle to prevent escape.

Forty-five miles later he arrived with his captives in Dickinson, some thirty miles east of Medora. Turning Finnegan, Burnsted, and Pfaffenbach over to the local sheriff, he was paid his fee and travel costs for three hundred miles, the total coming to about fifty dollars.

Returning to Medora on April 12, he chaired the meeting of the Stockmen's Association the next day with the Marquis de Mores in attendance. But there was no question now, Roosevelt was the primary leader in that room. He had captured the gunman Finnegan and now was regarded as somewhat a folk hero.

This became even more evident five days later when he went to Miles City, Montana, as a delegate to the Montana Stock Growers' Convention. (Harry Longabaugh, the Sundance Kid, was in Miles City at the same time. One wonders if they passed and nodded a greeting on the street).

Back in the Bad Lands, Roosevelt took part once more in the strenuous spring roundup. On July 4 he was back in Dickinson as the orator for Independence Day. A few days later he left again for New York.

But Roosevelt was back in Medora on August 5, noting that a vicious drought was plaguing his cattle country. He took a hunting trip to northern Idaho, going back to New York in the fall. Dark days were ahead for the rancher Roosevelt in the winter to come.

The winter of 1886-87 was to be known as the Winter of the Blue Snow. It turned bitter in mid-November after a summer of drought. The snow built day after day.

After a thawing turning all to mush in December, the real winter set in. Cattle were buried alive or frozen where they stood.

Ranchers froze in the late January blizzard and by spring all that was left was a grisly scene. Cattle bones covered the range and even the tarpaper sides of the building in Medora had been eaten by starving cattle that raided the town.

With warm Chinook winds the thaw came, bringing floods that washed away any good land left. All that could be salvaged were the bones for picking by fertilizer companies.

On April 4, 1887, Roosevelt went back to Medora to view the disaster. After two meetings of the Stockmen's Association, it was decided to sell out at great loss.

Some time earlier the Marquis de Mores had sold his four stagecoaches to Buffalo Bill Cody for his Wild West Show. Now he and his wife left Medora, abandoning the mansion, furniture and all, never to return. The mansion was to become a North Dakota tourist attraction. Roosevelt, too, bailed out at great financial loss, retaining only a small part of his holdings. Theodore Roosevelt went home to New York.

His Dakota days were included in his book, *Ranch Life and the Hunting Trail*, in 1888. The book was illustrated with sketches by Roosevelt's friend, Frederic Remington. Remington's early life in some ways paralleled that of Roosevelt.

His first set of drawings were done to illustrate Roosevelt's series of articles in *Century* magazine. Remington's sketches accurately showed the American cowboy described by Roosevelt.

This then was a trio who helped make the cowboy a real American western romantic hero: Remington in art, Owen Wister in literature, and Roosevelt in his verve and political position.

The West remained part of Theodore Roosevelt's life. In the winter of 1898 when the *U.S.S. Maine* was blown up and sunk at a cost of 262 American lives, Roosevelt, then assistant secretary of the Navy, quickly rose to the cause.

Shortly he became acting secretary, and one indeed of action. By late April he had won a commission from President McKinley as lieutenant colonel to lead three regiments of American "Frontiersmen" against the Spanish in Cuba.

On May 12, 1898, he left for San Antonio in a Brooks Brothers cavalry lieutenant colonel's blue uniform complete with spurs. He had already enlisted fifty Ivy League gentlemen in the First U.S. Volunteer Cavalry. Now he was off to sign up cowboys to ride and fight alongside his Knickerbockers.

The range of personalities in the Rough Riders was indeed great and included even Tom Horn, veteran cowboy, lawman, range detective and bounty hunter.

Roosevelt set up at the elegant Menger Hotel next to the Alamo, maintaining his flair for the dramatic. He then drove his men and whipped them into fighting shape at Camp Wood. What happened when they joined the war in Cuba is history.

Roosevelt as a nominee for U.S. vice president went back to the Bad Lands in September of 1900. After many whistle stops on his campaign he rode the train west of Bismarck. Past Dickinson Roosevelt rode alone on the rear observation deck, gazing with great sentiment at the scene he had once roamed. The train made another stop later near Little Missouri where Roosevelt borrowed a horse and rode off across the Bad Lands by himself. His sentimental ride completed, he returned to the train.

Roosevelt's infatuation with the great American West would never end. He returned many times to the part of the country he loved so well.

References

Dictionary of American Portraits, Dover Publications, New York, 1967.

McLoughlin, Denis. *Wild and Wooly, An Encyclopedia of the Old West*, Doubleday and Company, New York, 1975.

Morris, Edmund. *The Rise of Theodore Roosevelt*, Coward, McCann and Geoghegan, Inc. New York 1979.

Pringle, Henry F. *Theodore Roosevelt*, Harcourt, Brace and Company, New York, 1956.

Prindle, Barclay Ward, Sharon, Connecticut.

Roosevelt, Theodore. *Ranch Life and the Hunting Trail,* The Century Co., New York 1888.

Taylor, Lonn and Ingrid, Maar. *The American Cowboy*, Harper and Row, New York, 1983.

Robert G. McCubbin

Bob McCubbin was born in Stillwater, Oklahoma, 1937. His life-long interest in the history of the American West, especially out-laws, lawmen, and gunfighters, developed long before he received a degree in mechanical engineering from Oklahoma State University. He was fifteen years old when his interest was first stimulated by the works of Walter Noble Burns, James D. Horan, and Stuart Lake, pioneer writers in the field. As a teeneager he began collecting signed first edition books of the genre. Over the years he has known and corresponded with all of the giants in the field, including Stuart Lake, Homer Croy, M.G. Fulton, J. Evetts Haley, Walter Prescott Webb, William MacLeod Raine, Earl R. Forrest, Wayne Gard, W.A. Keleher, and many others. His collections have expanded to include original photographs and memorabilia relating to the outlaw-law-man field. He has authored no books himself, but has contributed introductions to several, including the 1961 edition of John Wesley Hardin's autobiography published by the University of Oklahoma Press. Bob has been very generous in allowing writers to draw upon his vast collection of original photographs for use as illustrations in their publications, and has been honored by having three books ded-icated to him. In early 1999 he retired as vice president of opera-tions for the El Paso Natural Gas Company. In the fall of that year, he, with two partners, purchased Western Publications, publishers of *True West* and *Old West* magazines. He currently lives in Santa Fe, New Mexico.

LONG LOST PHOTOGRAPH OF TONY NEIS AND BOB OLINGER IS FOUND

•

By Robert G. McCubbin

NOLA *Quarterly*, Fall-Winter 1990

Henry Antrim, alias Kid, alias William H. Bonney, was uncom-
fortably and impatiently languishing in the Santa Fe jail, hoping
Governor Lew Wallace would help him out of his situation. Wallace
resided only a short distance from the jail in the Palace of the
Governors on the north side of the Plaza. Two stalwart deputy
United States marshals paused on the west side of the Plaza at the
photograph studio of W. Henry Brown:

> Tony Neis and Bob Olinger, the twin deputies, have just had a photo-
> graph taken of themselves taken at Bennett and Brown's Gallery. The
> picture is a good one and shows the two men off to good advantage.
> They are both well grown boys weighing perhaps 240 pounds each,
> and are, what might be called, a heavy team. Bob had to sit down to
> keep his head in range of the camera. [*Santa Fe Daily New Mexican*,
> March 2, 1881.]

Only four weeks after having their picture taken together, these
two deputies were destined to escort Antrim, now known to the
world as Billy the Kid, down the Rio Grande to Mesilla for trial.
After the Kid received a death sentence, Olinger was selected to
guard the Kid in Lincoln while awaiting execution. On April 28,
1881, Olinger would fall victim to the Kid during his dramatic

escape and thus be propelled into immortality, making the photograph one of great historical interest.

Phil Rasch, the indefatigable researcher of the Lincoln County War and it's participants, made note of the above quoted newspaper item in 1963, with an added comment: "So far the writer has been unable to locate a copy of this picture."[1] As a collector of historical photographs, and a particular student of the visual record of western outlaws, gunfighters, and lawmen, I have been dreaming of finding that photograph since reading Rasch's account twenty-seven years ago.

In October, 1989, I traveled to Provo, Utah, to examine the Lily Casey Klasner collection which was being processed. The material had been used by Eve Ball in compiling the book *My Girlhood Among Outlaws*, published by the University of Arizona Press in 1972. The book contained a chapter entitled "Bob Olinger As I Knew Him" which was somewhat of a defense of the much maligned character of Olinger. In a footnote Mrs. Ball noted: "Reportedly they [Lily Casey and Bob Olinger] were engaged to be married."[2] Mrs. Ball also stated that "After Olinger's death Lily Casey was given his six-shooter, field glasses, and gauntlets."[3]

So, I reasoned that if the Neis/Olinger photo still existed, it might be in the collection in Provo. However, I was discouraged by a couple of factors. I knew Eve Ball and she never mentioned the existence of the picture to me. And I reasoned that if she had seen it she would have used it in the Klasner book. Further, I had seen a listing of the photographs in the collection and there was no mention of the Neis/Olinger photo.

But I made the trip to Utah anyway, because there was other material in the collection that I wanted to examine, including an original *carte de visite* of the famous Charles Bowdre and Wife photograph. I had acquired many years ago from the Pat Garrett family another original CDV of Bowdre and his wife, taken at the same time but a different pose. [This as yet unpublished picture was later published in Fred Nolan's *The Lincoln County War, A Documented History*, University of Oklahoma Press. Ed] I wanted to make a close comparison of the two originals.

In going through the Klasner picture collection, I had the advantage of knowing what Olinger looked like, for in 1985 I acquired an original cabinet card photograph taken in Santa Fe of Olinger and

Tony Neis and Bob Olinger. Robert McCubbin Collection.

James Dolan, which at one time had belonged to the Dolan family. [This picture also appeared in Nolan's book. Ed.] So when I came upon the original cabinet card photograph in the Klasner collection, which is now published for the first time in this *Quarterly*, I knew in an instant that it was the long lost, long sought after image of the two famous deputies! What a thrill that was!

It was labeled No. 12 and listed in the Eve Ball inventory as "two men unidentified." So Eve had never realized the significance of the picture. It is on the card of "W. Henry Brown, Photographer, West Side of Plaza, Santa Fe, N.M." Richard Rudisill points out that Brown was in partnership with George C. Bennett from early 1880 until February, 1881, after which time he advertised only under his own name.[4]

Very little is really known today regarding either of the two deputies. Lily Casey Klasner states very matter-of-factly that Olinger's full name was Robert Ameridth Olinger.[5] Utley calls him Charles Robert Olinger.[6] He was known in New Mexico as Bob and was appointed deputy sheriff of Doña Ana County on April 15, 1881, as Robert Olinger. Other official documents refer to him only as Robert, with no middle name or initial. Rasch suggests that he was born after 1850, but no birth record has been found. I would suspect that he was less than the age of thirty at the time of his death, perhaps as young as twenty-five.

Emerson Hough and Walter Noble Burns succeeded in making him the villain in the story of Billy the Kid, but testimonials in his behalf can be found.[7] As Lily Casey Klasner said: "One thing I do know, however, and that is that Bob Olinger went to his death bravely and courageously as became a worthy peace officer." She had a point. When he heard the shot that killed Bell, he didn't cower in the safety of the Wortley dining room, he ran to the courthouse...and to his death.[8]

Even less is known of Tony Neis, other than he was Chief Deputy in Santa Fe under U.S. Marshal John E. Sherman, Jr.[9] That seems to be all we know about him...but, then, he wasn't killed by Billy the Kid!

NOTES
1 Rasch, Phillip J. "The Olingers, Known Yet Forgotten." *Corral Dust*, Potomac Corral of the Westerners, Vol. VIII, No. 1. February, 1963.
2 Klasner, Lily. *My Girlhood Among Outlaws*. Edited by Eve Ball, University of Arizona Press, 1972. p. 185.
3 Ibid., p. 188.
4 Ridisill, Richard. *Photographers of the New Mexico Territory*. Museum of New Mexico, 1973. p. 17.
5 Klasner. See note 2. p. 184.
6 Utley, Robert M. *Billy the Kid, A Short and Violent Life*. University of Nebraska Press, 1989. p. 176.
7 Rasch. See note 1. Rasch quotes a number Olinger's detractors as well as his admirers.
8 Klasner. p. 190.

9 Ball, Larry D. *The United States Marshals of New Mexico and Arizona.* University of New Mexico Press. 1978.

Leon C. Metz

Born in Parkersburg, West Virginia, in 1930, Leon Metz joined the Air Force after high school graduation and served four years as a propeller specialist. Most of his tour of duty was spent at Biggs Air Force Base near El Paso, Texas. After leaving the service he spent several months back in West Virginia and in Los Angeles before returning to El Paso in early 1953 to settle permanently. For several months he held a number of jobs, including radio patrolman for the El Paso Police Department, before beginning work with an oil company where he remained for fourteen years. In 1967 he accepted a position as Library Archivist for the University of Texas at El Paso. He left the university during the administration of El Paso Mayor Tom Westfall to serve as the mayor's executive assistant. Returning to the university in 1981, he spent four years as an assistant to the president and another four years as public affairs officer for an El Paso bank. During all these years he had been researching, writing, and speaking on historical subjects. In 1989 he turned to this as a full-time occupation. He has written many articles and fifteen nonfiction books dealing with the American Southwest and averages 150 talks a year. His newspaper column and radio and TV shows are El Paso staples. He has been president of many organizations, including the Western Writers of America. Among his many awards was the prestigious Spur Award from the WWA in 1997. He and his wife, Cheryl, an autistic specialist, have four children.

AN INCIDENT AT CHRISTMAS

•

By Leon C. Metz

NOLA *Quarterly*, Spring 1990

This is not your usual Christmas tale, for there is nothing redeeming or uplifting nor even religious about it. It is a story of bitterness and hate and death that began with a soft snow falling in Socorro, New Mexico. Parishioners were preparing for the December 24, 1880, evening services at the First Presbyterian Church.

Down in El Paso and Ysleta, the Texas Rangers had hung up their six-shooters and gone home for the holidays. Sergeant James Gillett, author *of Six Years With the Texas Rangers*, and the most famous Texas Ranger of his time, had joined his pretty fifteen-year-old wife Helen at the home of her father, Captain George W. Baylor. The affable Baylor commanded the ranger battalion stationed at Ysleta.

Roughly 190 miles separated Ysleta/El Paso from Socorro, New Mexico. All of these communities started as ancient Spanish settlements. Each had populations of fewer than two thousand, and all were mining/railroad towns with lawless backgrounds.

The portly A.M. Conklin had not resided long in Socorro, New Mexico. He had edited the *Indianapolis Sun*, but after discharge from the Union Army he moved to New Mexico and edited the *Las Vegas Gazette*. From there he published the *Albuquerque Herald* before settling in Socorro with the *Socorro Sun*. In today's vernacu-

lar, he would be a "crusading editor," meaning he found a lot of sin
in his adopted city, and he was vigorously bringing it to battle.

Conklin stoutly supported the First Presbyterian Church, and as an
elder he sat near the altar during the Christmas Eve services, 1880.
To the rear, Onofre and Abran Baca entered. They were brothers as
well as local hidalgos, with powerful old family connections in New
Mexico as well as Ysleta, Texas.

Both sat down and one placed a muddy boot on a chair occupied
by an unidentified young lady, by some accounts, soiling her shawl.
A commotion started, and Conklin investigated. At this point, a little
more tact and a little less resentment on the part of both Conklin
and the Bacas might have calmed the situation. Instead, harsh words
erupted, and since Conklin had the most clout, congregation members ejected the Bacas.

When services ended at 11 p.m., the Bacas were waiting outside
the door. They shoved aside Mrs. Conklin and shot the editor twice.
Conklin slipped toward the earth gasping, "May the Lord have
mercy on my soul." He had worshipped during his last Christmas.

The murderers escaped, leaving the church a "house of weeping
and wailing."[1]

Following the funeral the day after Christmas, Colonel Ethan
Eaton, former Fort Craig commander, rode into Socorro from his
ranch and organized 400 Anglo vigilantes. They called themselves
the Socorro Committee for Safety.

The *Las Vegas Daily Optic*, with little interest in calming troubled waters, wrote a barely restrained editorial: "Every able bod-
ied American has armed himself to assist in the capture of the
murderers. The Mexicans have been apprised of the contemplated
movement and are prepared to resist the arrest of the young assassins [sic]."

The *Optic* mistakenly identified Jacobo Baca, a relative of the
brothers, as one of the slayers. When Sheriff Juan Maria Garcia,
also a relative, refused to place Jacobo Baca under arrest, and
threatened to swear in additional deputies to keep order, the vigilantes expelled him from office. In turn they incarcerated Jacobo
Baca, even though be was not involved. They planned to hold him
hostage until the Baca family made a swap for the murderers.

Late that night someone slipped a revolver through the jail window to Jacobo Baca. He attempted to escape, wounded a guard, and

was himself shot dead by the vigilantes.

Rumors now swept the town of a Hispanic uprising, and a panicked Eaton telegraphed City Marshal Hill at San Marcial, New Mexico: "Send immediately as many Americans, well armed, as you have to save the lives of Americans at Socorro."

A.A. Robinson, division superintendent of the Atchison, Topeka and Santa Fe refused to release a train, so locally organized vigilantes seized Engine No. 97. It careened into Socorro, with thirty-five Anglo reinforcements.

Hispanic and Anglo factions both wired the governor for assistance. "Leave the case for the District Judge," he responded. "Have referred telegrams to the District Attorney. Peace must be preserved, or it will be much worse for the guilty. Troops are in route to Socorro."[2]

Four days after Christmas, twenty soldiers of the 13th Infantry restored order. But while Anglos and Hispanics had been quarreling and fighting, the assailants had fled south.

A circular offering $500 reward for Abran and Onofre Baca reached Texas Ranger James Gillett in Ysleta, ten miles southeast of El Paso, Texas, and the seat of El Paso County. Gillett had barely finished his Christmas and New Year's turkey before putting a watch on the home of El Paso County Judge Jose Baca, an uncle of the fugitives. During late February, the rangers arrested two well dressed men squatting on the judge's front porch. One was Abran Baca. He was chained and returned to Socorro. His fate is unknown.[3]

A few days later, Onofre Baca was spotted clerking in a Zaragaza, Chihuahua store, directly across the Rio Grande from Ysleta. Gillett and Corporal George Lloyd eased their horses across the river, rode quietly into town, and through an open window watched Baca measuring dry goods.

While Lloyd held the horses, Gillett walked inside, put a gun barrel against Baca's ear (as a female patron fainted), and ordered him to step lively. A Mexican posse, firing wildly, nearly caught the rangers short of the river, but the rangers with their captive escaped into Ysleta. A furious Captain George Baylor said the Mexicans should have shot Gillett and Lloyd "into doll rags."

Gillett and Baca took the stage from Ysleta to Mesilla, New Mexico (about seventy miles), where Gillett checked into a hotel, chained Baca to him, and the two slept in the same bed.

The next day they proceeded by stage to Rincon, terminus for the Santa Fe Railroad, where Gillett wired Socorro authorities that he was bringing in his prisoner.

An answering wire came from the New Mexico governor, who wanted Baca brought to Santa Fe where there was less danger of a lynching. The problem was that the train went right through Socorro.

The train reached Socorro late at night, and Gillett was met by Deputy Sheriff Eaton and thirty armed vigilantes. After a brief argument, both Gillett and Baca were hustled into a "bus" and driven toward the jail. Gillett kept his Winchester rifle.

By now a hundred armed men had surrounded the vehicle. Gillett threatened them with his Winchester, but it was jerked from his hands and he was thrown to the ground. Gillett argued that he could not get the reward unless he delivered the prisoner to the jail door. So everybody got back on board the bus and proceeded to the jail.

This time a group of vigilantes took Gillett by the arms and walked him back down the street. Baca was hustled in the other direction to a nearby corral and lynched from a gate beam.

Early the next morning, Baca's relatives awoke Gillett at the hotel. They asked for keys so that they might remove the shackles from the dead Baca's legs. Gillett later wrote, "I felt both mortified and ashamed."

That afternoon, as Gillett boarded the train for the trip home, a group of vigilantes paid him $250 and thanked him for delivering the prisoner. They promised financial assistance if Gillett should get in trouble because of the Mexican kidnapping. [4]

And an international uproar did occur. The State Department put pressure on Texas Governor Oran Roberts, who sent word to Captain Baylor that Gillett must go.[5] James Gillett resigned from the Texas Rangers and found employment as El Paso city marshal, replacing the flamboyant Dallas Stoudenmire.

Meanwhile, Gillett's wife divorced him for adultery. His only son changed his name to Harper Lee, and became a popular Mexican bullfighter. Gillett could not even keep his job. He struck an El Paso alderman with a six-shooter, and the city council dismissed him as city marshal. Following this low point, Gillett moved to the Big Bend and became a respected cattleman as well as organizer of

Cowboy Camp Meetings. He died in 1937 and is buried in Marfa.

The physical outcome of this dramatic Christmas Eve incident is self evident: at least three men died violently. Several families were shattered, and numerous reputations destroyed. An international controversy troubled relations between the United States and Mexico.

The moral conclusion seems almost as clear: obstinate Anglo and Hispanic factions, each overreacting and practicing their own brand of racism, had proven that when goodwill, understanding, and compassion do not exist, there can be no peace even on the birthday of the King of Peace—even on Christmas.

References

1 The *Las Vegas Daily Optic*. December 27, 28, 29, 1880.

2 The *Daily New Mexican*. December 29, 1880.

3 James Gillett, *Six Years with the Texas Rangers* (Yale University Press, 1925), 212-222.

4 Ibid.

5 Adjutant General's Office, Capt. George W. Baylor to Adj. Gen. John B. Jones, Jan. 16, 1881; Baylor to Caldwell, April 23, 1881. Also see *Foreign Relations of the United States*, 1881, portion dealing with Mexico.

Rick Miller

Born in San Diego, California, in 1941, Rick Miller moved with his family to Dallas, texas, in 1947 and was raised there. Entering the army after high school graduation in 1958, he served in the 82nd Airborne Division and was discharged in 1961. He attended East Texas State College for two years and then joined the Dallas Police Department, where he spent twelve years, rising from patrol officer to lieutenant. While a police officer he earned a BA from the University of Texas at Arlington (1970), attended the FBI National Academy (1972), and received a master's degree in public adminis-tration from Southern Methodist University (1975). During the next six years he worked as a program coordinator for the Texas Organized Crime Prevention Council, chief of police at Killeen, consultant with the Texas Commission on Law Enforcement Officer Standards and Education, and chief of the Denton, Texas, police department. He resigned in 1981 to enter Baylor Law School, where he received a juris doctorate in 1983. He maintained a private law practice until 1992 when he was elected to the office of Bell County Attorney, a position he still holds. His writing credits include *The Train Robbing Bunch* (1983), *Bounty Hunter* (1988). *Bloody Bill Longley* (1996) and *Sam Bass & Gang* (1999). A NOLA member since 1980, he has served on the board of directors, held the office of president for two terms, edited the *Quarterly*, and is currently NOLA's secretary. His wife Paula is membership secretary for the organization.

LONGLEY LETTER SURFACES AFTER BOOK PUBLISHED

•

By Rick Miller

NOLA *Quarterly*, January-March, 1997

One of the problems with finally committing your research to a published book is the information that pops up after publishing occurs. *Bloody Bill Longley*, published in the spring of 1996, was no exception. With the pages still warm from the presses, noted El Paso collector Bob McCubbin turned up an original photograph of Longley that surpassed the copy used in the book. Also, the following letter was recently discovered in an April 28, 1878, issue of the *Illustrated Police News*. In a letter to the editor from his Galveston jail cell, Longley, still awaiting the outcome of his appeal after being convicted of the 1875 murder of Wilson Anderson in Lee County, Texas, forcefully urged his continuing effort to rewrite the history that he created, perhaps in a last ditch effort to impress the appellate court. Despite his claims that the stories of his bloody deeds were fabricated by the press, the facts indicate that Longley himself spread the tales. And it was to no avail; Longley hanged on October 11. 1878.

"The following interesting letter from William P. Longley, frequently referred to as the 'King of Texas Man-Killers,' and now under death sentence in Galveston Jail, is published in full in accordance with the condemned man's request, and will well repay perusal:

181

"GALVESTON JAIL, Texas, "March 25, 1878
"EDITOR POLICE NEWS:

"*Dear Sir*-I see in your POLICE NEWS that some one is continually writing sketches about me which do me great injustice. But, sir, I do not mean to insinuate regarding any of your correspondents, for I believe that they are misinformed by men who are very prejudiced toward me. Now, I do not intend trying to justify myself in everything, but I am undoubtedly justifiable in some things that I have done; and there is one thing that I do stoutly deny, and that is that I am a cold blooded, wilful [sic] murderer, as the NEWS correspondent often says. I have always acted in self-defence [sic]. I have not been dodging the law for the past ten years. It is the high-toned mobs here in Texas that I was always afraid of, for there has never been any law in Texas but mob law—that is, in western and middle Texas—and there has been two parties here ever since 1860 which [was] about the time of the rebellion. I was a small boy then, but it is well I remember the heart sickening murders that were perpetrated by the secession party upon as good men as the sun ever shone on, simply because they differed in politics. If all

THE BLOODY DEEDS

that were done in Texas during the war could be written down on paper, without any exaggeration, it would chill the blood of every human being; it would be a shame to the civilized world. It was nothing uncommon in those times to see from two to seven men hanging on one live-oak tree, with a card pinned on their backs which said, 'These chaps came to their death by supporting black republicanism.' The meaning of that was that they had voted for the Union. I have known mobs to go to houses and pull the very best of men out of their beds, and shoot them while on their knees praying to God, and their wives and children pleading with the leader of the murderers to have mercy; but mercy was unknown to them and they would shoot men to death and leave them laying on the floor. I suppose that is how Evergreen got the name of being a sort of

TRAINING SCHOOL FOR MURDERERS.

"My father voted a Union ticket and came very near being murdered on the spot. All that saved him was his being one of the oldest settlers in Texas, and because he had served in the Mexican war and was under Gen. Houston at the battle of San Jacinto, and he still lives, but he is very old. He lives now in Bell county, Texas. They

William P. "Bloody Bill" Longley. *Courtesy R.G. McCubbin*

talked very strong of hanging him, and did abuse him every way they could. And now I will show you why they got so down on me. Soon after the war the sons of those murdered men grew up into manhood, and of course they wanted revenge for the blood of their fathers. Well, then because I befriended them in some little things people became embittered against me, and I was waylaid and shot at and the boys were getting killed on every side, and then what on earth could I do but keep out of the way? I knew perfectly well what my fate would be if they succeeded in getting their hands on me; but well they knew that

I NEVER STOLE

anything, for my father kept me and there is not a man on earth that can say that he ever traced a stolen horse to me.

"Well, now this killing negroes, as they say, for pastime, is the most ungodly falsehood of all of it. It was those fellows themselves that did all the negro killing and laid it on me in order to get the United States troops turned against me, and they succeeded in doing it, too, and caused General Griffin to offer $1000 reward for me, dead or alive. Then they had me where they wanted me, for I had no protection, and my father advised me to leave the State. So I left and went to Wyoming territory and enlisted in Company B, Second United States Cavalry. After serving two years there, a lieutenant by the name of Norwood got in command of the company, and he was always drunk and he treated us very bad, and on that account

I DESERTED

and came back to Texas, and all those reports about my killing a soldier in Gonzales county, and the cattle drover, Rector. and the Osage Indians and then the soldier at Leavenworth, Kansas, and the quarter-master, in Wyoming, is all a conglomerated, damned lie. There is not one word of it true, and they can not produce any proof of it, but I can easily prove it to be a lie. An editor in Lee county wrote my 'life,' as he calls it, and wrote up such stuff as would sell his books; and then there was an interview with me here, on the 16th of last September, by a *Galveston News* reporter, and after a little talk he went off and wrote out a great long piece, which he got from reports that had been circulated up the country, and he just called it 'an interview with Bill Longley,' when I had

NO SUCH TALK

with him at all. Now, sir, all in the world I want is justice, for there was no possible chance on earth for me to do any other way than the way I have done; for if I had ever given myself up, or had ever been captured at any time previous to the time that I was I would certainly have been shot or hung without a trial. But I might as well have been mobbed as to be hung by the jury that tried me, for it was no trial at all. It was the greatest mockery of a trial that ever was known on earth. The jury was stocked [sic] on me, and every witness of mine was run off, and I had no lawyer. My father received letters with no names to them, telling him that if he assisted me in getting a lawyer he would surely be killed, and my father and mother were not allowed to come and see me while I was in Giddings jail. It has been three years since I have seen them. It has been ten months since I was captured. I was tried for

KILLING WILSON ANDERSON

in Lee county. I would tell you all about that but you have published the particulars. I see that you have been informed that I killed
my uncle, Caleb Longley, in Lee county, but that is not true; it was
the killing of his son by Anderson that caused me to kill Anderson.
It has been stated that he was not armed when I killed him, but that
is told to influence people against me. Anderson was well-armed
and on the lookout for me when I came upon him, and had a fair
chance, for there was not a tree nor anything near us, and it was
about one o'clock in the daytime in an open field when I rode on
him.

"Now, you have law in your country, and you try criminals by law.
But let me say to you that you haven't the least idea of things in
Texas. I will just relate one little circumstance out of many hundred
similar cases: Once in Washington county, before Lee county was
made, near Evergreen, where I was raised, the mob hung an old man
and his son and son-in-law, and in a few years his youngest son
grew up to the age of sixteen years, and there never was a single
charge against him. He worked hard to support his widowed mother,
but he was regarded as a brave, determined boy, and of course he

HAD A BITTER FEELING

toward the men who murdered his father and brothers, for he
knew they had been hung for their politics. So one evening he got a
little too much whiskey in and made the remark, as he passed the
tree where his father and brothers were hung, in company with a son
of one of the mob who did the hanging, that justice 'would yet overtake the cowards that did that deed.' This boy went on home, and the
son of the widowed mother went to his home, and in a few nights a
crowd of masked men went to his mother's, and, pulling him out of
bed, took him to the same tree on which his father had been hung, to
hang him. Of course he

PLEAD HARD FOR HIS LIFE

and they knew they were hanging him for nothing, only because
they were afraid of him, and one of the mob proposed to him that if
he would go before the court and plead guilty to theft, so they could
send him to State Prison, they would not hang him, and of course he
agreed to it. He told them that he would say that he had stolen a
beef steer, and they told him that one beef steer would not be sufficient to send him to the penitentiary, because it did not amount to

twenty dollars. 'Well,' the boy says, 'I will say that I stole two beef steers.' So they told him that would do, and they would now put him in jail until court on that charge, and if he told anything while in jail, they would take him out and hang him; and that when court set, he must not object to any one on his jury, and must plead guilty. So he agreed to this, and court came on and the poor boy went to the penitentiary for ten years. He hoped some day to bring the truth to light, but in about three years he

DIED FROM BRUTAL TREATMENT

and exposure, and his poor grief-stricken mother had died about one year before him. Thus ended the once happy family, just because they were Union men. They were not what was called 'Abolitionists;' they never troubled any one, nor influenced any negroes. The long and short of it is this—that the whole family was exterminated simply because they loved the old Union that their fathers had long ago fought and died for. Now, sir, this is true, and thousands of more heart-sickening things than this are true that have been done here in Texas, and which will never come to light. But we have one consolation, and that is that God knows it all. These are the men that have condemned me to death—my very worst ene-mies—and I have

HAD NO SHOWING

for my life and I have so many enemies, that it is no use for me to say anything. But I am not afraid to stand before God who knows all things, for he will give us all a fair trial. Now, sir, I do not ask you to publish this for me. I only write to you to let you hear my side of the question; yet if you should deem any parts of this letter worthy of publication. or all of it, I would be glad to see it. Of course it will do me no good any way, now, but it hurts me to see so many things published against me that I am not guilty of. I suppose you think that I am one of the most cold blooded murderers in Texas, but sir, if you do you are wrong, for I never wanted to kill any one, and what few men I have killed, I thought I was doing right in finishing, and still think so. Every piece that comes out in the NEWS winds up by saying, that 'the most terrible crime that Longley ever committed was the killing of one Rev. Mr. Lay,' because he interfered in my courtship. That is another grand mistake. I do wish you just knew everything I have ever done, and all the circumstances attached to each case. I am satisfied you would form a different opinion of me.

I hope you will think on this matter, and think of the condition that I am now in, and how many enemies I have got, and when you hear such unreasonable tales of what they call the 'king of Texas man-killers,' just think for a moment, and satisfy yourself that

THEY ARE NOT TRUE

I know you don't believe that I have killed thirty-two men. You cannot believe it.

"Well, I will bring my long and badly composed letter to a close, but I hope you will permit me to write you one more letter just before I am executed. I will be executed about next October. There is no day set yet by the governor. I am in good health and in as good spirits as a man could be under the circumstances. Of course I am well aware of my dreadful condition, and can have no hopes of a commutation, because I have no friends; but then I don't see any use in a man's dying until his time comes, and therefore I am in good spirits, and if I must die on the scaffold I think I will die game. So please accept my kindest respects, as I remain your humble servant,

WILLIAM P. LONGLEY."

Frederick Nolan

Born in Liverpool, England, Frederick Nolan was educated there and at Aberaeron in Wales. Long interested in the American frontier, he was a founder of The English Westerners' Society. A move to London in the early sixties enabled him to pursue the other consuming interest of his life, the American musical theatre. While employed as a reader, and later editor, of Corgi (Bantam) Books in London, he began writing western fiction as Frederick H. Christian. While working in the publishing field for Transworld, Penguin, Collins and Granada in London, and later Ballantine Books and Warner Communications in New York, he produced fourteen western novels. Between 1971 and 1975 he also edited and co-published a widely-read and influential international book trade publication. On July 4, 1973, he made his own "declaration of independence," quit his job as a highly-paid publishing executive and signed a contract to write eight full length novels in a year. the first of these became a best-seller on both sides of the Atlantic and was later filmed by MGM as a starring vehicle for Sophia Loren. Since then he has written many successful thrillers, biographies, childrens' books, and translations from French and German, as well as many radio and television scripts. His lifelong interest in outlaws and gunfighters of the Old west has led to his highly acclaimed trilogy, *The Life and Death of John Henry Tunstall*, *The Lincoln County War: A Documentary History*, and *The West of Billy the Kid*.

THE SHORT, UNHAPPY LIFE OF WILLIAM SEYMOUR DOUGLASS

•

By Frederick Nolan
NOLA *Quarterly*, January-March, 1996

The short, unhappy life of Seymour Douglass is a veritable paradigm of those moral fables so beloved of Victorian times, that of the young man who forsakes the paths of righteousness early in life, and pays the bitterest of prices. How bitter that price could be may be judged from a letter Seymour wrote to his nephew Maurice shortly after his second incarceration in the State Penitentiary in 1886. In it, Seymour recalled how the "roots of evil crept into my heart and ruined my life" during boyhood.

> I was not content to spend my evenings till bedtime with my mother's children, around a happy fireside and the purity of that home circle. But I would run off to the next door neighbor, when they would lend me a pipe to smoke, and gave me tobacco to chew. And after these bad habits had got a good hold upon me, these people told me I must get them so and so, in return for the tobacco I used. In fact, I was set to stealing sugar, coffee, vegetables, meat and some little amount of nearly everything my mother had. This life of guilt and shame was carried on for a long time, and my mother never had a thought that she was being robbed, and that too, by her own boy. This went on till my moral sense was so dulled and outraged, that I did not feel any guilt: And I would go into my mother's trunk and steal all the small change I could find; and by this means she found me out; and the bitter shameful truth,—truth worse than death—pierced that dearest of all hearts.
>
> I nearly troubled that dear mother to death, and at last she deter-

mined to send me away from my early associations; and I went to
Romney [West Virginia] to learn to be a printer. I resolved that I
would do better. I spent my evenings with good young men, at a
boarding school, debating society and in many ways to my profit. I
made rapid advance in my work, and was liked by everybody. I was
careful and honest in all my ways, but did not realize that sense of
honor which should rule the life. I attended Church regularly, and
after some months, was awakened by the spirit of God to a just sense
of my wicked and lost condition if left to myself. He called me to
give up my life in printing and study for the ministry. The Pastor's
daughter, Miss Mary Belle Foote, talked to me many times about it,
and finally mentioned looking up a place for me in a suitable school.
Then I thought, I must tell Dr. Foote and his family all about my
shameful conduct at home. I thought this over for months, fighting
against it; and I gave the devil the victory over me, by packing my
valise and running away...

   After I left Romney, and up to the time I was sent to this prison,
my life was mostly wandering and aimless. I had little regard for
anybody. I could make money easily at printing, as I was rapid and
correct. But my life was not correct, as my gambling and drinking
bore testimony; and three times after I ran away from Romney, I
committed crimes for which I deserved imprisonment.[1]

What these crimes were, and where he committed them, we shall
probably never know. There is no question that he repented them;
the letter to Maurice exhorts that young man to "think soberly, think
seriously, think *manly*! What are you going to be? I can tell you out
of a heart which has passed through the bitter waters of sin and
shame, if I could commence life where you are now, I would, like
Jacob, wrestle with God until He blest me."[2]
   William Seymour Douglass said he was "born and raised in West
Virginia" which is somewhat misleading, since that state did not
come into existence until 1861. When he was received at
Moundsville Penitentiary in West Virginia on August 24, 1878, he
was 27 years of age, indicating he was born in 1861, but since
statewide recording of births did not begin until two years later,
further detail is unavailable. The 1860 census for Hardy County,
Virginia, from which Grant County, West Virginia was formed,
reveals that Seymour, as he was always known, was the third child
and first son of innkeeper Thomas P. Douglass, 46, and Mary F.
Douglass, 36, of Luneys Creek in Milroy Township.
   There were five children, all Virginia-born like their parents: Sarah
Virginia, fifteen in 1860; Ann C., a year younger; William Seymour,

9; Thomas B., age 5; and Adam, age 2 at the time of the census, July 19, 1860. The family was comfortably placed, with real estate valued at $1,500 and personal estate at $600. A decade later, by which time Luneys Creek was in Grant County, West Virginia, their circumstances had been severely reduced. Thomas Douglass does not appear in the census taken on August 31. His widow, Mary, has personal estate of only $200. Virginia, 26, is a housekeeper; Anna, 24, a schoolmistress; Seymour, 19, Thomas, 15, and Adam, 12. All three boys had attended school within the last year.[3]

Of Seymour's boyhood and the fate of his family during the Civil War, there is no record, but he must have seen a great deal of violence—Romney changed hands more than fifty times during the course of the conflict. In one account of his life, he stated that at age 15, i.e., in 1866, he went into a newspaper office as a "printer's devil," learned to set type, became a compositor, afterwards a "jour" and finally, finding the field of journalism too narrow for his special talents, emigrated to Texas.[4]

"Being a man of pleasant address, and apparently a gentleman, he formed the acquaintance [of] and married an estimable young lady, by whom he had one child, which lived but three or four years and was shortly followed by its mother. He left that portion of Texas, went to Lampasas, and started a newspaper called the *Lampasas Advertiser* [sic]. Here he again married."[5]

He arrived in Lampasas around 1872. The tradition there is that he got a job on the *Lampasas Dispatch,* probably as a typesetter. On December 31, 1873, he married Sara Ann "Sally Ann" Horrell, youngest daughter of a family notorious, in the words of the attorney general of Texas, for "the branding, killing, and skinning of other peoples' cattle." From what little is known about them, it is safe to assume the Horrells were not an easy clan to become intimate with, so there can be little doubt, if Seymour was permitted to court Sally Ann, that he was aware of all this: he must have been around in March, when the "boys" killed State Police Captain Thomas G. Williams and four of his men, and in September when the brothers and a number of their kin fled Lampasas to avoid trial.

Sam, Tom, Merritt, Mart, and Ben Horrell betook themselves to Lincoln County, New Mexico, where in short order they became embroiled in a race war that cost many lives, including that of Ben, the youngest of the Horrell brothers, and they were eventually forced to flee New Mexico and returned to Lampasas in February 1874.[6]

Meanwhile, Douglass had been appointed a deputy sheriff, "and performed the duty so well, especially that portion of it connected with catching the wild outlaws of the frontier that when his time as deputy sheriff expired he was elected marshal."

> As a Marshal there is no doubt that Douglas[s] made his mark on more than one occasion, principally inscribed no doubt with 40 caliber bullets. He always brought in his man, but as often feet foremost as with perpendicular, but one day he went out to arrest some one on a warrant, he followed probably his last trail (but one) of death. He returned with the prisoner strapped to the back of a horse. But the prisoner was as dead as cold lead could make him. One story goes that the dead man had many friends who believed that he had been deliberately murdered and swore to avenge him. Another, but somewhat less plausible one, was that the score keepers of the coroner's jury disagreed as to the number of bullet holes in the dead man, and the coolness that arose on that occasion gradually centered upon Douglas[s]. Be that as it may, Douglas[s] directly after the above occurrence left Texas for the mountains of West Virginia.[7]

Perhaps the case referred to was one that happened in November 1875. In his capacity as a deputy sheriff, Douglass was ordered by the Lampasas grand jury to arrest a Dr. I.W. Hudson for questioning. Hudson was a former dentist who had abandoned his profession to run a gambling house. Douglass and his posse found Hudson about two miles from Lampasas and arrested him. On the way back to town, Hudson broke away and was pursued about a mile. Douglass ordered the fugitive to stop, but Hudson refused to do so, drawing his pistol. Douglass, armed with a Winchester, exchanged fire with Hudson, who was fatally wounded. He died in the Star Hotel (now the Keystone Hotel) at Lampasas the next day.

In a bizarre chain of events following Hudson's death, a man named Bryant, claiming he was the dead man's cousin, attended the funeral and began to make arrangements to collect Hudson's effects. Deeming his actions suspicious, citizens organized an impromptu court which charged Bryant with attempting to obtain property by false pretenses. Bryant escaped custody and disappeared.[8]

An alternative, and perhaps likelier reason for Seymour's needing to leave Lampasas is that he became involved in the affairs of his dangerously volatile brothers-in-law, once more practicing their wild ways in Lampasas. Soon afterwards, he was slightly wounded in a street fight there involving Merritt Horrell, who let it be known he was going to whip local rancher and former county commissioner John C. Cooksey. "Cooksey had gone on Merritt's bond and then surrendered him," recounted a contemporary. As the rancher came into town, his friend Dick Hughes managed to warn him. "Cooksey was unarmed, but soon got a gun and met Merritt. Merritt was going to whip him in a fist fight, but Cooksey opened fire and shot at him two or three times. One shot hit Douglass who was standing around, but the wound was slight. Some thought that Cooksey fired at Douglass on purpose as [there was] an irrelation between the two."9

Douglass, described as "a good-looking, bright fellow," seems to have been cursed by ill-fortune. His wife Sally Ann died in child-birth in 1876, and soon thereafter, Douglass returned to West Virginia. According to George B. Moomau of Petersburg, to whom the story was passed down by his father, William Moomau (1875-1940), and to him by Grandfather George Moomau (1829-1880) who was a juryman at Douglass' trial, the Douglass family lived in "the second house north of the main intersection of the four roads leading into Petersburg. The Moomau house was the fourth one. Seymour was said to be a rather unruly boy and young man."10

[T]he day of the murder several registered letters were put in the pouch carried by the boy and this knowledge came to the ears of Douglas[s], who waylaid and shot the boy, inflicting a serious but not fatal wound. The boy in endeavoring to escape the assassin ran his horse into St. Johns run and swam across, only to meet his murderer, who ran across a bridge and headed him off and deliberately mur-dered him as he came out of the water.11

On testimony rendered by George S. Harney and others (which was later suggested to have been perjured), Douglass was indicted for murder by the grand jury on June 5, 1877. Although the details con-tained in the indictment (prosecuting attorney F. M. Reynolds) gave no indication of the cause or motives for the killing, the Petersburg tradition, as recounted by George Moomau, confirms that:

Seymour heard that the mail contained money for a local busi-ness. The temptation was too much for this young outlaw so he planned an ambush and murder. He selected the Petersburg Gap, one mile east of town, where the South Branch of the Potomac river goes through a narrow gorge in the mountain. He hid in the rocks above the road and shot Hiser as he approached on horseback. He then pil-fered the mail, crossed the river, and returned to Petersburg through brush and forest growth. He left Hiser on the road. No mention of any loot, so I am assuming it [the robbery] was unsuccessful. Hiser's horse, who had made this trip many times, came wandering into Petersburg without mail or rider.

Much excitement insued [sic] and a posse was formed, which
included about every able-bodied man in town and it was followed
by a number of young people on foot. Seymour joined one of these
groups. I can't remember the circumstances leading to the arrest of
Douglas[s], but I think he was seen coming into town from south
Petersburg not long after happenings began.[12]

William Seymour Douglass went to trial on Monday, September
17, 1877, in the Circuit Court at Petersburg, Judge James D.
Armstrong of the 12th Judicial District presiding. The defense
opened with a request for a change of venue, claiming the accused
could not get a fair trial in Grant County; prosecutors Reynolds and
Dyer "produced large number of affidavits of prominent men from
all over the county, to prove that he could." Judge Armstrong
reserved a decision until it could be ascertained if a legal jury could
be obtained.

On Thursday [September 20], Sheriff Smith summoned about forty
qualified jurors, in addition to the panel of thirty jurors, out of which
eight had been found qualified. On Friday evening a jury was made
up and sworn in, comprising the following gentlemen: W.F. Tucker,
Daniel Shell, Moses Feaster, Lloyd Kitzmiller, John Vest, John
Swires, John Simmons, Jacob Lee, Solomon Clark, Henry Berg,
Allen Michael and Isaac Taylor. On Saturday [September 22] testimony, including the finding of the body and the post mortem examination, was taken, and the same was proceed[ed] with on Monday
[September 24].[13]

Evidence was introduced by prosecutors Reynolds and Dyer that
an army pistol with four loads in it had been in the possession of
one Peter Welton, a brother-in-law of the prisoner, [suggesting (a)
Douglass married again subsequent to his return to Petersburg or (b)
Welton was married to one of Douglass' sisters]. Welton kept the
pistol in a bureau drawer in his house at Petersburg. The State based
its case on the fact that four shots were known to have been fired,
that Douglass had been seen to go into the house "before he started
in the direction of the place and on the day the murder was committed," that a track in the mud at the scene had been identified by a
witness as having been made by Douglass, that the aforesaid pistol
was found at the scene of the crime.

When the pistol was offered in evidence, Douglass' attorney, Mr.
Norment, of the firm of Sprigg, Flournoy, Norment and Pugh,
objected on grounds that the pistol had been a privileged communi-

cation between the prisoner and his counsel, improperly and by force obtained from said counsel. The court overruled the objection and allowed the introduction of the pistol as evidence.[14]

The trial concluded on Wednesday, October 3. "The jury remained in consultation for about two hours and rendered a verdict [of guilty] on Wednesday night."[15]

Upon his being sentenced to life imprisonment in the Moundsville Penitentiary, Douglass' attorney moved for a new trial, which the court refused. The prisoner then entered six bills of exception, two concerning the refusal of the court to agree to a change of venue, one concerning the court permitting a witness to testify to a track [footprint] allegedly made by the prisoner when he had no measurements of said track, and the others challenging the means by which the State had obtained the pistol.[16]

At the time of his imprisonment in 1878, Seymour was a fraction over 5'9" tall, with light blue eyes, light blond hair, and a fair complexion. He had a scar in the center of his forehead and two more under his left ear, caused by scrofula [tuberculosis of the lymph glands in the neck]. In addition, he had two gunshot wounds above the hip.[17]

Some time shortly thereafter, Douglass somehow escaped custody. "While he was a fugitive from justice," says George Moomau, "he spent much time in and around Petersburg and he was constantly being pursued by law-enforcement people. On one occasion it was reported that he was hiding in the barn behind his mother's home. The search revealed nothing, but later Seymour told that at the time, he was hiding under the hay in the hayloft when a Sheriff's Deputy drove a pitchfork between his body and arm, but missed him."[18]

Eventually Seymour fled to Texas. He must have returned more or less immediately to Lampasas, because on July 3, 1878, he was arrested there by Sheriff Albertus Sweet and his deputy, Doolittle, whose finger Douglass almost bit off in the struggle. George Moomau says the Petersburg tradition is that Seymour "was arrested in Texas sleeping on a hill with a six-shooter in each hand." Subsequent to the arrest, Sweet escorted him back to Virginia and collected a $1,100 reward which he shared with his deputy.[19]

On August 24, 1878, Douglass was incarcerated once more in the State Penitentiary at Moundsville; he appears in the 1880 census as being 29, married, and assigned to work in the wagon shop.[20] On November 18, 1882, however, the Supreme Court found the record showed that Douglass had "put in a plea to the indictment, and the jury tried the case and rendered a verdict, when no issue had even been made. The Attorney-General admits very properly, that this is a fatal error and that court could not, on such a verdict, render any judgment. The judgment rendered must therefore be set aside, reversed and annulled, and the case remanded to the circuit court of Grant [County] to be further proceeded with."[21]

Douglass was discharged from the penitentiary November 25, 1882, and sent for a new trial. He was collected from the Wheeling, Ohio County jail by Sheriff Scherr and Jailer Bauer and brought to Maysville, ten miles north of Petersburg, where he was placed in the same cell he had previously occupied. "He will be brought before the Circuit Court that convenes on the 27 inst. for trial" said the report, adding that the prisoner, who "after being shaved presented a very genteel appearance," looked "pale and thin and has very little to say. He shows the great pressure and wear of prison life...[and] says if he has to return to the penitentiary he don't think he could live long."[22]

His trial commenced in the Grant County court on Tuesday, March 27, 1883, Judge Armstrong again presiding. The State was again represented by F.M. Reynolds and W.F. Dyer, the defendant by Colonel Robert White, S.I. Flournoy and A.B. Pugh. After motion to quash the indictment, a motion for change of venue was made by the defendant and a number of witnesses examined by both sides. On the evening of Friday, March 30, after argument of counsel, Judge Armstrong granted change of venue and directed that the trial would be held in Mineral County commencing April 24. Douglass was taken to Keyser, just a few miles from his home town of Romney, the following day.[23]

On Saturday, May 5, 1883, he was again found guilty of murder in the first degree and sentenced to life imprisonment. "The verdict," said the *South Branch Intelligencer,* "seems to have given general satisfaction to the public. The opinion is that it was a plain and clear case of murder." Noting that on the first ballot the jury divided eight for hanging, two for penitentiary for life, and two for acquittal, the newspaper then reproduced Seymour's words in his own defense.

> Your Honor: When you have spoken, it will have been the second time you have pronounced the sentence of the law upon me for the same offence [sic], and also a like sentence of imprisonment for life. On the former occasion I had nothing to say, because I was under the influence of liquor, and consequently to a great degree insensible to the grave surroundings. But I feel thankful that I stand before you all and before God this morning, in full possession of all my faculties, and can declare to you and to all the world that I am innocent— wholly innocent— of the fearful, heinous crime with which I stand

twice convicted. In all the mass of evidence produced by the State in the former trial, through 80 or 100 witnesses, but one material circumstance was testified to that I know to be false. But not so on this occasion! No less than six witnesses have come upon that stand and have sworn blackly false, false, false! and that, too, in the most damaging circumstances of this case.

With but two exceptions these witnesses stand high as good and true citizens, and I am disposed to believe they were honestly mistaken, notwithstanding the fearful consequences to me. I know that you regard me as a guilty man beyond a doubt, but I thank God that does not make me so. The prosecution in this case have often referred to the hand of Providence pursuing me at every step and pointing me out as the guilty man. How far this is true the circumstances of the case fully show...I cannot explain them. Would to God I could! My innocence would be established. And though I am now sent away to a living tomb, there is a great, a good, and an all wise God who will not forsake me but will, in His own good time, provide a way of deliverance. Have the eloquent gentlemen on the prosecution noticed the hand of the loving Father on my side of the case? Have they, in all the annals of criminal procedure through the ages, or in their own experience, known of a man charged with so foul and dastardly a crime as that with which I stand twice convicted, whose neck has been twice saved? Did they vent their spleen and pursue and urge my blood to be taken? These very walls almost yet resound with their cries for blood, blood, blood! Have they ever reflected as to what ruled the minds of men at this moment? Yes, sir; there is an all-wise and good God who will never let me die for this crime! I hope to bear the burden now to be placed upon me with such patience and fortitude of soul that His smiles may go with me and strengthen me all the lonely hours of my prison life.

I am covered with shame and confusion when I look back at the abused and blasted opportunities of my life! But out of it all how glad I feel that I can stand before God, who knows all things, and declare that my hands are not stained with the blood of this good man.

And now, sir, I will only say that you can proceed with your duty and send me away.[24]

The judge did just that. Seymour was returned to Moundsville, and it was from there that he wrote that long, sad letter to his nephew Maurice, dated Sunday, December 12, 1886. Exactly when Seymour Douglass died we may never know; his name does not appear anywhere in the death records of Marshall County, where the prison was located (although there are numerous instances where prisoners are known to have died or been executed who are not in those records). More specifically, he does not appear in the census for 1900, so it is probably safe to assume the short, unhappy life of William Seymour Douglass ended before the new century began.[25]

Notes

1 Seymour Douglass to "Maurice," Sunday, December 12, 1886. Courtesy George B. Moomau, Petersburg, West Virginia.

2 *Ibid.*

3 U.S. Bureau of the Census, Census for Luneys Creek Post Office, District No. 2, Hardy County, Virginia. July 29, 1860, by Assistant Marshal John J. Shipley. Census for Luneys Creek Post Office, Milroy Township, Grant County, West Virginia. August 31, 1870 by Assistant Marshal Arnold Schen. Courtesy Conley M. Edwards, Head, Archives Public Services Section, The Library of Virginia' Richmond, Virginia.

4 Wheeling, West Virginia, *Sunday Register,* April 21, IX86.

5 *Ibid.*

6 The full story of the lives and feuds of the Horrell family may be found in Nolan, Frederick. *Bad Blood: The Life and Times of the Horrell Brothers.* Barbed Wire Press, Stillwater, Oklahoma. 1994.

7 Wheeling, West Virginia, *Sunday Register,* April 21, 1886, *op cit.*

8 *History of Lampasas County,* Lampasas Historical Commission, Lampasas, Texas. 1991, p. 27.

9 J. Evetts Haley, interview with John Nichols, May 15, 1927, at Lampasas, Texas. Haley History Center, Midland, Texas.

10 Personal communications, George B. Mooma';, Petersburg, West Virginia, January 23, 1995.

11 *State of West Virginia vs. William Seymour Douglass,* Indictment and True Bill of the Grand Jury, William F. Tucker, Foreman. Courtesy Betty C. Moomau, Clerk of the Circuit Court, Grant County, Petersburg, West Virginia. Wheeling, West Virginia., *Sunday Register,* April 21, 1886, *op cit.*

12 George B. Moomau to Nolan, *op* cit.

13 Romney, West Virginia, *South Branch Intelligencer,* Friday, September 28, 1877.

14 Watts, Cornelius C. *Reports of Cases Argued and Determined in the Supreme Court of Appeals of West Virginia at the June, August and Full Special Terms,* Vol. *XX,* 1882. Wheeling, West Virginia: C.H. Taney, 1883. 771- 792.

15 Romney, West Virginia, *South Branch Intelligencer,* Friday, October 5, 1877.

16 Watts, *op cit.*

17 Prison records, West Virginia Penitentiary, Moundsville, West Virginia. Courtesy John Massie, Moundsville State Penitentiary, West Virginia.

18 George B. Moomau, *op cit.*

19 Nolan, *op cit.*

20 U.S. Bureau of the Census, Census for Moundsville, Marshall County, West Virginia by Assistant Marshal O. A. Manning, June, 1880. Courtesy Debra Basham, Archivist, West Virginia Division of Culture and History, Charleston, West Virginia.

21 Watts, op cit.

22 Petersburg, West Virginia, *South Branch Gazette,* Friday, March 9, 1883.

23 Romney, West Virginia, *South Branch Intelligencer,* Friday, April 6, 1883.

24 Romney, West Virginia, *South Branch Intelligencer,* Friday, May 11, 1883.

25 Research by Debra Basham, Archivist, West Virginia Division of Culture and History, Charleston, West Virginia.

Chuck Parsons

Born near Laurens, Iowa, in 1940, Chuck Parsons grew up on a farm in southern Minnesota, only twenty miles from Madelia, where the Younger brothers were captured after their failed raid on the Northfield Bank, a fortuitous fact that he credits for his life-long fascination with the history of Western outlaws and lawmen. After high school graduation in 1958 he attended the University of Minnesota and received a degree in education. He taught eight years and then moved into school administration in Minnesota and Wisconsin, holding posts as high school principal, athletic director, and director of transportation. From 1983 to 1999 he wrote the "Answer Man" column for *True West* magazine, fielding questions from various readers on Western history. He has served on the board and in various executive positions for NOLA and has edited the *Quarterly* and *Newsletter* for the past decade. He has written many articles for the *Quarterly* and other magazines, as well as books and pamphlets on such figures of the West as gunfighters Clay Allison and John Wesley Hardin; gambler Phil Coe, last victim of Wild Bill Hickok; Texas Sheriff Jim Brown, who hanged Bill Longley; and Texas Rangers T.C. Robinson and C.B. McKinney, the latter biography co-authored with Gary Fitterer. Parsons is currently completing biographies of Texas Rangers L.H. McNelly and N.O. Reynolds. The father of two successful sons, he says a highlight of his life has been helping to raise a grandson.

DESTROYING THE HARDIN GANG
•
By Chuck Parsons
NOLA *Quarterly*, July, 1980

L ittle has been published on Texas Ranger Captain John R. Waller and his Company "A" Frontier Battalion, composed of Erath and Comanche County men. The few references giving attention to this particular body of men usually emphasize the desperadoes pursued, but seem reluctant to provide positive recognition to the rangers themselves. This is certainly not a striking revelation, as traditionally the outlaw has received more attention than he deserves in the literature dealing with law and order problems of the post-Civil War American West.

One of the first published works giving any attention to Waller's rangers was, ironically, the autobiography of Texas mankiller-convict-author John Wesley Hardin. Hardin wrote at some length how he and cousin Jim Taylor evaded capture or death after their killing of Charles Webb in late May, 1874.

Although his account contains some factual material it is highly colored and attempts to transform Waller's rangers from a legally constituted force of lawmen into a murderous mob. Hardin's *Life*[1] has been readily available over the years. Possibly because of its availability and the lack of serious research in this period and location, writers have not been concerned with comparing it with other accounts written by contemporaries of Hardin.

These writings are very few. A lengthy newspaper account of the Webb killing and its immediate aftermath appeared in the *Houston Daily Telegraph* of June 3, 1874. This article, the earliest I have located, is essentially a description of the killing provided by an

201

unidentified gentleman from Brown County who may have been an eye-witness.

In the twentieth century William M. Green prepared an account of Company "A's" efforts against the Hardin gang which was published in the *Frontier Times* history magazine.[2]

Green's memoir is valuable as he was a member of Waller's company and participated in much of the action he described.

In addition to squads of rangers pursuing Hardin and his associates, respectable citizens of the county were also in arms. A Brown County official, name not provided, later informed the *Houston Daily Telegraph* of events in the county after the killing of Webb via a letter which read in part:

> Former murders by this same killing party are not wanting to probe their lawless and bloody nature. This time they went too far in their dark career. Webb was known as a brave and honest man, and the people were not to brook his slaughter in silence and awe.
>
> Their vengeance was swift and terrible. The people arose as by one impulse, and assumed in their sovereign capacity the functions of judge, jury and executioners. Vigilance committees were organized and sent in search of the desperadoes, with instructions to shoot all who refused to surrender and hang all who did submit.[9]

In the aftermath of the Webb killing a total of eight associates of Hardin and Taylor lost their lives to either mob action or the rangers. During the night of May 31-June 1 Hardin's brother, Joseph G. Hardin, and two cousins, William A. and Thomas K. Dixon were taken from the Comanche jail and lynched.

On Tuesday, June 2, another cousin, Alec Barackman,[10] and his brother-in-law Hamilton Anderson, were shot and killed by a squad of rangers which included Andrew L. Taylor.

During the night of June 21-22 three other associates, A. "Kute" Tuggle,[11] Rufas P. "Scrap" Taylor,[12] and James White were taken from the Clinton jail in DeWitt County and lynched. They, with other prisoners, had been delivered to Clinton by a squad of Waller's rangers under the command of Sergeant J.V. Atkinson.

The most dramatic incident described in the John H. Taylor letter is certainly the killing of Anderson and Barackman. John Taylor barely missed being a part of the squad which attempted to capture the pair, because his horse was lame. Brother Andrew was there, however, and most likely John learned of the details from him. It is fortunate that Taylor's version of the events was recorded and preserved.

John Henry Taylor as he appeared in May 1939. *Author's Collection.*

The Taylor brothers' length of service to the State was relatively brief, both having enlisted May 25, 1874, and serving until April 30, 1875. Although they performed no spectacular deeds, they certainly deserve more recognition than what history has accorded them.

Here follow the two letters of John H. Taylor describing the events in the days after the killing of Charles Webb. They are presented exactly as written, with misspellings and grammatical errors unchanged: [some punctuation has been added for clarity, Ed.]

41 1-3-7- Grimes - Okla - [Route] #3 Harraet Smither your letter with request to write something about my service as a texas Ranger [has been received and] I will try to say something about the general work of the Boddy of Men I fear you will find it poor stuff as I have no education to speak of only about four months of schooling in the latter part of the civil war in a little log school House & out of an old Blue back speller[. I] have picked up the rest as I went along—I

Joined the Rangers on the 23d of May 1874[13] at Comanche texas &
was discharged in April 1875 having served just 11 Months[.] our
Company was A. & was comanded by Capt John R Waller of
Stephensvill[e][,] Erath Co[.] our Lieutennant was Jim Milican[14] of
Comanche Co[.,] Frontier Batallion. Co A was verry active rite from
the start[.] the Country was overr Run with lawless caracters &
among them was that notorious Killer John Westley Hardin[.] the
evening before Capt Waller arrived Hardin & two of his men Killed
Charley Webb a Deputy Sheriff from Brownwood rite on the street of
Comanche & defyed arrest & rode out of town with Pistols pop-
ping[.][15] our Work comenced at once & continued for three weeks
we had at one time seventeen Prisoners at one time in a rock building
there in town[.]some of them was turned loose some went to the Pen
& three was Mobbed[16][.] it took us just 3 weeks to clean out that part
of texas but we done a finished Job[.] there was lots done in those 3
weeks[.] I will tell of incidents that happened where I was present[:]
there was 80 men & I was only one among them[.] There was a great
deal done men wounded[.] two Men Killed resisting arrest. some
Horses Shot but I will tell only where I was Present[.] there was at
least 40 Men in the saddle all of the time both day & Night[.]
comanche was Just a small Frontier town & the lawless element
threatened to Burn the town[.] the People was verry uneasy. We were
camped 5 miles west at ranger Springs[.] So one night a small House
in the North west part of town Mysteriously Caught fire & the
People was almost Panic stricken[.] A Runner was sent after us[.] it
was about 11 oclck[.] Seargent Halstead[17] gathered up about 30 men
& in a few minutes we were off for town on the run[.] it was a false
alarm but we Patroled the town the rest of the Night[.] the Next day
we Moved in town & camped on the Public square[.] from then on
the square was a buisy Place[,] S[c]outs going out & others coming
in both day & night[.] We had been camped there about 3 days when
one morning a Man Named Hesley rode in & reported That his
Father in law Mr Campbell had 5 Horses stolen & he could put us
rite on the trail of the thieves[.] Seargent Bundy[18] drew out his note
Book & took down the names of the first ten Rangers in sight & told
us to get our Horses & saddle up at once[.] Some of the Boys had
had Breakfast & some had not but in our hurry we forgot about it &
in a few minutes we Were off with Hensley[19] leading[.] He took us to
where the thieves had torn down the Rock fence & led the horses
out[.] there was a dim wagon road that ran along leading down into
San Saba county[.] the thieves would not ride in the road but rode
parilell to it on the grass trying to cover Their trail[.] they went about
five miles & then took the Road[.] They were rideing hard & So was

we[-]they was Just a little handicaped with the stolen stock[.] about 4 oclock we sighted them & they saw us & quit the stolen Horses & started to a Brush mountain about a mile & a quarter off[,] but we rode them & When they saw that they could not make it They Jumped down off of their Horses & put them Side by side & stood between them with Their Backs together & their guns across their saddles[,] swearing that they would die before they would give up[.] We had them surrounded[,] our guns on them[.] the Seargent reasoned with them for half an hour[.] finally they laid down their arms[.] we went back a few Miles to a Watter hole & camped for the night[.] it was a dreary camp[.] we were tired & hungry havin Rode 65 or 70 Miles in the heat & no supper & some had no breakfast & no breakfast comeing[.] We were Riddng long before daylight & got to camp about 3 oclock[.] us & our Horses tiard out but Mr Campbell had his Horses & the Lay [law?] had the Thieves[.] such was part of the life of the Texas rangers 63 years ago[.] we indeavored to make life & Property saffe regardless of the hardships that we had to under go—Lady I doubt verry much whether you can read this if you can & wish me to write again I will do so[.]

J H Taylor Co A Frontier Bat Texas Rangers

I am 80 years old[.]

Mrs. Smither did request Taylor to write again and this second letter described the killing of Barackman and Anderson:

29-37 - Grimes - Okla - #3

Harriet Smither Archivist Austin Texas

I received yours & I feel Just a little bit flattered at what you said about my little Squib—While we was buisy contending with the outlaw gang around comanche they kept spies that Kept them informed as to our movements & in the meantime we had citizens in different parts of the county that was helping the best they could but they had to be verry care ful[.] among the out Laws was two Killers from Navarrow county[.][20] they were wanted for Murder & a $1500 reward was offered by the widdow of their victim.[21] they had relatives in Comanche county[22] & it was natural for them to drift out there. it was a natural harber for criminals[.] the eastern part of the county was almost a dense thicket & only a few Settlers on the streams & some of those settlers was favorable to the outlaws & fed them & their Horses. the Rangers had run them twice[.] the last time a few shots had been exchanged but no one hurt on either side. There was a settler that lived on the Leon creek 12 miles east of comanche near the mouth of Walnut creek. There was an almost dense thicket

extending nearly a mile & Walnut Creek came down from the east it
was a small dry creek. these two outlaws got in with the settler & he
was feeding them & their Horses & they thought he was all right &
they got him to go to Comanche & find out what he could about the
movements of the Rangers[.] but instead He reported evearything
concerning them to the rangers[.]²³ of course we got buisy at once
Sergent C Y Pool made a detail of nine men[.] I was on the detail &
when I went to get my horse he was a little lame in one fore foot & I
was taken off of the list & My Brother A L Taylor was put on [A.L.
was a ranger] the Boys got all of the Cold Chuck they could find in
camp[,] put it in their saddle pockets & was off[.] This informor lived
close to the creek in a double log house & a thicket ran up close to
the House[.] the plan was for the rangers to slip in one of the log
houses & be ready when the outlaws came for information from
town[.] then they would step out & make the arrest but only one of
them showed up he & the settler talked about 30 minutes we were in
80 feet of him[.] the Seargent would not chalenge him as he wanted
both of them[.] he Knew that he could get this one but the other one
would get away[.] so he let him go back in the thicket to his
Partner[.] after dark the seargent with his 5 men slipped out of the
house & down to where he had left the horses in charge of 4 rangers
in the bottom. Lieutennant Milican had left camp a little before the
informer came in[.] he had 20 men & was aiming to make a drag that
night down in the south east part of the county[.] a runner was sent to
over take him & tell him what we had found higher up the creek[.]
So he turned & arrived at Seargent Pools camp about midnight[.] that
made a Bunch of 30 Rangers[.] this thicket was a long thicket & run
to almost a point on the east & on the north & South was opin Post
oaks & the land was somewhat sandy[.] Lieut Milican took 10 men
on Horses a little while before day to surround the thicket on the
point & two sides[.] Sergent Pool took the others over & Spread
them out to drag the thicket[,] which they did clear through & found
nothing[.] about that time one of the rangers rode up & told the
Lieutenant that he had circled the thicket & found where two Horses
had went in & had not come out[.] the Lieutennant said[,"]Boys they
are in there spread out & go back all except three men[.] they must
follow the meanders of the creek[.] Keep close together & be sure do
not get in the bed of the creek[.] Keep on the Bank & close together
[."] the order to all of the men was to Keep absolute silence & if a
shot was heard for eavery man to get to the spot as quick as possible[.] they had went about half way back when those three men came
to a small opening & a horse snorted & the two outlaws Jumped up
from their Pallets & shot[.] (they were asleep & the horse woke

them)[.] They shot two shots at the Rangers but they was shot to death immediately by the Boys[.] They made Their words good[.] they said they would not be taken alive.[24]

(Lady) this is badly written & the composite is faulty[,] also the manner[.] if you accept this story fix it up[.] correct all defciences So it will be readable[.]

J H Taylor Co A F.[rontier] B.[attlion .]

I have a Particular Friend in your town[,] Judge C[.]M[.] Cuerton[.]

Little additional information has been learned of the Taylor brothers. William M. Green recorded, in a letter to J. Marvin Hunter, that one of the brothers, which one not indicated, was the first man to be bound over to the grand jury of Eastland County. From Green's description it is apparent that Taylor was acting under unclear orders from Captain Waller, and that he was later reinstated without any loss of time. Green described Taylor as "a credit to our company and there was not a man in Company A but that regretted the action of the captain."[25] Both John and Andrew were discharged from the ranger service on April 30, 1875.

A rare pamphlet[26] recording the Taylor family history suggests that as a boy Andrew had a violent temper and the social unrest of the reconstruction period tended to reinforce this aspect of his nature. By joining the ranger company, it is quite probable that an outlet was provided for this characteristic of his temperament, allowing his violent nature a release in a socially acceptable manner.

There are no details provided, but family history indicates that during his early years Andrew was forced to kill three men. In addition there is belief that he later served on the El Paso police force. Since the name A.L. Taylor does appear on a 1903 police roster there may be truth to this claim.[27] At times Andrew assumed the name of Smalley, his mother's maiden name.

Andrew married Mary Jennings Ball, a widow, and they had three children: Mary, 1881; John, 1884; and Bessie, 1892. Although no document has been located relevant to Andrew's death, family history records that he died in 1936, somewhere in Texas.

John Henry Taylor also lived a long life. Born January 22, 1857, in Fayette County, Texas, near the town of Round Top, his nature developed quite differently than Andrew's. John was exceptionally bright, of a "sunny disposition," and very dependable. His formal education was brief, but with a bright mind and excellent memory he educated himself.

After service with the Texas Rangers, he worked on several large sheep ranches. In 1883-84, with a crew under him, he drove a flock from Colorado to central Texas, spending the winter where the Palo Dura and Palo Alta Canyons meet, some five miles east of present day Canyon City, Texas. Taylor became an expert sheepman.

He married Nancy Elizabeth Beck September 1, 1892. She was considerably younger than her husband, being born August 22, 1871. They had eight children. She died January 3, 1951. John preceded her in death, on July 4, 1942, of heart failure.[28]

An informative sketch of Taylor's life appeared in his obituary, published in the *Cheyenne* (Oklahoma) *Star* of July 16, 1942:

> John Henry Taylor was born near Round Top in Fayette County, Texas, Jan. 22, 1857, that locality at that time the Texas frontier, and departed this life July 4th, 1942, at the age of 85 years, 5 mos. and 14 days.
>
> He was old enough to remember seeing the young men leave for service in the Civil War. In 1874 he enlisted with the Texas Rangers for service against the Indians and outlaws of West Texas. He visited Ft. Elliott, now Mobeetie, Texas, the year it was established [1874] and was present at the arrest of John Wesle[y] Hardin, the noted Texas outlaw.[29] He narrowly missed being at the battle of Adobe Walls[30] on the upper Canadian valley as he was recovering in the North Panhandle at that time.

References

1 Hardin. John Wesley, *The Life of John Wesley Hardin, as Written by Himself*, Smith and Moore, Seguin, Texas, 1896. Reprinted by the University of Oklahoma Press, Norman, 1961, 1966. See in particular pages 93-108 (Oklahoma edition) for Hardin's interpretation of the Webb killing and subsequent events.

2 Green, Major William M., "Breaking Up the Lawless Element in Texas." *Frontier Times*, May 1924, Vol. I, No. 8, pp. 3-6.

3 Harriet Wingfield Smither was Archivist from 1925 until her retirement in September, 1953. Her major contributions to the field of Texas history were in the editing of manuscript collections. On her retirement in 1953 the State Library and Historical Commission adopted a resolution stating that through her efforts, the Library "...had acquired one of the most complete Texana collections in Existence." She died in Austin, March 20, 1955. For further biographical information see *The Handbook of Texas*, edited by Eldon Stephen Brands, Vol. III.

4 John R. Waller has received attention from historians mainly in relation to John Wesley Hardin, the desperado he almost captured. His Civil War record in the National Archives shows he was mustered into service

April 14, 1862, at Dallas, enlisting for the war's duration. The following appeared in an article describing the organization of the Frontier Battalion: "[Waller] was captain of a company in the Thirty-first Dismounted Cavalry, Harrison's brigade; [he] was one of the best fighters in the Confederate army, and is a frontiersman of large experience and one of the truest and bravest men in the State." (*Daily Democratic Statesman*, Austin, May 9, 1874.) G.A. Beeman, editor of the *Comanche Chief*, referred to Waller's "known pluck and energy" in directing the company while pursuing the Hardin-Taylor gang. (*Daily Telegraph*, Houston, June 3, 1874.) No doubt if more details of Waller's career were known his life would appear as adventuresome as many better known western figures.

5 General Order No. 1, issued by Major John B. Jones from Headquarters, Frontier Battalion, May 7, 1874. Original in Texas State Archives, Austin.

6 "Memorial of Citizens of Comanche County," dated May 28, 1874. Other signers were G.A. Beeman, Rufus Beal, J.R. Fleming, J.D. Stephens, B.A. Wright, J.A. Wright, C. Childress [?], C.C. Campbell, A.H. Tuggle, G.L. Wright, McLane & Campbell, William Barnes, J.D. Wright, M.D., James Carnes, Sr., M.R. Green [?], Carnes, W.T. Sands, O.W. Young, Buchanan & Hamilton, M.V. Fleming, George Vernon, J.B. Green, Dickson A. Green, R.P. McCrary & Son, John G. Stand [?]. This document was certified by N. Yarborough, J.P. Precinct No. 1 of Comanche County. The original is in the Texas State Archives, Austin.

7 Waller to Jones, May 28, 1874. This letter was written on letterhead of Comanche attorneys J.R. Fleming and J.D. Stephens. It was Stephens who later introduced a bill which resulted in the State offering a reward of $4,000 for the arrest of Hardin.

8 *Daily Democratic Statesman*, Austin, June 17, 1874. This article, mainly a quotation from a letter written to W.B. Simpson from an unidentified resident of Brown County, had originally appeared in the *Denison News*, date undetermined.

9 *Daily Telegraph*, Houston, June 3, 1874.

10 The spelling of this individual's name has posed a continuous problem as each writer seemingly chose a different spelling. However, an examination of the 1870 Navarro County census record, where he lived prior to coming to the Comanche County area, shows his name "A.H. Barackman." He was 27 years of age, his occupation farming. He was a native of Indiana. His real estate was listed as $700 and personal estate as $450. His wife, "S[usan] S." was 19 years of age, and a native of Texas. They had a daughter, eleven months of age, "A.R." Reel #553,099, page 45 of Census Record, enumerated by A. Hanson, Assistant Marshal. Genealogical Library, Church of Jesus Christ, Latter

Day Saints, Salt Lake City, Utah.

11 One of the signers of the May 28 petition was an A.H. Tuggle. Whether this individual was a relative, or possibly the same man as "A. Tuggle" has not yet been determined. It is certainly not beyond credibility that a Hardin associate may have, for the sake of appearance, signed a petition requesting aid to combat lawlessness in the county.

12 Rufus P. Taylor was a brother of the noted William Taylor, the slayer of Gabriel Slaughter at Indianola, Texas, March 11, 1874. At the same time Jim Taylor, with Hardin at Comanche, killed William A. Sutton. These Taylors were not related to Rangers John H. and Andrew L. Taylor.

13 The names of the Taylors appear as number 72 and 73 on the "muster and Pay Roll of Company A Frontier Men, Erath & Comanche County, Mustered into the Service of the State of Texas on the 25th Day of May 1874." The document is a muster roll only, as no amounts of payment are shown. A total of eighty-eight names, including Waller's are given, although some were entered as having been mustered into service prior to May 25. Both Taylor brothers gave eleven months, eleven day service to the State of Texas. Their enlistment ended April 30, 1875. The most familiar name on this muster roll is that of Dallas Stoudenmire, later El Paso marshal.

14 This was Lieutenant James W. Millican. He was probably one of the oldest members of the company, having been born in the early 1830s. He had married Mary L. Ellis on December 22, 1855, the same year A.L. Taylor was born. He died July 3, 1909. (*Texas Ranger Indian War Pensions*, Robert W. Stephens, Nortex Press, Quanah, Texas, 1975, p. 72.)

15 The May 28 petition stated that Webb had been killed May 25. The *Daily Telegraph* of Houston of June 3, receiving the report from "a gentleman of Brown county," also stated that the killing had taken place "…last Monday in front of a saloon on the public square of the village of Comanche," which also set the date as May 25. Strangely enough, Hardin, writing his *Life* some twenty years later, wrote that the killing had taken place on May 26, his twenty-first birthday. Did Hardin deliberately change the date of the Webb killing to coincide with his birthday for a dramatic effect?

16 The mobbing of three men is probably a reference to the lynching of Joseph G. Hardin, William A. and Thomas K. Dixon the night of May 31-June 1 in Comanche. The men imprisoned may be a reference to a group of prisoners delivered to the Clinton, Dewitt county jail, by Sergeant J.V. Atkinson and a squad of Company A. This group of prisoners included James M. Bockius, G.W. Parkes, J. Elder, Thomas Bass, Rufus P. "Scrap" Taylor, James White, and A. "Kute" Tuggle. The

Daily Democratic Statesman of June 16 printed this item regarding the prisoners: "PRISONERS—Thirteen men belonging to Capt. Waller's frontier company have arrived in Austin from Comanche, having in charge seven prisoners, charged with cattle stealing. The prisoners are from Comanche and DeWitt counties, and are to be turned over to the State authorities. Some of them are supposed to belong to the Hardin-Taylor gang of cattle thieves. The rangers report that there seems to be a systematized plan organized for stealing cattle on a gigantic scale, and that recently Hardin and Taylor were overhauled while en route for Kansas with a large drove of cattle, and a lot of blank bills of sale of cattle taken from them; or rather, picked up after their flight from camp." A report in the *Daily Express* of San Antonio of June 19 provides a few additional details. The prisoners reportedly had in their possession 700 stolen cattle and 33 horses when captured. The party which captured them was commanded by Comanche attorney J.D. Stephens.

17 This was Sergeant S.T. Halsted who served from May 25 to August 25, 1874.

18 This was 3rd Sergeant Z.T. Bundy who served from May 25 to November 7, 1874.

19 This was Private J.H. Hensley who served from May 25 to August 25, 1874.

20 The "two killers from Navarrow [sic] county" were Anderson and Barackman.

21 The victim of Anderson and Barackman was Colonel W.M. Love who had been shot and killed in 1873, supposedly by Barackman. On the night of June 21, 1874, Alb Love, the colonel's son, was shot at, presumably by friends of Barackman. This was the third attempt on the life of Alb Love. (*Daily Express*, San Antonio, June 28, 1874, based on bulletin from Corsicana, Navarro County, June 28, 1874.)

22 The Comanche County relatives were Joseph G. Hardin and family, as well as the father, the Reverend J.G. Hardin and his family. Other relatives included the Dixon brothers. Ranger Green wrote that it was supposed that Barackman and Anderson came to Comanche county "...to get with the leaders and to be protected from charges then pending against them at Corsicana." (Green, as cited, pp. 3-6.)

23 According to Hardin's *Life*, William Stones was the man who betrayed Anderson and Barackman. Wrote Hardin: "When we got [to our companions] I told them that Jim [Taylor] and I were going to leave the country, and if they wanted to go with us to say so quickly. They wanted us to stay and go to Bill Stone's house, a man whom they had lately helped out of trouble and whom they looked on as a friend. They said they had done nothing and no one would hurt them. So they said they

would stay and go to Bill Stones'. I told them to leave the country as Jim and I were going to do, that they did not have to go with us, but to go anywhere, so that they got away from this country. I told them that Bill Stones would betray them if they went there; that these were no times to trust such men. They still said they were going, so I pulled out five $20 gold pieces and told them to divide it among them, and so we bade them good-bye. It proved to be a last farewell. They went to Stones', who betrayed them, and they were shot to death." (Hardin, as cited, p. 98.) It was Hardin's belief that Waller's rangers murdered the pair as they lay asleep. Taylor claimed they were awakened by a horse and then killed when they refused to surrender.

24 In his letter of June 6 to Governor Coke, Captain Waller provided this terse comment on the deaths of Barackman and Anderson: "The Sheriff of Comanche County [Frank Wilson] While trying to arrest Bareckman [sic] & Anderson [,] the murderers of Col[.] Love of Navarro County were compelled to Kill them[.] His posse was composed of Citizens and some of the members of Company 'A'."

25 Green, William M., to J. Marvin Hunter, in *Frontier Times*, Vol. 3, #8, p.8.

26 Taylor, Nat M., *The Taylor Family Brief History*, compiled in 1960. No date, no place, 17 pages. Nat M. Taylor was a son of John Henry Taylor.

27 Examination of El Paso records are inconclusive. An Andrew L. Taylor is listed as a miner in the 1898-99 *El Paso City Directory*, and an A.L. Taylor is listed on a police roster in 1903. It is not known if this is the same as Texas Ranger Andrew L. Taylor. Correspondence from Leon C. Metz to author, April 3, 1978.

28 *Taylor*, as cited, pp.7-8.

29 Since it is known that Taylor was not involved or present at the capture of Hardin, it is presumed that the writer means that Taylor may have seen or visited him in Austin, where he was jailed after the Florida capture. Hardin was visited by many people while in the Travis County jail.

30 On June 27, 1874, a group of buffalo hunters were attacked at Adobe Walls, on the Canadian River in the Texas Panhandle. The attack lasted five days and was conducted by about 500 Comanche and Kiowa warriors. William Dixon and "Bat" Masterson were two well known scouts involved in this significant battle.

Philip J. Rasch

   Born at Grand Rapids, Michigan, in 1909, Philip J. Rasch moved
with his family to a southern California farm in 1914. Eight students
were in his graduating class at the one-room grade school he attended. After high school he worked for an oil company and attended
Fullerton Junior College. Marriage to Mary Kirk of British
Columbia, Canada, in 1939 produced two children. Having joined
the U.S. Navy Reserve, Rasch was called to active duty in 1940.
During World War II he captained a picket ship, served on an admi-
ral's staff, and saw action in the Battle of Leyte Gulf. After the war
he taught Naval Science and Tactics at the California Maritime
Academy and pursued studies which eventually earned him a doctorate degree in physical education, a master's degree in education,
and a bachelor's degree in anthropology. Dr. Rasch became an international authority in the field of corrective physical therapy and was
included in *Who's Who in Science*. He retired from the U.S. Naval
Reserve as a lieutenant commander in 1969 after thirty-three years
of service, and in 1972 left his profession to pursue personal interests, one of which was his avid interest in frontier history, especially
outlawry in territorial New Mexico and Arizona. For fifty years he
meticulously researched the violent events of the period and published his findings in historical magazines and journals. His collected articles are currently being published in a series of books by
NOLA. Dr. Rasch died at his home in Ojai, California, in 1995 after
a long illness.

THE OTHER ALLISON
•
By Philip J. Rasch
NOLA *Quarterly*, October 1979

The name Clay Allison is known to every *aficionado* of western gunfighters. But one of his contemporaries was another once noted Allison, Charles, who today is known to almost no one. Adams lists only a single entry opposite his name in the index to his exhaustive bibliography, *Six-Guns and Saddle Leather*; Kelly's *Encyclopedia of Gunmen* does not even mention him. Yet for a brief period in 1881 he and his gang terrorized southern Colorado and northern New Mexico, in the process garnering more newspaper space than was devoted to Clay during his entire lifetime. There ought to be some sort of a moral here, if only we could figure out what it is.

Allison, whose real name was Annis, although it more generally appears as Ennis, was born in Virginia c. 1851. According to the Denver newspapers[1] he was raised in Chicago and moved to Nevada in 1878 as an agent for an Eastern firm which manufactured manacles and handcuffs. He got into some sort of trouble in Carson City, pawned his samples for $50, and became a brakeman on the Central Pacific Railroad, making his home in Eureka. It is a good story; it would be an even better one if there were some documentation to substantiate it. As it is, neither the Ormsby Public Library at Carson City, the Nevada State Library, nor the Nevada Historical Society know anything of this individual.

We do know that for some reason on April 28, 1879, Allison found

215

it desirable to depart from Eureka in something of a hurry. Walking
into a local livery stable he did "feloniously steal take and drive
away" the owner's best horse. Charlie was soon overtaken—which
does not speak well for the quality of the stable's horseflesh. On
June 16 he was convicted of grand larceny and sentenced to seven
and one-half years at hard labor in the state penitentiary at Carson
City. A few days later he was ironed with one of the handcuffs he
had pawned at Carson City and started for the prison in the custody
of Sheriff Matthew Kyle.

En route he succeeded in unlocking the handcuffs and made his
escape by plunging through a window in the moving car.
Unfortunately, no file of the *Eureka Sentinel* for May and June has
survived and we lack all details.

In the spring of 1880 Sheriff Kyle was advised that a man had
been arrested in Portland, Oregon, who was "supposed to be Ennis,
who escaped from him, by jumping out of the car-window, about a
year ago, while enroute for the State Prison"[2]—an identification
which the sheriff quite justifiably questioned.

En passant there is no Charles Annis or Ennis in the List of
Registered Voters in Eureka Township for 1878, although there are a
P.M. and a J.T. Ennis. What relationship, if any, they bore to Charles
is unknown. One of the outlying precincts is referred to as Allison's
Ranch. One wonders whether Annis took his *nom de guerre* from it.

Charlie is said to have made his way to Arizona, where he joined a
gang of notorious outlaws known as the Cow Boys. This would
seem to indicate that he was in the Tombstone area, but I have found
no record of him there. In any event he soon transferred his operations to Colorado and was appointed a deputy sheriff of Conejos
County by Sheriff Joe Smith. He was rumored to have been
involved in five stage coach robberies before moving on to Durango
some time in 1880.

About the middle of February, 1881, Allison accompanied Ike
Stockton, James W. Garrett, Tom Radigan, Gus Hefferman
[Hefron], and three other men to the vicinity of Farmington, New
Mexico, to round up some cattle. Stockton and Garrett had been driven out of that country by the Farmington Stockmen's Protective
Association, who believed that they were rustling cattle and warned
them that they would be killed if they returned. As luck would have
it, two members of the Association, Tom Nance[3] and Aaron Barker,
chanced to ride up while the Durango men were camped at Garrett's

Ranch. Both parties opened fire without any preliminaries. Radigan was hit in the knee; later he had to have his leg amputated. Barker was killed.[4] Allison apparently made a poor impression on his peers. Later Stockton was to tell C.O. Ziegenfuss, city editor of the *Denver Republican*, "Allison was with us only one trip—the first. The whole party was so disgusted with him that all declared they would-never go out again if he went along."[5]

Allison apparently escaped from this fight without a scratch, but once safely back in Durango he was less fortunate. On the night of March 17 Andy Guinan, a carpenter, and a friend visited Larsh's Old Dance Hall, on lower F Street. What happened there depends on whose story you choose to believe.

According to Allison, Guinan gave the bar girl a bill too large for her to change. She asked Charlie to go out and get the bill changed. This he did. On his return he was sitting quietly in the front room when Guinan suddenly struck him with a pistol, he said. Allison pulled his own revolver, clubbed his assailant on the head and then shot him through the wrist. Somehow in the melee Allison was shot in the left thigh, the bullet coursing down and around the leg, inflicting a serious wound.

Guinan, however, was never known to carry a pistol. Durango Marshal Healthly searched the room and the combatants and found only Allison's weapon. The general opinion—in which Stockton concurred—was that Charlie had done all the shooting and had been wounded by the ball which passed through Guinan's wrist.

The following month a grand jury at Tierra Amarilla, New Mexico, found indictments for murder, assault with intent to kill, and horse stealing against Allison, Stockton, Harge Eskridge, Garrett, Radigan, Wilson Hunter, and three others, and placed warrants for their arrest in the hands of Deputy Sheriff Moses Blanchard for service.

Governor Lew Wallace issued a notice offering $500 for the capture and delivery of Stockton and $250 each for Allison, Garrett, Eskridge, Radigan, Lark Reynolds, Wilson "Texas Jack" Hughes, and Bill "Tex" Hunter, and sent a representative of the Rocky Mountain Detective Association to Governor F.W. Pitkin, of Colorado, with a requisition for their extradition.

At that time Allison, Stockton, and Garrett were hanging around Amargo, 18 miles west of Chama, New Mexico, and now known as

Lumberton. Eskridge was at Conejos, Colorado. The Stockton gang
split into two groups, one led by Stockton and the other by Allison.
With Allison were Thomas "Little Tommy" Seeley, Lewis Perkins,
Henry Watts, and two other men. Apparently additional recruits
joined them later.

These road agents instituted a veritable reign of terror in the
Costilla-Amargo-Durango-Antonito-Chama-Pagosa Springs area.
On May 26 they robbed the passengers on the J.I. Sanderson & Co.
stage between Amargo and Durango obtaining $600 in cash, four
gold watches, and $2,400 in bank drafts. On May 31 the town of
Chama was held up, the gang getting about $60 in cash and a supply
of ammunition.

The *Pueblo Colorado Chieftain* indignantly called for Judge
Lynch to take a hand in the situation. It bemoaned the fact that the
hanging of LeRoy and his accomplice[6] had not stopped this sort of
thing and commented that "the sooner a little more lynching is
indulged in that section the sooner the decent portion of the people
will be rid of that festive class who 'never worked and never will.'"[7]

In desperation Sheriff Smith sent the following message to
Governor Pitkin:

"The county is powerless against armed desperadoes. C. Allison,
late deputy sheriff, is the leader. Life and property are in danger;
stages, stores and ranches are being robbed of money and stock.
Threatened with an attack on Antonito and Conejos. Assistance is
wanted. Have good men but no arms."[8]

"There is," said the *Colorado Chieftain*, "little doubt that the devil
has broke loose in the lower country..."[9] The governor promptly
dispatched a supply of weapons and ammunition and posted a
reward of $1,000 for Allison and $200 for each of the other members of the gang.

About June 14 Little Tommy was captured and jailed at Alamosa.
Deputy Sheriff Frank A. Hyatt immediately went to work to scare
him into giving the gang away. The officer soon succeeded. Little
Tommy confessed he had held the horses while Allison and his gang
held up Sanderson's stage coach and robbed the mail. He said that
Allison had gone south through the Rio Grande Valley and that if
the officers hurried they could overtake him at Albuquerque.

Hyatt engaged the services of Miles Blain, S. Afton, and H.G.
Dorris. The party stopped in Santa Fe and obtained Governor Lionel

Sheldon's permission to capture the outlaws without waiting for a requisition. On their arrival at Albuquerque, however, they could learn nothing of the men they were seeking.

The following morning, June 16, Hyatt decided to go to Bernalillo in search of information. He sat down at a table in a restaurant there and started to talk with the owner, telling him that his name was Perkins and he was the son of a wealthy stockman. At that point Allison walked into the room, followed by two other men later identified as Perkins and Watts. The leader took a seat just opposite Hyatt, drew his pistol and laid it in his lap. The two men ignored his action and calmly continued their conversation. The meal proceeded without incident. Later Allison told the deputy that if he had made one move to put his hand below the table edge, even to pick up his napkin, he would have shot him.

As soon as the outlaws had ridden out of town Hyatt telegraphed his men, "Come meet me with good men and horses. Allison gang coming on same side of river as Albuquerque." Hiring a Mexican to guide him, he followed the robbers at a safe distance. Becoming uneasy when Hyatt's party failed to appear, they rode around the gang and entered Albuquerque ahead of them. Here he learned his men had just received his dispatch and were preparing to join him.

Hyatt obtained the services of a number of other men, including one Jeff Grant, owner of a livery stable. They watched the road agents riding up and sent Grant out to meet them. He engaged the travelers in conversation, during which they mentioned that they were headed south. Grant responded that he was going to Lincoln in a day or two himself to see about filling a beef contract and would be racing a string of fine horses there.

Finally he invited the party to come up to look the horses over and to put up at his barn for the night. Allison objected that they could not do this because they were all wearing six-shooters. Grant replied, "Button your coat and no one will see."

At the barn Grant dismounted and took Allison's rifle to put it away, or so he said. At that moment the possemen, who were secreted in all parts of the building, demanded the outlaws' surrender. The robbers had no real choice; they could only comply.

Going up to Allison, Hyatt said, "Well Charlie, I took breakfast with you this morning."

"Yes, g-d d—m you, and I was dead on to you all the time. I had a notion to take you prisoner then, and was a fool for not doing it, but

I watched you pretty close and didn't think you knew me or were on this lay."[10]

The three men were locked up, but Justice of the Peace Sullivan, who had been one of the posse, announced that since they had been captured in New Mexico he would not release them to Hyatt until the rewards offered in New Mexico for their arrest had been paid to him. Governor Sheldon instructed Sheriff Armijo, of Bernalillo County, to aid Hyatt. When Sullivan still refused to surrender the prisoners, the governor dispatched Adjutant General Max Frost with writs for their arrest and transfer to the jail at Santa Fe. Hyatt and Grant relinquished their claims to the New Mexico reward and the governor awarded it to Sullivan.

Curiously, when Hyatt set down his recollections of this affair some years later he identified the man he had captured as Clay Allison.[11]

Great precautions were taken in transferring the prisoners to Colorado. False information was deliberately allowed to leak out to mislead both sympathizers who might attempt to release them and irate citizens who might respond to the *Colorado Chieftain*'s urging that they be lynched. At Antonito a gang of roughs led by Catron and Anderson, whoever they may have been, had assembled for the purpose of liberating them, but the train passed through the village without their learning that Allison and his fellows were aboard.

Strange as it may seem, the gangsters had some highly vocal supporters. When the editor of the Alamosa paper ventured the mild comment that, "Since the Stockton gang and the Allison gang of robbers have been gathered in, it would appear that southern Colorado is an unhealthy location for such gentry,"[12] the editor of the *Rico Dolores News* replied with startling vehemence:

"The above is from the *Conejos County Times*, five-eights [sic] patent and the other three-eights [sic] , smotched, blurred and medded [?] out in Alamosa.

"You poor, idiotic, stupid fool, Mr. Editor of the above named paper, what you call the Stockton gang is at large, four of their number are in the Grant Valley, fighting the murderous hell-hounds who killed May, Smith and Thurman, a better cause than you were ever identified with.

"The above absurd little bit of ignorant and cowardly abuse to Stockton, Eskridge, and others, simply shows how much the average surmiser and rumor grabber cares for truths."[13]

The prisoners were transferred to the Denver jail for safe keeping. The *Denver Tribune* reported that a crowd of at least 300 curious citizens met the train and watched Hyatt turn the men over to Deputy Sheriffs Charles T. Linton and Barney Cutler. These two Arapahoe County officers were to carve another niche in outlaw history for themselves on May 15, 1882, when they would assist Perry M. Mallon in arresting John Henry "Doc" Holliday. For his part Hyatt received $1,700 reward.

Allison professed not to be worried. He was, he said, on crutches at the time of the stage robbery, hardly able to crawl. He predicted that as he had never done anything wicked he would soon be set at liberty. The force of this pious declaration was somewhat weakened when he gave Linton a map showing a site in Archuleta County where he had hidden the loot from a robbery of the Denver and Rio Grande Railway. The stolen goods were later recovered by W.C. Black, special officer for the railway.[14]

At this point we encounter one of those infuriating "throw away" stories which seem designed specifically to tantalize the researcher. The *Trinidad Daily News* commented quite casually that, "Allison feels some little satisfaction in the knowledge that the Justice of Peace who held him for trial for a shooting scrape at Antonito has since been lynched."[15]

No file of contemporary papers for this area is known to exist and the Colorado Historical Society is unable to identify either the shooting scrape or the lynching of the J.P. If any of our readers has this information or comes across it in the future, we would be pleased to learn the details.

When Conejos County decided that it could not afford to pay $3 a day each for the prisoners' keep, it became necessary to return them to Alamosa. Once again elaborate precautions were taken to insure that the move was made in secrecy. Shortly afterward Sheriff Kyle appeared on the scene with a requisition from the Governor of Nevada for Allison, but the county officials refused to deliver him.

The desperadoes came to trial at Conejos on October 19, 1881. They were said to have expected fairly light sentences, perhaps four or five years' imprisonment. If so, it must have come as a considerable shock when each of them was sentenced to thirty-seven years in the penitentiary at Canon City.

It could have been worse. Hamilton White, alias Henry W. Burton, had the misfortune to be tried in Pueblo the previous month on a charge of robbing the stage near Alamosa on June 28. He received life at hard labor.

Perhaps a bit carried away by it all, or possibly reacting to the urgings of the *Colorado Chieftain*, the citizens of Amargo entered into the spirit of the occasion by lynching Dell Lockhart, a man named Coulter, and Slim Jim on October 29. Lockhart and Coulter are unknown to me, but according to Secrest[16] Slim Jim was James Bruce, a professional gambler who had shot another gambler in Leadville.

Perkins was discharged from the penitentiary on September 21, 1885, Allison and Watts on September 21, 1890. There is a report that Allison ended his days as a bartender in Butte, Montana, but I have been unable to confirm this.

Appendix
The following physical descriptions of the men arrested by Hyatt were furnished by Ms. Lisa Stahle, Records, Colorado State Penitentiary, formerly the United States Penitentiary for Colorado:

Charles Allison—Age 30, height 5' 7-1/4", dark complexion, gray eyes, brown hair. The *Denver Tribune*[17] mentioned that he weighed about 160 lbs.

Lewis Perkins—Age 20, height 5' 9-1/2", dark complexion, gray eyes, brown hair. The *Tribune* mentioned he was cross-eyed.

Henry Watts—Age 23, height 5' 6", dark complexion, black eyes, black hair.

The similarity of the descriptions of Allison and Perkins strongly suggests a confusion in the records. Ms. Stahle has written that she is disturbed by the coincidence but that it cannot be resolved from their records. I have found no other descriptions of the trio.

Acknowledgments
The writer is indebted to Mrs. Catherine T. Engel, Colorado Historical Society; Ms. Lisa Stahle, Colorado State Penitentiary, and Mrs. Angie Evans, Third Judicial District Court, Eureka, Nevada, for their assistance with this paper.

References
1 *Denver News*, quoted in *Pueblo Colorado Chieftain*, June 19, 1881; *Denver Tribune*, quoted in *Las Vegas* (New Mexico) *Gazette*, July 1, 1881.
2 Eureka, Nevada, *Daily Sentinel*, March 4, 1881.
3 Rasch, Philip J., "Re: Billy Le Roy." Los Angeles Westerners *Branding*

Iron, 36:n. p., December 1956.

4 Rasch, Philip J., "Feuding at Farmington." New Mexico *Historical Review*, XL:215-232, July 1965.

5 Denver *Republican*, August 12, 1881.

6 Rasch, Philip J., "Re: Billy Le Roy." op. cit.; Rasch, Philip J., "A Tree, a Rope, and Billy LeRoy." Los Angeles Westerners *Branding Iron*, 65:8, June, 1963.

7 Pueblo *Colorado Chieftain*, June 2, 1881.

8 Ibid, June 5, 1881.

9 Ibid, June 7, 1881.

10 Santa Fe *Daily New Mexican*, June 21, 1881.

11 Hyatt, Frank A., "The Capture of the Allison Gang." *The Colorado Magazine*, 12:222-224, November 1935.

12 *Conejos County Times*, quoted in Rico *Dolores News*, July 2, 1881.

13 Rico *Dolores News*, July 2, 1881.

14 Lincoln, Chas. T., "An Experience with Horse Thieves." *The Trail*, 1:27-28, September 1908.

15 *Trinidad Daily News*, August 20, 1881.

16 Secrest, William B., "A Gamblin' Man." *Real West*, 22:21 et seq., March 1979.

17 *Denver Tribune*, June 26, 1881.

Nancy B. Samuelson

Born Nancy B. McDonough in 1940, in Dent County, Missouri, she received a BA in Elementary Education in 1963 from Harris Teacher's College in St. Louis and an MBA from Syracuse University in 1968. She served as logistics officer in the U.S. Air Force for twenty years. A graduate of the Armed Forces Staff College and the Air War College, she was posted at a number of bases in the United States and in England and Thailand. Before retiring as a lieutenant colonel in 1984, she was named Outstanding Supply Officer of the Year and awarded the Bronze Star and the Meritorious Service Medal with two Oak Leaf Clusters. She taught management and marketing courses for Park College and for five years was an Assistant Professor of Aerospace Studies at the University of Connecticut. She married the late Reid Samuelson, a retired Air Force lieutenant colonel. Since her own retirement, Nancy has kept busy with research, writing, and civic activities. Research and writing projects have focused on western history, genealogy, and women in the military. Articles and book reviews have appeared in over a dozen publications including *Air University Review*, *Armed Forces and Society*, *The Herb Quarterly*, *Oklahombres*, the NOLA *Quarterly*, and the *Journal* of the Western Outlaw and Lawman History Association. She has authored a cook book and two outlaw and lawman books, *The Dalton Gang Story* (1992), and *Shoot From the Lip: The Lives, Legends, and Lies of the Three Guardsmen of Oklahoma and U.S. Marshal Nix* (1998).

CHRIS MADSEN'S ELASTIC MEMORY
•
By Nancy B. Samuelson

NOLA *Quarterly*, October 1979

C hris Madsen has gone down in history as one of the famed "Three Guardsmen" of Oklahoma. There is no doubt that Chris served as a U.S. deputy marshal for many years and that his service was honorable. Chris was, however, an excellent press agent for himself and his multiple accounts of how he won the West for law and order contain a lot of questionable material and a fair amount of outright fiction.

Madsen's memoirs were dictated to Harold L. Mueller and were serialized as "Four Score Years A Fighter" in the *Daily Oklahoman* from November 17, 1935, through March 15, 1936. A typed manuscript of Madsen's memoirs titled "Oklahoma Outlaws" was used extensively by Harold Preece for his book *The Dalton Gang* and was also the basis of Homer Croy's biography *Trigger Marshal*. Frank Latta also consulted Madsen when he was working on *Dalton Gang Days* and Latta appears to have accepted Madsen's version of events as gospel. Chris also wrote a number of letters to a Miss Hixson in 1939 after her request for information about Oklahoma outlaws. These letters were printed in the *Going Snake Messenger* during 1988 and 1989 under the title "Some Recollections of Oklahoma Outlaws."

Chris was well up in years when most of these memoirs were dictated or written and one could certainly excuse a few glitches as due to failing memory. Confusion of dates or minor details would be

225

understandable, but Chris went well beyond confusion of minor details. He tells completely contradicting stories about some events and people and takes credit for actions performed by other lawmen on more than one occasion. Furthermore, several stories can be proven to be complete fabrications.

Both Preece and Latta relied heavily on Madsen as a source of information about the female outlaw Flora Quick Mundis, or Tom King as she was commonly called. Flo was branded "Bob Dalton's Bandit Bride" and was described as "the smoothest, shrewdest woman outlaw who ever popped out of the sage brush." Flo was supposedly a regular part of the Dalton Gang and spied and stole horses for them. She reportedly rustled the horses the Daltons rode during the Coffeyville raid.

Flo was reported to be living with a supposed husband named Munday (Chris didn't even get her married name correct, it was Mundis) in Guthrie. She allegedly fought often with Munday and repeatedly obtained money from him which she turned over to the Daltons.

Madsen claimed to have arrested Flo several times and on one occasion he said he took her to Oklahoma City in a buckboard. During the trip she reportedly cursed, swore and called Madsen every vile and obscene name in the book.

Another tale about Flo and Bob Dalton told by Madsen supposedly happened in June 1892 right after the Daltons robbed the train at Red Rock. Flo found herself back in Guthrie and short of funds so she decided to collect some of the reward money offered for Bob Dalton. She notified the Guthrie city marshal that Bob Dalton would be at her house on a certain date and the marshal could arrest him there. She only wanted a mere $1,000 for betraying her lover. The marshal made the arrest but he did not know Bob Dalton by sight and telegraphed Chris to come and identify Dalton. Madsen arrived from Winfield, Kansas, to discover the man in question was a very embarrassed farm boy who was six inches taller and a great deal heavier than Bob Dalton.[1]

Flo, or Tom King, was a notorious female in the Oklahoma Territory but there are several problems with Madsen's accounts of her. First of all, the Dalton Gang was wiped out during the raid on two banks in Coffeyville, Kansas, on October 5, 1892, but Tom King's name does not appear in territory newspapers until nearly mid 1893, several months after Bob and Grat Dalton and two other

Chris Madsen. *Author's Collection.*

members of the gang were dead. There are several newspaper accounts of arrests of Flo but Chris Madsen is never mentioned in any of the newspaper stories about her. It is highly unlikely that he ever arrested her or took her to jail. The tale about the arrest of the fake Bob Dalton is almost surely pure fiction. No account of this incident has ever been found in any newspaper and the supposed arrest of Bob Dalton in mid 1892 would have been "Big News."[2]

Flora Quick is known to have been the daughter of Daniel Quick of Johnson County, Missouri. Probate records of that county show that a guardian was appointed for Flora in 1890 after the death of her father. Flora married John O. Mundis July 15,1890, with the consent of her guardian as she was yet under the age of eighteen. In the summer of 1893 newspaper stories began to appear in the territory about Flo's horse stealing and jail breaking escapades. In August 1893 a dispatch from Holden, Missouri, appeared in some of the territory newspapers claiming that Mundis was a worthless young man whose main objective in marrying Flo was to obtain her share of her father' estate. The final settlement of the estate of Daniel Quick was made in mid-1892 This probably allowed Flo time to collect her share of the estate and for her and Mundis to have spent it before she turned to outlaw activities.[3]

Flo Quick as a member of the Dalton Gang is only one of many tales Chris told about the Daltons that can be shown to be questionable or entirely false. Some basic chronology about the Daltons is necessary here in order to make it perfectly clear how ludicrous some of Madsen' stories really are. The Dalton family is clearly identified on the Bates County, Missouri, census in 1880. According to many sources they moved to the Indian Territory, near what is now Vinita, Oklahoma, sometime in 1882. Some time later the Daltons moved to a location near Coffeyville, Kansas, and then returned to Oklahoma in 1890, settling in the Kingfisher area. In 1884 an older brother of the gang, Frank Dalton, became a U.S. deputy marshal working out of Fort Smith. In November, 1887, Frank Dalton was killed in the line of duty. Shortly after Frank's death Grat Dalton became a deputy marshal and a bit later Bob Dalton also hired on as a federal lawman. Emmett Dalton sometimes rode as a posseman with his brothers. No questions arose about which side of the law the Daltons were on until Christmas Day of 1889 when Bob and Emmett were accused of selling whiskey to a group of Indians.[4]

During the summer of 1890 Bob, Emmett, and Grat were all accused of stealing horses in the Cherokee Nation. Bob and Emmett did not stick around to face any of these charges. Grat did have a hearing in September of 1890 and later the charges against him were apparently dropped.[5] These three Dalton brothers then went to California to join Bill, who had been living in California since 1884.[6] Brothers Ben, Cole, and Littelton were also in California at this time.

In spite of the lack of any clear and specific evidence as to the guilt of anyone in the case of the Alila robbery, four of the Dalton brothers were indicted for it. Bob and Emmett left the state and avoided arrest but Grat and Bill were arrested. Bill was released on bond and was latter arrested for the fourth robbery at Ceres on September 3, 1891. Bill was shortly released for lack of evidence in the Ceres robbery but his bondsmen for the Alila robbery charges now withdrew their bond and Bill was placed back in jail in Visalia. Grat was tried during the summer and convicted of the Alila robbery, in spite of some very good evidence that he was in Fresno playing cards at the time the robbery took place. Grat was still in Visalia awaiting sentencing when he broke out of jail and disappeared in September 1891. Bill was tried and acquitted by a jury that was only out for about fifteen minutes. Bill's trial ended on or about October 15, 1891.[7]

These four Daltons all returned to the Oklahoma Territory in one fashion or another. Bob and Emmett were back in the Territory by May 9,1891 and participated in a train robbery at Wharton on that date. In September the same two Daltons were involved in the train robbery at Leliaetta, and by June 1892 Grat was back and assisted with more of the train business at Red Rock. Further negotiations were transacted between the Daltons and the railroads at Adair in July 1892. On October 5, 1892, the Dalton Gang made their final raid and attempted to rob both of the banks in Coffeyville, Kansas, at once. The results of that raid are well known and need not be detailed here.

Bill Dalton also returned to Oklahoma, but the exact date of this return is not known. As his trial ended in mid October 1891 he could not have been back until after that time. After Bill Dalton's death his wife stated he returned to the Kingfisher, Oklahoma, area around November 15, 1891, and letters were also found after his death showing him to be in the Kingfisher area in early July 1892.[8]

How much Bill Dalton was involved in his brothers' activities before the Coffeyville Raid may never be known for certain, but it is clear that Chris Madsen is the source of a couple of the most often repeated tales about Bill Dalton.

Chris Madsen was born in Denmark and had been in the Danish Army before coming to America. He reportedly served in the U.S. Army in the Indian wars from 1876-1879. In 1885 he had served as a quartermaster sergeant in the Indian Territory. He married in 1889 and farmed near El Reno, Oklahoma, until he became a U.S. deputy marshal in January 1891.[9] In spite of the fact that Chris was proba-

bly not in the Indian Territory until 1885 and did not become a
deputy marshal until January of 1891 he claimed in almost all of his
memoirs to be personally acquainted with all of the outlaw Daltons.
(Especially remember here that Bill Dalton had been living in
California since 1884). Chris also claimed in all but the Latta
account that he was sent to California in October 1891, to help track
down Grat Dalton. When he arrived in California he was able to
inform the railroad and other officials that Bill Dalton was back in
Oklahoma because he had talked to Bill in the train station in
Kingfisher while en route to California. Madsen related, even to
Latta, that Bill Dalton was closely watched by detectives who
believed that Bill would lead them to Grat. Bill supposedly escaped
to Oklahoma by purchasing a very "loud" suit of clothes and wearing this suit while taking his wife for a buggy ride every evening.
One evening he had a friend don the "loud" suit and take his wife
for the usual ride. Bill meanwhile left for Oklahoma.

Chris also reported that he went out with various lawmen and railroad detectives to attempt to arrest Grat Dalton while in California.
However, there is no evidence whatsoever that Madsen went to
California in October 1891 or at any other time in connection with
hunting the Daltons. Madsen's account of tracking down Grat does
not match in any way the accounts by Sheriff Kay and Deputy Ed
McCardle. These two men were involved in the attempt to capture
Grat near what is now known as Dalton Mountain around Christmas
1891. Madsen also reported that molded silver money wrapped as it
had been shipped, was dug up on the Dalton premises in Oklahoma
and produced as evidence at Grat's trial. Recovering such money
would have been a very clever trick indeed, as nothing had been
taken in the Alila robbery attempt.[10]

Another Bill Dalton story that is probably one hundred percent
fiction is as follows: On the night of the Red Rock train robbery,
Madsen states that he and Judge Burford and U.S. Attorney Horace
Speed were all in a Kingfisher hotel. These three gentlemen were
reportedly attending a session of the court in Kingfisher at the time.
Supposedly Bill Dalton joined the trio, talked with them for some
time then pointedly departed at 10:00 p.m. saying it was his bed-
time. Early the next morning news of the Red Rock robbery was
relayed to Madsen and associates. In a short while Bill Dalton again
appeared at the hotel and made comments to the effect that he certainly had a good alibi for the Red Rock robbery. Here it should be

pointed out that Madsen also claimed to be recalled from Winfield, Kansas, right after the Red Rock robbery in order to identify "Bob Dalton" who had been arrested by the Guthrie city marshal. The towns are about 150 miles apart, but these two stories certainly make it sound like Chris was in two places at once. Or maybe it was three places at once, for Chris also reports he went to the Riley Ranch near Taloga, in Dewey County, Oklahoma, right after the Red Rock robbery. Taloga is at least 100 miles west of Guthrie.[11]

Possibly Chris had some kind of magic or perhaps a flying carpet at his disposal; if so, it didn't work for him at Coffeyville. Madsen claimed he had received information on October 1, 1892, that the Daltons were planning to rob two banks in either Van Buren, Arkansas, or at Coffeyville, Kansas. Madsen also stated that he had deputies detailed to intercept the gang on the way out of Coffeyville and that the town of Coffeyville had received ample warning that the Daltons might strike.[12] If Coffeyville had been warned, it is very difficult to understand why the citizens armed themselves on the spot, mostly from the local hardware store, when they realized the twin bank robbery was underway. It is also very difficult to understand why the editor of the *Coffeyville Journal,* who witnessed the events of the day firsthand would say: "The people of Coffeyville were never in the enjoyment of more peaceful or comfortable surroundings than on the eventful Wednesday morning of October 5, 1892. The prospects for a day of lively trade had inspired the merchants and business men to renewed activity. At an early hour the streets were filled with men and women, moving about in the transaction of business and in pursuit of their usual vocations. [Then] the most remarkable occurrence that has ever taken place in the history of our country came upon the peaceful city like a flash of lightning from a clear sky."[13] Even Marshal Connelly, who died in the gun battle, was unarmed when the robbery began. He had left his revolver at his residence that morning.[14]

In conclusion, one last example of Madsen's misinformation will be cited. Many other examples can be found if the various Madsen memoirs are examined carefully and compared to known and documented facts. This final episode shows that Madsen was not at all opposed to claiming credit for the deeds of other lawmen long after the details of the event had been forgotten by many others. Chris provides two accounts of when and how he shot and wounded Bill

Doolin. In one account he has this occur after the robbery at Spearville, Kansas, and in the other account he says it happened after a robbery in Cimarron, Kansas. Here surely one could be generous to the aging lawman and just pass this off as fading memory. However, it turns out that it was Sheriff Frank Healy, at the head of a posse of farmers, after the Cimarron robbery who was actually responsible for wounding Bill Doolin in the foot.[15]

Perhaps the moral of the story should be, beware of even "Famed Guardsmen" when they recount their adventures many years later; their memories are likely to be very elastic indeed.

References

1 Preece, Harold, *The Dalton Gang*. Hastings House, New York, 1963; pp. 151, 155, 159, 161, 180, 181, 183, 211. The quote is from p.155. Also, Harold Preece, "Bob Dalton's Bandit Bride" in *Real West*, March 1965, 10-12, 61-63; Frank Latta in *Dalton Gang Days*, Bear State Books, Santa Cruz, CA, 1976. p. 193, 196-198, 200-202.

2 Croy, Homer, *The Trigger Marshal*. Duell, Sloan and Pearce, New York, 1958, pp.160-161relates the story of the arrest of the phony Bob Dalton and also state Madsen arrested Flo Quick several times. Also, in Latta, op. cit., 193, Madsen claims arresting her and delivering her to Oklahoma City, and in Preece, op. cit., 183-185 he relates the arrest of "Bob Dalton."

3 Probate record of Daniel Quick. Box 12 and Box 61. Probate Index Johnson County, Missouri. This shows actions of the estate from August 13, 1889 to May 14, 1892. Marriage record of Flora B. Quick and John O. Mundis, July 15, 1890, Johnson County, Missouri. Newspapers: *Daily Oklahoma State Capital* (Guthrie) May 23, June 20, 27, July 17, 27, August 7, 11, 16, December 5, 9,1893, August 7, 16,1894; December 14, 1909; *Oklahoma Daily Times Journal,* August 10, 17, 1893; *Edmond Oklahoma Sun,* July 20, 1893; *Guthrie News,* December 12,1893; *Indian Journal,* August 24, 1894; *Norman Transcript,* March 16, 1894; *Eagle Gazette* (Stillwater) August 16, 1894; *Coffeyville Daily Journal,* January 26,1895; *Magum Star,* December 16, 1909.

4 Documents concerning the "Introducing" charge against Bob and Emmett are located in the Kansas City branch of the National Archives. On March 26, 1890, Emmett was released from the case and on September 5, 1890, a true bill was returned against Robert Dalton in spite of the fact that the evidence against him was extremely questionable. About ten different witnesses had testified at the hearing that they had not seen Bob Dalton sell any whiskey or accept any money from anyone for whiskey that was sold in the vicinity where Bob and Emmett had been seen that Christmas Day.

5 Documents concerning the charges of horse theft can be found in the Fort Worth branch of the National Archives. Grat had a hearing on September 18, 1890. The hearing conclusion was that there was probable cause to believe him guilty and Grat was ordered held on bail of $1,000. There is no indication of belief of guilt of Bob and Emmett. The records are not clear about when or why Grat was released, but clearly he was released not long after the hearing.

6 Repeated testimony in Bill Dalton's trial for the Alila train robbery recorded in the *Tulare County Times,* October 15, 1891, make it clear that Bill had been residing in the Merced, California, area since 1884.

7 *Tulare County Times.* Grat's trial was reported in much greater detail in a number of issues of this newspaper during June and July, 1891.

8 McCullough, Harrell, *Selden Lindsey U.S. Deputy Marshal*, Paragon Publishing, Oklahoma City, 1990, pp. 124-127.

9 Shirley, Glenn, *Guardian of the Law,* Eakin Press, Austin, Texas, 1988, Pp. 195-196.

10 Slightly varying versions of the trip to California are to be found in Croy, op. cit., 156-157, and in the *Daily Oklahoman,* January 26, February 2, 1936, and in the *Goingsnake Messenger,* November 1988, 104-107, February, 1989, 16-21. The story of the money used as evidence in Grat's trial is from *The Messenger,* November, 1988, 106. Madsen appears to have omitted the trip to California in the information furnished to Latta. Latta lived in California and would have known Madsen had not been there. Latta, op. cit., 151-177, gives a detailed account of Grat's escape from Sheriff Kay's posse in December, 1891. *The Republican,* a central California newspaper, of December 26, 1891, "Ed McCardle's Christmas Party With Gratton Dalton," also gives details of Grat's escape. Madsen is not mentioned in either account.

11 Latta, op. cit., 202-204. Croy, op. cit., 157-159.

12 Latta, op. cit., 224-229. Preece, op. cit., 202-221.

13 Elliott, D.S. and Ed Bartholomew. *The Dalton Gang and the Coffeyville Raid*, Frontier Book Company, Fort Davis, Texas. 1968, 13-14.

14 Ibid., 34.

15 Shirley, op. cit., 207.

William B. Secrest

Born in Fresno, California, in 1930, William B. Secrest served in a Marine Corps guard detachment and a rifle company during the Korean War. Returning to college after his military service, he received a bachelor's degree in education, but his career took a different direction; he was for many years art director for a Fresno advertising firm. He is now retired. Bill began researching and writing Western history in the 1960s. He first delved into a wide range of interests, but with the realization that the history of outlawry in his native state had been neglected, he decided to concentrate on early California subjects. He has published seven monographs on California themes, and has written articles for *Westways*, *Montana*, *True West*, and *The American West*. He is a contributor to the Fresno City and County Historical Society's journal, *Fresno Past & Present*. His book, *I Buried Hickok*, was published by the Early West Publishing Company in 1980, followed by *Lawmen & Desperadoes* (The Arthur H. Clark Company) in 1994, and *Dangerous Trails* (Barbed Wire Press) in 1995. Another book, *Throw Up Your Hands*, an account of eight early California outlaws, is about to be released by World Dancer Press. His research of many years on the life and adventures of noted San Francisco police detective Isaiah Lees has resulted in a forthcoming biography. Current projects include a biography of Harry Love, the leader of the California Rangers who tracked down the legendary Hispanic outlaw, Joaquin Murrieta.

FOUR LAWMEN AMBUSH TWO CALIFORNIA OUTLAWS

•

By William B. Secrest

NOLA *Quarterly*, Summer 1977

No frontier lawman lived a life of continual gunfights and excitement as characterized by the Wild Bills, the Earps and Pat Garretts of popular concept. Even to these worthies, the keeping of the peace was a grinding and thankless task, a routine of arresting drunks, serving papers, enforcing ordinances and attending boring courtroom appearances. It was indeed a risky occupation at times, and when it was over only a comparative few could look back and remember that they had touched history. One of the few was Frederick Eugene Jackson.

Born in Wyalusing, Wisconsin, November 4, 1861, Fred Jackson was a descendent of "Old Hickory," President Andrew Jackson, and showed it in his craggy good looks. Little is known of his early years, but in the 1880s he was a lawman in Nevada. Later he moved to California where he served as an officer in various parts of the state. About 1890 Jackson became acquainted with Eugene Thacker, son of a noted Wells, Fargo detective, John Thacker, and the two young men became good friends.

In August of 1892 two Visalia, California, farmers were suspected of a local train robbery. When officers went to Chris Evans' home to question him and his friend John Sontag, a gunfight resulted and the suspects fled to the nearby hills. When they returned home that night for supplies, there was another shoot-out and this time an officer was killed.

Evans always maintained that the officers had insulted his daughter and this initiated the shooting. But whatever the circumstances, the men were now outlaws with a price on their heads. Wells, Fargo and the Southern Pacific both had detectives in the field and local lawmen were quickly ranging the Sierra mountains and forests. When a deputy U.S. marshal and a posse cornered two outlaws in a mountain cabin, a fierce battle took place in which the deputy marshal and another deputy were killed. Again the fugitives escaped.

All winter the newspapers heralded the colorful badmen who allegedly had tilted against the mighty and hated railroad. A devoted family man and an expert mountaineer, Evans regularly visited home that winter under the very noses of the lawmen and bounty hunters. In the spring a campaign was again launched to track him and Sontag down. By now the lawmen knew they were dealing with desperate killers.

Late in May of 1893 U.S. Marshal George E. Gard received a wire from John Thacker and the two men met in Fresno to discuss a plan to capture the outlaws. It was known that Evans made regular trips to Visalia, and Thacker proposed to put several good men into the hills and lay an ambush. Recommended for the job were Hiram Rapelji, a Fresno deputy sheriff; Tom Burns, a detective from San Diego; and Fred Jackson, the former Nevada lawman, staying with a sister in Fresno. Whether Jackson got the job on his reputation or due to his friendship with Thacker's son isn't clear, but the choice was a good one.

Early in June the three men, now serving as deputy U.S. marshals, were smuggled out of town in a wagon late at night and dropped off in the hills east of Visalia. Gard was to join them later. The men were to stay out of sight in the daytime and at night keep on the alert for signs of the outlaws. They subsisted on sardines, crackers and water.

Much of the officers' time was spent on hilltops surveying the surrounding country with a telescope. When Gard joined them on June 7, he suggested they move closer to the road and they took up residence in an empty cabin which blocked the route from Willco Canyon. They still scouted the hills at night.

On the evening of June 10, Gard, Rapelji and Burns were sleeping while Jackson watched the road in front of the house. About twenty minutes before sundown Rapelji woke up and went to the back room where he happened to glance through a crack in the wall and

John Sontag, the mortally wounded bandit, lies in the foreground in this famous photograph Hi Rapelji is the portly figure, second from the left. Marshal Gard is third from the right with Tom Burns standing next to him. The others are officers and reporters who returned to the scene with Rapelji.
Author's Collection.

saw two men walking toward the cabin. He called to Jackson. The two officers saw that the approaching men were armed, and Burns and Gard were immediately alerted. When the two figures were identified as Evans and Sontag, the lawmen quickly took up positions for a deadly ambush.

"We prepared for a fight, and went out the front door," Jackson told a reporter of the *Visalia Weekly Delta.* "Burns went to the northwest corner of the house and the rest of us on the other side. Evans saw Rapelji and fired. I shot at him and he fell, firing as he went down. After he fell he began scrambling to get behind a rock and fired again.

"Sontag dropped behind what appeared to be a straw pile. I could not see him and went to the other side of the house where Burns was. I was trying to get a better position. I saw Evans' hat and did not think he was in a position to fire. He was about a hundred yards distant. I turned back and just then he fired and hit me in the left leg, near the ankle.

"The others kept up the fire and Evans did the same. In the dusk they observed him crawling off and reopened fire. He left his gun behind and carried a pistol in his left hand as he ran. His right arm appeared to be disabled. The others followed, but he soon disappeared. After returning to the house Rapelji and two others living in that neighborhood brought me to town..."

During the several hours of the fight, the outlaws had been critically wounded. "There was no intention of trying to capture Sontag and Evans alive," growled Hi Rapelji later. "...It was our intention to kill them without giving them any show whatever ..." Three officers had already died. That was enough!

Did Fred Jackson fire the opening shot at what came to be called the Battle of Stone Corral? In both Wallace Smith's study of the outlaws' careers and the book by C.B. Glasscock, Jackson is credited with this first shot, and a newspaper obituary also gives him this dubious distinction. Jackson himself, however, consistently declined the honor. "Gramps always disavowed the fact that he fired that first shot that set off the battle," wrote a granddaughter. A careful sifting of the evidence seems to bear out her claim.

The *Visalia Weekly Delta* published the first account of the fight in its June 15 issue and featured interviews with most of the participants. Jackson, Burns and Rapelji all stated that Evans fired the first shot. Sontag himself stated that, "When Chris fired at the officers last night I thought his gun had gone off accidentally." Let's let it go at that.

The wounded Evans had escaped after making Sontag as comfortable as he could. Late that evening a wagon was commandeered from a nearby rancher and Rapelji drove Jackson into Visalia. There were few people on the streets when they arrived and after securing a room for his wounded partner at the Palace Hotel, Rapelji obtained a doctor. Word of the fight spread quickly and soon people were gathering on the streets passing along what news was available. Tulare County Sheriff Hall was out of town, but Rapelji gathered together several deputies, a photographer and some reporters.

Several buggies full of reinforcements were soon on their way.

Early the following morning Sontag was captured and photographed with his captors standing behind him. Evans was later found at the nearby home of a relative; and within a few hours the two most famous fugitives in America were in the Visalia jail. Sontag died a few weeks later, of tetanus, rather than of his wounds.

Evans too was badly shot up and later had an arm amputated.

That Sunday afternoon Doctors Bernhard and Patterson examined Jackson's left leg which was shattered about six inches above the ankle. Another surgeon assisted when it was decided later to amputate the lower portion of the lawman's leg. Jackson came through the operation with no complications.

There was over $11,000 in rewards offered by the railroad, Wells, Fargo and the state, but just how this was divided is unknown. The *Merced Star* quoted Marshal Gard as saying Jackson "who lost his leg in the encounter should receive the largest share of the reward" and also "life employment by Wells Fargo or the Southern Pacific..." Jackson evidently did receive a nice portion of the reward and was afterward employed by Wells, Fargo for many years.

On June 22 Marshal Gard arrived from Los Angeles and visited Jackson in his hotel room. Tom Burns dropped in that same day and showed Jackson a new 45/90 rifle presented him by Harry Morse in San Francisco. Morse, a famous California lawman, at this time operated a detective agency and had employed Burns to hunt the two outlaws. On this day too, Jackson received the sad news that his old friend Mike Tovey, a Wells, Fargo shotgun messenger, had been killed during a stagecoach robbery.

On July 15 the *Delta* reported that Jackson was "making a good recovery." Four days later the *Fresno Republican* noted that he was in town and had visited Chris Evans who had by this time been transferred to Fresno for his trial. Jackson "took a chair beside the grated door, set his crutches against the wall and then shook hands with Evans. They sat there for a long time, Evans nursing the stump of his left arm and Jackson the stump of his left leg, and talked over the incidents of the fight that crippled them both for life."

Various sidelights of the Stone Corral fight helped emphasize these closing years of the Old West and the new, emerging era. The Bacon cabin, from which the posse had ambushed the outlaws, had been taken down by July 6 and shipped to San Francisco where it was displayed in a stage play, "The Train Wreckers." Too, both Eva Evans and her mother later played themselves in another drama so as to raise money for Chris' defense.

One of the more incongruous aspects of the battle was the fact that on the day the wounded outlaws were brought in, a Wild West show was playing in town. "The idea of a Wild West show holding forth in a .44 calibre town like Visalia" commented the *San Francisco*

Call "is much the same as carrying coal to Newcastle."

Even more fascinating was the report that Evans' description of the Stone Corral fight had been recorded phonographically and was being played in Fresno and Visalia as a benefit for Mrs. Evans and the children. What a discovery if one of these old cylinders could be located today!

Jackson was working for Wells, Fargo as late as 1900, but by 1905 was a deputy sheriff in Amador County. Later he returned to Nevada, although he reportedly spent some time in Arizona. He spent the last years of his life in Los Angeles, where he lived in a small frame house.

"That little place was truly haunted with memories," wrote Marilyn Allen, a granddaughter who moved in after his death. "I could still smell Gramp's old pipeful of Prince Albert and picture his cribbage board on the old oak dining table and imagine the old wooden leg tucked into a corner as it used to be, and the old coffee can he used as a spittoon! The spitting was always a kind of signal that some horrendous tale was about to unfold when we were little kids..."

Fred Jackson died January 27, 1949, and is buried in North Hollywood, California. "Here forever lies a part of the Old West," declared the minister at his funeral. It seemed a fitting tribute to a lawman who had helped close the door on the outlaws and desperadoes in the far west.

C.L. Sonnichsen

Charles Leland Sonnichsen was born at Fonda, Iowa, in 1901 and raised on a Minnesota farm. After graduation from the University of Minnesota in 1924 he went on to Harvard where he received a master's degree in 1927 and a doctorate in 1931. That year he began teaching at the Texas College of Mines (now the University of Texas at El Paso) and became head of the English Department at that school. His interest in western history was awakened when he was directed to teach "The Life and Literature of the Southwest," a course designed by J. Frank Dobie. After forty-one years of teaching at El Paso, he retired in 1972 and moved to Tucson, where he was editor of the *Journal of Arizona History* for five years and later senior editor and editor emeritus. Between 1942, when he published *Billy King's Tombstone*, and 1982, when his *Tucson: The Life and Times of an American City* appeared, he authored twenty-six books, many of which are considered classics of western history. Those who shared his love for the field of outlaw and lawman history and researched it deeply he called "grassroots historians," and he was famous for the encouragement and assistance he provided them. He was married twice and had a son, two daughters and a stepson. When he died on June 29, 1991, at the age of 89, memorial services were held for him in both Tucson and El Paso, but he was mourned far and wide by members of what Fred Nolan has called "The Doc Sonnichsen Fan Club."

Long, Long Trail
of Baldy Russell

•

By C.L. Sonnichsen
NOLA *Quarterly*, Summer 1977

This is the true story of a tough frontier American who spent thirty-seven years keeping ahead of the law in Texas, New Mexico, and Arizona, setting some sort of record for years spent on the dodge in the American West. He was still a fugitive when he died, on his feet, in the Douglas, Arizona, hospital in 1928.

We pick up the story in 1875, just after he became an outlaw. His name was Bill Mitchell, and his father, Nelson "Cooney" Mitchell was about to be hanged for a killing in which Bill did the shooting.

Sheriff Wright and his deputies had erected a gallows on the northern outskirts of Granbury, county seat of Hood County, thirty miles southwest of Fort Worth, Texas, and about mid-morning they drove up to the jail on the bluff above the Brazos River to take Cooney to his death. He sat on his coffin in the bed of an ordinary farm wagon and started his last ride.

He was calm now, though he had been desperate and rebellious during his months behind bars. He had not killed anybody himself or even tried to, and he protested bitterly that he was being railroaded to the gallows in the face of reason and justice.

He had tried everything he could think of to get the people in power to listen—had even written and printed a pamphlet pleading his innocence, but nothing could save him.

His family had tried to help by smuggling a loaded pistol into his cell, but the guards had found it, and when his young son Jeff tried

243

to crawl up the bank from the Brazos Bottom and bring him a lethal dose of laudanum, the three men on duty outside had shot him dead.

All that was past history now, and Cooney was back in self-control. He kept his head up as he rode and observed the great gathering of friends and foes who had come to see him die. The newspapers estimated their numbers at 5,000.

The old folk story told about others in his situation is told of him: A group of cowboys hurried past the wagon, intent on getting a good place to observe the proceedings, and Cooney called out to them: "Don't hurry boys! Nothing can happen until I get there."

The wagon pulled up under the gallows and the sheriff put the rope around Cooney's wrinkled neck. Then he asked if the condemned man had anything to say. "Yes, I have," Cooney replied, and proceeded to say it. No stenographer was present to record his remarks, but the people of Granbury remembered them:

He stood up in the wagon, a thin, dried-up old man with a long white beard and white hair hanging down to his shoulders, and made what Hood County historian T.T. Ewell called a "bold protestation." He reminded the spectators that he was an honest man and had always paid his debts.

He didn't say much about the crime of which he had been accused. Instead he talked about the death of his son Jeff and what it meant to him—how proud he was that "there was not a cowardly bone in that boy's body."

He looked George Wright, one of the three deputies who had blasted Jeff out of existence, straight in the eye and accused him: "You knew all the time who was coming up that bluff and you murdered the boy in cold blood."

Then he called on his absent son Bill, wherever he might be and however long it might take, to make his father's murderers pay.

Then he looked out across the intent faces of the crowd and saw the Reverend James Truitt, whose testimony at the trial had put the noose around Cooney's neck. He motioned to Jim to come nearer but Jim did not move so he spoke to him, according to Granbury tradition, across the multitude:

"Jim, when you didn't have nothing but one pony and a wagon, didn't I take you in and feed you? Didn't I?"

Jim made no reply.

"When you wanted to go to preaching, didn't I buy you the first suit of clothes you ever had?"

Jim said nothing.

"Didn't I buy you a Bible—a good Bible —to start you out?"

Still Jim said nothing

It seemed to the sheriff that this had gone on long enough and he drove the wagon out from under the gallows so that Nelson Mitchell swung like a pendulum and choked to death at the end of the rope.

The sight of the old man, so thin and frail but as bold in his own defense, standing up there in the wagon with the rope around his neck while the last seconds of his life drained away, left its mark on the mind of every spectator.

Seventy years later D.C. Cogdell (ninety-six years old when I interviewed him in 1944) shuddered as he recalled that scene and said he hoped never to have to watch such another.

The hanging—the only one ever to take place in Hood County— touched off a revolution which continues to this day in the country where it all happened. It seemed to almost everybody, after the excitement was over, that justice had been overdone.

The Mitchell family never doubted it, and Bill Mitchell, following the code in which he had been raised, vowed to even the score. That hanging changed the course of many lives.

Behind Cooney Mitchell's death was trouble between the Mitchells and the Truitts, neighbors in what is still known as Mitchell's Bend, a few square miles of land surrounded by a great loop of the Brazos River. The bottoms were fertile and heavily timbered, a good place to settle if one didn't mind clearing brush and grubbing stumps.

The two families lived comfortably in log cabins shaded by live oaks, and made out well enough by fishing, hunting and farming. It was still dangerous country, however. Indians were often active in the vicinity and desperadoes and thieves were a menace.

But civilization was creeping in as the 1870s came up on the calendar. There was law and commerce at Granbury, twelve or fourteen miles away, and a store and blacksmith shop at Mambrino, a couple of miles north of the narrows, where the river almost closed its loop. Life could have been pleasant and rewarding if the two families had not fallen out.

The Truitts, including P.M. Truitt, his wife and ten children, lived within sight of the Mitchell cabin, where Cooney, his wife and seven of their nine children lived their lives. They had been friends, even close friends, after their arrival in the late 1860s or early '70s, but the two families were headed in different directions.

Their differences were visible and personified in the two older sons, young men of nearly the same age:

James Truitt was a good looking boy, very blond, slender, thin-faced, sensitive and intelligent. Country living had given him a wiry strength, but he was eager to earn and improve his mind. In a nearby town he found an old man who taught school and was willing to accept him as a student. Jim did well. His teacher told him, "You have a mind like a tar bucket. Everything sticks to it."

To pay for his education, Jim split rails to make ties for the railroad and taught school. His dream was to be a Methodist minister, and just a few months before the trouble broke out, he was admitted to preach "on trial" in the Weatherford District near Fort Worth. He was now the Reverend James M. Truitt.

Bill Mitchell, on the other hand, was almost illiterate, though he was well schooled in the skills needed in his daily life. He could not read books, but he could read sign, and he was more than competent in the art of survival. In 1874 he was twenty-four years old. His mother was part Cherokee and his Indian blood showed in his dark skin, his high cheek bones, and his slightly slanted eyes.

He had a powerful, wiry body, a big nose, a grim mouth and a serious disposition. He looked hard and straight at anyone he happened to be talking to and was positive in his opinions. He was capable of love and loyalty, but he would not run from anybody and he would not let anybody "run over" him.

Hard feelings developed over a few acres of bottom land which the Truitts bought from Cooney. P.M. Truitt said he had paid for it. Cooney said he had not and took him to court. All friendship ceased thereafter. The boys quarreled and said unforgivable things to each other. They all had guns and were accustomed to using them. A showdown was inevitable.

On March 27, 1874, the showdown came. Cooney's case against P.M. Truitt was scheduled at the Granbury courthouse and both sides were there in force. Only P.M., who had pneumonia, was absent. They waited all day for the case to be called, and when it was not, they started for home.

Three and a half miles down the Mambrino road the two parties had to cross Contrary Creek, where the bottoms were heavily timbered, and there they had a bloody three minutes. When it was over,

Bill Mitchell and Mit Graves, who worked for Cooney, had killed Sam Truitt and his seventeen-year-old brother Ike and had put a load of buckshot into Jim's shoulder as he fled. The Truitts say their boys were unarmed. The Mitchells asserted that Ike had a derringer which he snapped at Bill. The issue was never resolved.

The posse which invaded Mitchell's Bend brought in four men. Cooney was one of them. Although he was not armed, he was said to have been the "instigator" of the murders, shouting "Give 'em hell, boys," as the shooting began. The judge sentenced him to hang.

After the shooting, Bill had headed for the wildest country he could find and took cover a hundred miles west of San Antonio and north of Bracketville in a parched universe of rock and brush with great, gray limestone hills rolling away toward the end of the world, their slopes so thickly thatched with rock that scrub oak, juniper, and mesquite were hard pressed to find a foothold. Bear and mountain lion were still at home there, but people were better off somewhere else.

For some years Bill lived a wandering, footloose life in his lost and lonely country, hunting wolves and lions for a living, camping out, and staying as much as he could away from people. The few human beings who lived there, however, were the kind Bill understood. In a few favored spots families had settled, drilled wells with horsepower equipment, and gone to cattle raising.

The tribe of Calamese Beckett was one such family. Calamese had migrated from Tennessee to Texas in 1859 with a wife and eight children (four more were born in the new home). A grown daughter was Mary Jane, recently divorced from George Holliday after two children.

She was a slender, quiet, rather pretty young woman who became Mrs. Bill Mitchell on March 28, 1884. She was probably the only woman in the world who could have loved and cherished dour, cantankerous Bill Mitchell (or John King or John Davis or Henry "Baldy" Russell, as Bill was also known). She was patient, sturdy and efficient, and never, so far we know, complained of her hard lot.

She took care of gloomy, bitter Bill as long as she had him, living in dugouts and shacks, going to town once in four or five years, rearing her children far from schools and churches and kinfolk, dreading the lawman's knock on the door.

This life continued for thirteen years and might have gone on for the rest of their days had Bill not located Jim Truitt and hunted him down.

Jim had picked up the pieces of his shattered life in 1874 and built a new one. In 1875 he was removed from "trial" statue and admitted to "full connection" as a Methodist minister. In 1884, after serving in several Texas conferences, he left the active ministry at his own request to provide for his growing family.

He had married clever and talented Julia Phifer and was the father of a boy and two girls. Julia was a successful writer and journalist and this fact no doubt influenced Jim's decision to become an editor.

In 1885 he was in business as editor end publisher of the *Timpson Times*, serving an ambitious community which had been born in a cotton patch beside a new East Texas railroad two years before. He and Julia acquired a "box house" without rugs or curtains or a front porch. They improvised furniture and felt that the future was theirs.

The shadow of Bill Mitchell still hung over them after thirteen years, but when Jim's friends urged him to carry a six-shooter, he would laugh and say, "It would be a waste of time. If he ever shoots me, it will be in the back."

He could not know that Bill had somehow learned that Timpson was 400 miles north and east of Bracketville, but the distance meant nothing to Bill. He filled a bag with coffee, bread and bacon, tied blanket and slicker to his saddle, added a small coffee pot, and hit the road. Probably he did not tell Mary where he was going. He had been heard to say, "Women should not know too much."

At Stephenville, out west of Fort Worth, he borrowed a fine horse from his brother Dan and on July 21, 1886, he was close to Timpson, waiting beside the road for night to fall. Several people saw him and remembered the fine horse and the little coffee pot. As dusk was gathering, he passed the town limits and paid a little black boy fifteen cents to show him the Truitts' house.

Inside Jim and Julia were preparing for the evening's work. They had lighted the Rochester lamp, their one fine possession, and Jim was getting ready to dictate an article to Julia. Their little daughter Hallie (who described the scene to me many years later) was playing nearby. At that moment a dark-faced stranger entered the front door, took three or four quick steps through the room, and as Jim turned to look, shot him through the head. Then he turned and walked out, mounted his horse, and rode off into the early night.

It took forty-eight hours for Sheriff Spradley, a famous man hunter from Nagodoches, to get on the trail, and Bill was out of reach. Spradley learned about the feud killings in 1874, however, and scared Bill's brother Dan into revealing the location of Bill's hideout in south Texas.

In his memoirs the sheriff tells of his attempt to flush Bill out of his hiding place. He located Beckett's camp but Bill was not at home. As a last resort Spradley sent Calamese Beckett a note asking him to persuade Bill to give up. The reply came back: "Go to Hell."

It was obviously time for Bill Mitchell to move on, and he headed for Three Rivers New Mexico, on the Pecos, where his sister-in-law Arrie Therrell lived. He arrived just in time to join the Therrells in a move to untamed country west of the Rio Grande. By 1892 Bill and Mary and their three children (two by Mary's first marriage, one by their own) were living, more or less permanently, on the Jornada del Muerto near the spot where the first atomic bomb was exploded half a century later.

The Jornada (meaning day's journey of the dead man) was named for hundreds of good reasons, all of them "dead"—of thirst, of exhaustion, of the arrows and lances of lurking Apaches. The Rio Grande swings away from the mountains on the east fifty miles above Las Cruces, running through rough and impassable country, and swings back again ninety or a hundred miles to the north.

Travelers from earliest times had to traverse those ninety waterless miles because there was no other way north and many of them left their bones. In the early 1880s the Santa Fe ran a branch line from Albuquerque to El Paso through this howling desert, and several almost imperceptible hamlets sprang up at points where drillers could reach water. But the country was still rough and forbidding— just the place for Bill Mitchell, who was now known as Baldy Russell.

He dug a hole back into a foothill, threw a wagon sheet over it, and moved his family in. With pick and shovel he sank his first well, sending the dirt up in a bucket while the women turned the wind-lass. At sixty-five feet he struck water, and although he did not own an inch of ground he was at home.

Little by little he got ahead, first with horses, then with cows. He moved around some—dug more wells and built houses, the last one made of stone. The two girls—half sisters—grew up there and were not aware that their lot was hard. They could not go to school but they learned to read and consumed books and magazines. There were neighbors—at some distance—and social intercourse was possible.

Baldy was really their only link with the outside world. Four or five times a year he went to San Marcial, fifty miles north on the river, for supplies, taking two days each way to make the trip. The women never went. If Mary or Belle or Maude got a new dress, Baldy picked it out. When he got back, the neighbors would drop in to see if he had picked up any mail.

This less-than-idyllic existence continued, with shifts in location (Baldy dug five wells before he finished) until March 24, 1907, when his past finally caught up with him. The family was now living on the east side of the mountains at a now-vanished hamlet called Estey City where Baldy was working at odd jobs and fooling around with a few mining claims, not expecting any trouble.

When it came, it was brought on by his daughter Maude, who ran away to San Marcial with a cowboy named Riley Caldwell and got married. Riley told her she would have to give her right name on the marriage license so she did —Maude Mitchell. Somebody who knew about it put two and two together and the word went back to Granbury.

In due time Sheriff H.M. Denny and Ben Wooten, his deputy, drove Wooten's buckboard from Alamogordo out across the malpais to Estey City—a two-day trip. They posed as potential buyers of mining property and asked Baldy to show them his claims.

For once unsuspicious, Baldy obliged, and when they were far enough away from the house the two men got him by the arms and wrestled him into submission—no easy task, even for two big strong lawmen.

Sheriff John Swofford and Deputy Sid Powell came out from Granbury and picked up the prisoner at El Paso. Baldy told his friends that he was glad the long years of suspense were over at last.

He was tried at two places for two crimes—at Granbury for the killing of the Truitt boys; at Timpson for shooting Jim Truitt. Admitted to bail at Granbury, he was taken to Timpson to face Julia Truitt, now Julia Truitt Bishop, who identified him positively. But others were not sure, and the trial ended in a hung jury. So it was back to Granbury. When three major witnesses for the prosecution (including Bill Mitchell's brother Dan) failed to appear, the judge refused to continue the case and turned the prisoner loose.

Back in Timpson a new trial began in March, 1908, and again the jury could not agree. Bill went free on $20,000 bail and headed back to New Mexico after almost exactly a year's absence. Mary was waiting. She had been staying with Maude at Capitan.

Now she and Baldy took off in Baldy's old wagon behind his team of little weather-beaten mules, and fell into the old wandering life, looking for odd jobs, seeing the few friends they had left, always on the outskirts of everything.

The new trial loomed up ahead as 1910 drew to a close and once again the old man had to go back to the world of cells and bars and jail routine. A grim fate for this seeker of lonesome valleys and uninhabited deserts. He never tried to run away from his accusers, for whatever his sins, ingratitude to the friends who had financed his bond for bail was not among them.

Two days before Christmas, 1910, the judge gaveled the courtroom at Rusk, Texas, into silence, and lawyers and witnesses went through the familiar charges and rebuttals again. This time the verdict was "guilty"; the punishment, life imprisonment. Appeals were unavailing, and Baldy disappeared behind the walls of the Texas State Penitentiary at Huntsville on March 16, 1912.

Two years later, on July 13, 1914, he "escaped." One story says he walked away from a work detail of trusties. Another says the warden told him to go home for Christmas and come back when and if he felt like it. Apparently no attempt was made to recapture him.

Baldy could never be sure he was safe, however, and being on the dodge was so much his natural way of life that he went into the routine almost automatically. Mary was waiting for him back in New Mexico. They got into the old wagon again and drove off into new anonymity.

Baldy was now John Davis, and John Davis he remained for the rest of his years. His wanderings really brought him to Steins, or Steins Pass, a hamlet on the El Paso-Tucson highway where the railroad crossed the Peloncillo Mountains. A few ruined buildings, visible from Interstate 10, still mark the spot.

In due time he and Mary moved fifteen miles west to the village of San Simon, a major metropolis to them. But they still liked to take the old wagon and go camping in the hills.

It was at San Simon that Baldy had his last heart attack, in April, 1928. They took him to the hospital in Douglas, Arizona, and he lived two days more. They said then, and they say now, that he refused to die lying down and was actually on his feet when the call came.

The story was almost true. Baldy absolutely refused to use bedpans and urinals and was on his way back from the bathroom, supported by Mary and an orderly, when he collapsed and died. The story, as it was passed around, did, however, fit his character. In all his life he never took anything lying down.

Phillip W. Steele

Born in the historic frontier city of Fort Smith, Arkansas, Phil Steele developed an interest in the Old West and Ozark regional history listening to stories his grandfather told. Growing up in the Springdale/Fayetteville region of northwest Arkansas, he attended Springdale schools, Kemper Military Academy, U.C.L.A., and the University of Arkansas where he earned a BSBA degree. Over the past thirty years he has authored eight books and over a hundred newspaper and magazine articles. He has also written and narrated three documentary films, produced two Old West albums, and an album of pure delta blues music. A long-time member of Western Writers of America, he is a past president of NOLA and a founding member of the James-Younger Gang, Inc. He currently serves on the board of NOLA, as well as Friends of the James Farm, Arkansas History Commission, and the Arkansas Film Commission. He has interviewed dozens of old-timers with links to figures of frontier history, preserving their stories and memories for future generations. Having written extensively about Jesse James, Steele was selected by the James family to be a forensic team member when the remains of Jesse were exhumed for DNA analysis in 1995 and to serve as a pall bearer at the reburial ceremony. Steele is currently president of a food processing company of Springdale and Little Rock. He and his wife Charlotte have two children and five grandchildren.

JAMES BROTHERS' DEATH HOAX
·
By Phillip Steele
NOLA *Quarterly*, Winter 1983-84

T ales of Jesse and Frank James by far head all other subjects in Ozark folk tales. Few Ozark caves have escaped once being a James Gang hideout. Few Ozark banks, trains, or stages have escaped being robbed by the James boys. An estimated four thousand books have been published about Jesse and Frank James, each claiming to be the one and only true account of their lives and exploits.

One might then ask, with all this material, what else of interest could ever be said about the Jameses? Why are we attempting to present new material one hundred and one years after Jesse's death?

William A. Settle's book, *Jesse James Was His Name* I consider to be the best and closest to reality of all James histories. By no means will I attempt to question the James facts recorded in Settle's work. Settle himself, however, stated that after spending years researching James, many questions still exist. He further stated that fact and fiction are so intertwined that it is almost impossible to separate them.

Jesse and Frank James would lead all others in the race for America's greatest folk heroes. It was Settle who also perhaps best described the reason for this: "Jesse and Frank James continue to be fascinating because the average American relives their exploits and releases something of their outlaw spirit and suppressed rebellion against the restrictions of modern society."

With this background I would like to present relatively new theo-

255

ries on James history as it was told by one Jesse Woodson James, alias J. Frank Dalton, and by Franklin Alexander James, alias Joe Vaughn.

History tells us that Jesse James eluded the law for sixteen years after the Civil War. Jesse, who stood nearly six feet tall, supposedly found it necessary to stand on a chair to dust a picture in his Saint Joseph home where his trusted friend Bob Ford shot him in the back of the head with his .44 on April 3, 1882.

Frank James shortly thereafter walked into Missouri Governor [Thomas] Crittenden's office, handed him his guns, and became his prisoner. Frank was soon pardoned of all crimes and lived a peaceful life as a race starter, and a theatrical spectacle, and in Wild West shows for income.

The American public simply could not accept the fact that the greatest of all American bandits ended their careers in such a simple unromantic way. Great mystery and speculation have thus always surrounded the James story.

Some twenty-six men have been documented as impersonating Jesse James and some ten or more as being Frank James long after their death. Hundreds of stories exist of men claiming to have seen Jesse James after he was killed.

Jesse attended his sister's funeral in Wichita Falls, Texas in 1889, according to Dr. William Tunstill. The *Dallas Morning News* featured an article about a man who was with his father at the Dallas County Fair in 1906. The man's father had grown up next door to the James farm and had known the Jameses well. While at the fair the boy's father ran into Jesse and Frank in the crowd and spent some time in conversation.

The last two to claim to be the Jameses were J. Frank Dalton and Joe Vaughn. Dalton died in Granbury, Texas, in 1951 and Vaughn in Wayton, Arkansas, in 1926. The stories they told were quite creative and so convincing that their children and grandchildren today still believe and tell of their famous ancestors who played a great "hoax on history."

First, let's look at Frank James, alias Joe Vaughn.

I first became aware of the story in 1976 when I learned that a girl in my city claimed her great-grandfather was Frank James. A quick review in my library proved this could not be accurate, as Frank who had married Annie Ralston only had one child, Robert, and Robert had no children.

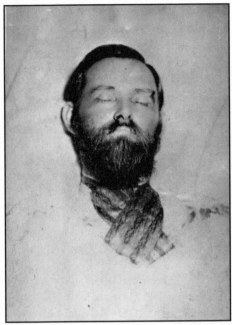

Jesse James in death, April 4, 1882.
Author's Collection & James Farm Museum

Finding the girl, I questioned her on this and she told me that her grandfather, Ebb Vaughn and his sister, Sara Vaughn Snow, were still alive in their 90s in a Carroll County, Arkansas, nursing home and claimed to be children of Frank James. There I recorded interviews with them that would change all James history if proven factual. Both firmly believed that their father was the one and only Franklin Alexander James and was a half-brother to Jesse.

Here is their story: Joe Vaughn called his family together on his death bed at his home on the Buffalo River near Jasper, Arkansas, in 1926. There he told them they were actually Jameses and not Vaughns. He directed his children to an old hand written manuscript describing in detail the true and authentic life of the James boys. He further requested his children to see that the truth was published and requested that his true name be inscribed on his grave marker.

Columbus Vaughn, a former college instructor in Iowa and now retired in the Ozarks, self-published a very poor book about his grandfather Frank James based on the old manuscript, entitled *This was Frank James*. Only a few copies were printed and it is no longer in print.

Basically the story tells that Frank James was a base-begotten child and his real father was Jim Reed.

Reverend Robert James married Zeralda Cole in Kentucky and soon thereafter they left for Missouri. Leaving Zeralda in Missouri with her mother who had preceded them to Missouri, Reverend James returned to Kentucky to finish seminary school at Georgetown University. During the months he was away, Zeralda had an affair with Jim Reed, who later married Belle Starr, and Zeralda became pregnant by Reed.

Reverend James soon returned and raised Frank as a James.

Thus, Frank was a half-brother to Jesse. Interestingly, several older books about the Jameses refer to Jesse and Frank as half-brothers but no explanation is ever made. We further find that all books describe Jesse and Frank as having completely different personalities, nature, and appearance. The Vaughn story would possibly explain this. We further find many books describing Zeralda James as being promiscuous and hard for Reverend James to handle.

Mystery has always surrounded Reverend James, leaving his family to go to California when Jesse was only three and Frank seven. It is unreasonable, especially for a minister, to leave a wife and three small children to make out for themselves on a frontier farm. Vaughn claims that Reverend James left because in the heat of an argument Zeralda told her husband that Frank was not his son.

The Vaughn story also tells that Frank returned for Jesse's supposed funeral and actually served as a pallbearer under the alias of Jim Vaughn. This Jim Vaughn pallbearer is mentioned in a great many books as a mystery man no one knew. John Ross, superior court judge for Orange County, California, is Jesse James' grandson. Ross believes Jim Vaughn was Frank James.

Frank James shortly thereafter found a way out of his sixteen years of running. A neighbor to the James farm, Sam Collins, was the same age as Frank. While Frank was away in the brush over the years, Frank's wife Annie had fallen in love with Collins. Frank made a deal through Sam's sister, Mattie Collins, and Governor Crittenden to finally rid Missouri of the James gang and help Crittenden's political ambitions.

Frank gave Collins the James farm, $25,000 cash, and all rights to his wife, Annie. Governor Crittenden had agreed to pardon James in the event any court convicted him. Once Frank was pardoned Collins became Frank James. Frank then took the name of Joe Vaughn, an ex-Quantrill guerrilla friend who had been killed.

Frank moved to Arkansas seeking peace and quiet, built a log home along the beautiful Buffalo river in North Arkansas. He soon married a neighbor girl and they raised nine children there as Vaughns.

Sam Collins, as Frank James, used his new found notoriety to earn money at carnivals, Wild West Shows, and horse races around the country. He died on the James farm in 1915 and is buried as Franklin Alexander James in Independence, Missouri.

Joe Vaughn died in 1926 and is buried in the Snow Cemetery on the top of a beautiful mountain near Wayton, Arkansas, as Frank James, alias Joe Vaughn.

Facts we have found are that Joe Vaughn was known to often quote Shakespeare. All histories of Frank James refer to this personality trait.

Although poor photos, those existing of Joe Vaughn have resemblance in facial structure to known photos of Frank James. The Vaughns, however, refer to most Frank James photos as being photos of Sam Collins.

Census records show that a Sam Collins was living on a farm immediately adjacent to the James farm near Kearney, Missouri. Sam Collins does not appear on any census after 1880.

Joe Vaughn was known to be an excellent marksman and won all kinds of shooting contests in Arkansas. The favorite gun, which his family still has, is of the same type Frank James used and preferred.

Ebb Vaughn, Frank's son, told that his father would leave home for weeks at a time. When he came home he would dump a sack of money on the kitchen table. He would never tell his wife from where it came. The Vaughns assume Frank left to dig up money he and Jesse had buried at various locations during their outlaw days.

Joe Vaughn admitted to the physician treating him a few days before his death in 1926 that he truly was Frank James, that his brother Jesse did not die in 1882, and was in fact still alive.

We have found several books mentioning that Jesse and Frank often used the alias of Vaughn. We have found a direct relationship between the James and Vaughn families. Dr. Reuben Samuel married Zeralda James after learning that Reverend James had died in

California. Dr. Samuel's brother, Fielding Samuel, had a daughter who married Ed Vaughn. The Vaughns moved to Clifty, Arkansas. Fielding Samuel is buried in Clifty. Grandchildren recall that stories were often told about their nephews Jesse and Frank James visiting the Arkansas Vaughn home.

One good physical piece of evidence also exists: Shortly before he died, Joe Vaughn told his children where to find a stone hidden in a cave near the Vaughn home. One of the Vaughn grandchildren still has the stone. Carved on it is:

1871-J. James, F. James, Bob, Jim, Cole.

Its age has been verified by the University of Arkansas.

This leads us to the tie-in with the last man to claim to be Jesse Woodson James. His name or alias was J. Frank Dalton and his story is even wilder than the Vaughn claim.

In Lawton, Oklahoma, in 1948 Dalton revealed himself as being the famous outlaw Jesse James. His story made national news, *Time*, *Life*, trips to New York, Los Angeles, and extensive interviews until his death in 1951 in Gladewater, Texas, at age one hundred and seven.

Dalton's story is this:

There are two sets of Jesse and Frank Jameses, a set in Kentucky and a set in Missouri. Reverend Robert James and Zeralda Cole in Missouri had Jesse Robert James and Franklin Alexander James. Robert's brother, George James, in Kentucky married Matilda Dalton, a sister of Lewis Dalton who was father of the Dalton Gang. George and Matilda had children in Kentucky, Jesse Woodson James and Sylvester Franklin James.

Thus we have two sets who were cousins. All fought together in Civil War guerrilla activities, and later together in outlaw gangs. Having these two sets would help explain the mystery of James Gang robberies so wide spread throughout the nation during short periods of time.

This would possibly help explain the widespread controversy over photography of Jesse, Frank and their mother. All photos could be authentic, depending on the set being referred to.

J. Frank Dalton's story now even becomes more complicated: Charles Bigelow was a Missouri outlaw who had been robbing banks, trains, and stores, using the alias of Jesse James. His widespread activity angered both the Missouri and Kentucky Jesses and Franks.

Both Jesses were married and tired of living in the brush with some $50,000 reward for their death or capture.

Thus a plot was planned to end Jesse forever.

First, Bigelow was found and killed. His body was brought to a home in Saint Joseph, Missouri where the Missouri Jesse was living with his wife and young son Jesse Edward James. Bigelow's body was laid out on the floor.

Bob Ford, a family friend—and cousin, according to Dr. William Tunstill—needed money, so they planned for him to get the credit. Ford shot a bullet into the wall and ran out to tell the world he had killed Jesse James.

Jesse's mother, wife, friends and gang members were all in on the plot and sworn to secrecy as was Governor Crittenden. None were to reveal the story until one lived past one hundred.

The Missourian, Jesse Robert James, then went south to spend his life under the alias of George Hines in Pensacola, Florida.

We note from the James ancestry that Jesse James' grandmother was a Hines and his uncle was George. Thus the alias of George Hines.

The Kentuckian Jesse Woodson James, after attending the Missourian Jesse's funeral, left for South America for several years, then came back to Gladewater, Texas, using the alias of J. Frank Dalton, the J. for Jesse, Frank for his brother Frank, and Dalton from his mother's maiden name.

J. Frank Dalton's photo was shown to Ebb Vaughn who is still alive at age ninety-five. Ebb identified the man as a man that visited his father Joe Vaughn often at their Arkansas home when Ebb was a child.

During J. Frank Dalton's two-year tour it was found that he knew dates, places and other facts corresponding to known James history extremely well. Three men well over the age of one hundred in 1950 who knew Jesse James were found and identified J. Frank Dalton as the Jesse James they knew during the 1870s.

Other facts we have found are these:

Many men reported seeing Jesse years after his 1882 "death."

The only Charles Bigelow on the 1880 census of Missouri never showed up on a later census.

Ten members of the Bigelow family in America have records of a relative being buried as Jesse.

J. Frank Dalton's index finger tip was missing. All Jesse James histories refer to his index finger tip as missing.

In 1978 the original Jesse James grave was exhumed on the James farm near Kearney, Missouri. The bullet found there created a new question as to who was buried there: The bullet found was .38 caliber. The photo Bob Ford circulated holding the gun he used to kill Jesse was of a .44 caliber.

What happened to the bullet that supposedly killed Jesse James is a mystery. Some say the mortician, a Mr. Heddons, kept it in his family. A search in his family, however, turned up no knowledge of the bullet.

Known photos of Jesse differ considerably from those taken of Jesse's body. One source pointed out clearly that Jesse's receding hairline, mysteriously disappeared in the casket.

Again it is interesting to look at Jesse's pallbearers. One J.T. Ford was a pallbearer. He was the father of Bob and Charlie Ford, Jesse's supposed assassins. It is not reasonable to think Zeralda James would have permitted the father of her son's assassins to serve as a pallbearer.

We also find the 1850 census records of Missouri list a Jesse (R.) James, child of Robert and Zeralda James. This R. is important as it would support Dalton's story that he was Jesse Woodson James in Kentucky and his cousin in Missouri was Jesse Robert James. All histories refer to Jesse as Jesse Woodson.

The stories told by J. Frank Dalton who died in 1951, and by Joe Vaughn, who died in 1926, have many, many holes in them and leave hundreds of questions still unanswered.

On the surface they appear to be so far fetched that absolutely no truth can be found in them. Yet some weak evidence exists that perhaps some part of the mystery can be found here.

No, we cannot change the more documented histories of the James brothers with the Dalton/Vaughn stories. Just why these men would have fabricated such tales only they could have known.

The fact remains that two graves exist for Frank James: One in 1915 in Missouri and one in 1926 in Arkansas.

Two graves also exist for Jesse Woodson James: One in 1882 in Kearney, Missouri and one in 1951 in Gladewater, Texas.

The Vaughn descendants from Joe Vaughn's nine children will no doubt keep the folklore tale alive for years to come.

J. Frank Dalton's grandson, Jesse Lee James III, and his children, Woodson Lee James and Jesse Lee James IV, now living in Rogers, Arkansas, will further keep the Jesse James controversy alive.

Let me emphasize again, I personally regard the work of William A. Settle to be the most accurate and true accounts of the James brothers.

The attempts J. Frank Dalton and Joe Vaughn made to change history are at least creative and interesting. Research into their claims is still being done in hope we can at least somehow determine the real identity of these last two James impostors.

Sue C. Van Slyke

Sue was born in 1937 in Chevy Chase, Maryland, in her grandfather's house on Western Avenue, and now wonders if the street name influenced her long interest in the American West. She attended elementary school in Florida, junior high in Bethesda, Maryland, high school in Leesburg, Virginia, and studied accounting at American University in Washington, D.C. She has maintained an interest in the outlaws and lawmen of the West since she was a teenager and became especially intrigued by the controversy surrounding the so-called gunfight at the O.K. Corral in Tombstone. Always having sympathy for underdogs, she began researching the Clanton family, a study she has pursued for the last twenty-three years. Sue is a lifetime member of NOLA and has attended every annual meeting since 1979. She has served on the board of the organization for eighteen years, has held the office of treasurer, and is currently elections chair. Her article, "The Truth About the Clantons of Tombstone." was first given as a talk at the NOLA Rendezvous at Driggs, Idaho, in 1981. Since then she has written two other articles on the Clanton family in collaboration with Dave Johnson. Sue is active in her church, where she and her late husband Ed have been elders, and she has been treasurer for more than twenty-five years. She is also past president and current treasurer and creative arts chair of the Temple Hills Club of the National Association for Family and Community Education, and a member of the Prince George's County Genealogical Society.

THE TRUTH ABOUT THE
CLANTONS OF TOMBSTONE
•
By Sue C. Van Slyke
NOLA *Quarterly*, Spring 1982

Twenty-six years ago I happened to read an article in *Woman's Day* magazine entitled "Wyatt Earp Rides Again," which of course, included an account of the so called gunfight at the OK Corral.[1] Shortly after this I read a piece by William McLeod Raine, whose version of the gunfight was considerably different.[2] This intrigued me and I wanted to learn more about the participants, so I started reading every book and article I could find on the subject. After awhile, I knew more about the Earps than I really wanted to, but still very little about the Clantons. I finally concluded that if I wanted to uncover their background I would have to do it myself. However, it wasn't until I discovered a brief Clanton family history sheet at the Arizona Historical Society five years ago that I seriously thought that I could put together a study of the Clanton family. Though much of the information on this sheet turned out to be inaccurate, at least it gave me an idea of how to get started. My research is yet far from complete; this is a progress report up to this time.

Newman Haynes Clanton, the father of Phin, Ike, and Billy, was born in Davidson County, Tennessee, in 1816.[3] He was one of six children of Henry and Polly Hailey Clanton.[4] Henry Clanton was born in 1784 in Sussex County, Virginia.[5] It is said that he took part in the War of 1812 and was at the Battle of New Orleans.[6] I have not yet found when Newman's ancestors came to this country, but it seems that they were here quite some time before the Revolutionary War.

Newman married Mariah P. Kelso, the daughter of John Kelso and
Mary Snedicor, on January 5, 1840, in Callaway County, Missouri.
The marriage was performed by Justice of the Peace T.G. Jones.[7]
The bride was about sixteen.

In Callaway County, Newman and Mariah settled down to farming
and their first three children were born: John Wesley in 1841,
Phineas Fay in 1845, and Joseph Isaac "Ike" in 1847.[8]

It is often said that Newman went to California in the gold rush,
and it may well be true. Certainly he left his young family in
Callaway County and went somewhere. The 1850 census shows
Mariah and the three boys living with a young Kelso family,
undoubtedly relatives of hers. Wherever he went, he didn't stay
long; their first daughter, Mary Elsie, was born in Illinois in 1852.[9]
After a short stay in Illinois—or perhaps they were just passing
through—they settled near Dallas, Texas, where they again took up
farming. Poll tax records show the number of cattle owned by
Newman to range from six to thirty-eight during these years.[10] Two
more children were born to them in this period: Hester, born ca.
1854 and Alonzo, ca. 1859.[11]

In 1861 they moved to Hamilton County, Texas. The population of
Hamilton County in 1860 was only 463 and it was a wild unsettled
area with many hostile Indians. In this year the Civil War broke out
and since so many of the young men were taken into the regular
army there was little local protection. A company of Home Guards
was organized under Captain W.H. Cotton and included Newman
Clanton, a private, and his oldest son John Wesley, nineteen, a first
corporal.[12] Apparently this was too tame for young John Wesley
Clanton, so he left after about six weeks and went to Ellis County
where he enlisted, possibly without his father's consent, in the
Twelfth Regiment of Texas Cavalry, known as Parson's Regiment.[13]
About four months later he left and went home to Hamilton County.
Three men were sent to arrest him and return him to his regiment.
According to Sgt. J.H. Hodges, he gave no difficulty at first but, said
Hodges, "That night about three miles from where I arrested him, I
met his father and his father did not wish him to come back, he told
him to break custody. The prisoner then refused to come; he afterwards agreed to come after my telling him he was obliged to. His
father told him he was afraid his destiny was death, which I suppose
was the cause of his refusing to come."[14] John Wesley was returned

Newman Hayes Clanton.
Author's Collection.

to his regiment and in February, 1862, a court martial was held. He offered no defense and was found guilty of desertion. However, due to "extenuating circumstances"—his youth and the fact that he had not read the Articles of War and so was not aware of the seriousness of his crime—his sentence was a light one, a stoppage of pay from the time of desertion to the expiration of his term of enlistment and then to be dishonorably discharged.[15]

At this point the military records become very confusing. Though John Wesley should have been dishonorably discharged in August, 1862, it appears that both he and his father enlisted in Waco in March 1862, but Newman was discharged July 6, 1862, being over aged, and John Wesley seems to have left on March 2, 1863. Another record shows that Newman enlisted again at Fort Herbert, but was "Absent With Out Leave" since June 1, 1863.[16] He also enlisted in the Company for Second Frontier District at Hamilton and served twenty-three days at two dollars per day, but claimed that he was never paid.[17]

In 1862 in the midst of the Civil War, the Clanton's seventh and last child, William Harrison, was born, probably in Hamilton County, Texas.[18]

In 1865 came the end of the Civil War, and on August 26 John Wesley's name appears on a list of refugees who reported at Franklin, Texas.[19] On September 3, he, Newman, and Phin, who was nineteen or twenty by this time, are found on a list of persons at Fort Bowie, Arizona Territory, en route to California, who formerly belonged to the Confederate States Army. Their descriptions appear on this list. Newman was six feet, one inch, fair complexion, light hair and blue eyes; John Wesley was five feet, eleven inches, fair complexion, light hair and brown eyes; and Phin is described as five feet, eight inches, fair complexion, brown hair and blue eyes.[20]

The family left Fort Bowie and headed for California. In 1866, somewhere on the way, Mariah Clanton died, leaving Newman with seven children ranging in age from twenty-five-year-old John Wesley down to four-year-old Billy.[21]

In California, John Wesley married seventeen-year-old Nancy Rose Kelsey and settled on a farm in Inyo County near her parents. Phin lived with them and worked on the farm. Their first child, Mary, was born in 1870.[22]

Mary Elsie, the Clantons' older daughter, was also married in California, to John Franklin Slinkard, and the first of their five children was born there.[23]

The year 1873 found the family back in Arizona, and the *Tucson Citizen* described their farm under the heading "Another New Settlement":

"Newman H. Clanton and family settled on the Gila Valley, a few miles above old Camp Goodwin August 3rd of this year. He at once laid claim to water, located a line, and now has a ditch two and a half miles in length which carries 1880 cubic feet. There is one body of fully 25,000 acres of very rich land and Mr. Clanton feels sure that with proper management he has water enough to irrigate the whole tract. This year he has cultivated 100 acres and is now preparing and will sow and plant at least 600. He was in Tucson early this week procuring utensils and supplies. He says the settlement now consists of three families...in all, fifteen persons, and that more are coming. He is very anxious to have families settle there so that a public school may be opened just as soon as possible.

Families will be supplied with a water privilege at the actual pro-rata cost of the ditch, and accommodated with all the information and assistance Mr. Clanton can afford. We have passed over the land and know it to be as rich as can be found anywhere. The water of the river is of first quality and the locality is very healthy as far as known. The settlement is near Camp Grant, not very far from Camp Apache and Bowie, and within reasonable distance of the important mining camp of Clifton. All these places must have much grain, vegetables and all sorts of farm and dairy products."[24]

Again in 1874 the *Citizen* had this to say:

"All who live in the Gila Valley near old Camp Goodwin and at Pueblo Viejo are enthusiastic in their accounts of the richness of the soil and the ease with which a man may make a farm. N.H. Clanton gave us these items last week, but after our paper was filled. About 12 months ago he moved to a point near old Camp Goodwin and about 160 miles northeast of Tucson and within Pima County. The place is now called Clantonville. During the year he has been there, himself and three sons have cut a ditch from the Gila River; planted 120 acres with wheat, corn, barley and all kinds of vegetables; and from nothing of consequence to start with, now has a fine farm and plenty about him. All his crops have grown nicely and some of them unusually large. Portions of his corn grew to be twelve to fourteen feet high with two large ears on a stalk. It was so nearly matured two weeks ago that an ear could be obtained soft enough for table use. He reports grass plentiful and from five to six feet in height. The cattle are fat and everything is in fine condition. All parties east or west who desire a very fine place to make a good home easily and cheaply cannot do better than to go into the Gila Valley. Land is abundant at government price and the public surveys will be extended there during the present year. Anyone desiring more detailed information can get it by addressing N.H. Clanton, Camp Grant, Arizona.

"Last year we gave Mr. Clanton a quart of white winter rye, which the Commissioner of Agriculture had forwarded to Hon. R.C. McCormick. He sowed it, and it grew surprisingly. Fully one half was destroyed by the breaking of a ditch, yet he gathered one and a half bushels of beautiful rye. We lately gave him a few sacks of winter wheat, forwarded, as stated in the *Citizen* last week, from the Department of Agriculture. The best varieties may soon be had in abundance by carefully cultivating the seed received from Washington. The Agriculture Department distributes only the choicest kinds. A few sacks are still at the Territorial Secretary's office."[25]

During this time it is said that Newman also ran the Clanton House Hotel at Fort Thomas.[26]

It seems that, for all its promise, Clantonville failed to thrive, and so in 1877 Newman, with sons Phin, Ike, and Billy moved to a ranch on the San Pedro River near Charleston, some fourteen miles from Tombstone. Remains of this ranch can still be seen today, though they deteriorate a little more each year. The sturdy adobe house, corral and irrigation ditch were all built by Clanton hands. In addition, the Clantons sometimes drove a freight wagon.

Apparently John Wesley Clanton and his family returned to California about this time.

The cattle business was good in southern Arizona and the Newman Clanton family prospered. Soon they met the McLaury brothers, Frank and Tom, young ranchers in the Sulpher Springs Valley, and they became close friends as well as occasional business partners.[27]

But somehow during this time they made enemies of the Earp brothers, Tombstone gamblers and part-time lawmen, and their dentist-gunman friend, Doc Holliday. Just what started the feud is anyone's guess, but the story most often told is that it stemmed from the Benson stage robbery of March 15, 1881, when Billy Clanton supposedly witnessed the killing of driver Budd Philpot by Doc Holliday.[28] Apparently some of the other robbers were sometime friends of Ike Clanton. Wyatt Earp, who aspired to be elected sheriff of Cochise County, approached Ike and offered him the reward money if he would lure them into a trap so Wyatt could kill them and "get the glory." This plot became very complicated and created a burning hatred between the two factions.[29]

In August of this year, Newman Clanton was ambushed and killed in Guadalupe Canyon, New Mexico, with four others. He had freighted supplies in his wagon to the Animas Valley ranchers and was returning with a herd of cattle. Clanton and his friends were attacked at dawn while some were still in their bedrolls. Only two men escaped death.[30] Newman was buried in Guadalupe Canyon, but it is said that his sons later had him reburied in the old Tombstone cemetery.

A Tucson newspaper gave this interesting description of "The Clanton Boys" during this time:

"The Clanton brothers numbered three—Ike, Phineas (nicknamed Phin) and Billy. They lived on a cattle ranch on the San Pedro River, about twelve miles from Tombstone, with their father. Old man Clanton was murdered in August by Mexicans with five others. The Clantons then fell heir to all of the old man's cattle, and were pretty well fixed. They are fine specimens of the frontier cattle man. Billy,although only 17 years old [sic] was over six feet in height, and built in proportion, while Isaac and Phineas are wiry, deter-mined-looking men, without a pound of surplus flesh. They lived on horse-back, and led a life of hardship."[31]

On the morning of October 25, 1881, Billy and Ike Clanton and the McLaury brothers ate breakfast together at Chandler's milk ranch. Then they separated, Ike Clanton and Tom McLaury heading for Tombstone and Billy Clanton and Frank McLaury to round up stock on the McLaury ranch. Almost from the time Ike and Tom arrived in Tombstone, the Earps and Holliday seemed to be trying to provoke a fight. Ike was verbally abused by Doc Holliday and Morgan Earp who told him, since he was unarmed, to "heel" him-self and stay that way.

The next morning Ike was standing on a street corner with a rifle in his hands when Virgil Earp, who was then city marshal, came up behind him, hit him with the barrel of his pistol, disarmed him and took him to Justice Wallace's court where he was fined twenty-five dollars. While in the court room, he was again taunted by Morgan Earp, who tried to force a pistol on him.[32]

Meanwhile, Wyatt Earp met Tom McLaury on the street and, for no apparent reason, pistol-whipped him even though he was unarmed.[33]

At about this time, Frank McLaury and young Billy Clanton rode into town with a rancher named Major Frink, who was a neighbor of the McLaurys. They were in a saloon about to buy drinks when they heard what had happened to Ike and Tom. Frank said, "We won't drink," and they separated to search for their brothers.[34] Billy Clanton met Billy Claiborne and together they went to several cor-rals looking for Ike's horse. Billy told Claiborne he wanted Ike to go home. "I don't want to fight anybody," Billy said, "and nobody wants to fight me."[35]

About 2:30, the two sets of brothers, along with Claiborne and Sheriff John H. Behan, who was trying desperately to avert a fight, were standing in a vacant lot next to Fly's Photography Gallery, when the three Earp brothers and Doc Holliday approached. Virgil said, "Throw up your hands!" and someone, probably Wyatt, said, "You sons of bitches have been looking for a fight and now you can have one!" Billy Clanton put his hands in the air and cried out, "Don't shoot me! I don't want to fight!" Even as he said this, he was shot by Morgan Earp and fell against the house behind him. Before he could draw his pistol he was shot through the right wrist. Ike, seeing Wyatt's pistol pointed at him, grabbed Wyatt's arm and held it a few seconds. While he was doing this, Wyatt fired and Ike released his arm and ran for the cover of Fly's gallery. Several shots were fired after him.[36]

Meanwhile, Billy managed to draw his pistol with his left hand and fought back, wounding Virgil and Morgan Earp. He was still trying to cock his pistol for another shot, but lacked the strength to do it when Camillus Fly came out of his house with a rifle in his hand and said, "Somebody take that pistol away from that man or I will kill him!" He was told to take it himself if he wanted it. As Fly wrenched the pistol from Billy's weakened grasp, Billy said to him, "Give me some more cartridges."[37]

Wesley Fuller had seen the Earps and Holliday going down Fremont Street and had tried to reach Billy Clanton to warn him of impending trouble, but arrived too late and witnessed the fight from an alley. Now, seeing Billy "rolling on the ground in agony," he picked him up and carried him into a small house on the corner of Fremont and Third street. Billy said to him, "Look and see where I am shot." Fuller found one wound in the left breast from which the lung was oozing and one in the right side of the belly beneath the twelfth rib, and told Billy he could not live. Billy requested, "Get a doctor and give me something to put me to sleep."[38] Dr. Giberson, among the crowd gathering in the house, said it was no use to give him anything.[39] Thomas Keefe, a carpenter who helped carry the dying Tom McLaury into the same house, heard Billy screaming in pain and sent a man for a doctor, telling him to get the first one he could find. Billy said, "They have murdered me!" and as curious onlookers crowded into the little house, he pleaded, "Drive the crowd away from the door and give me air." And again, "I've been murdered." According to Keefe he was "turning and kicking and twisting in every manner with pain." Doctor Millar arrived and, with

Keefe holding Billy on his back, injected two syringes of morphine near his stomach wound. Billy died about fifteen minutes later.[40]

The *Tombstone Nugget* described the incident in this way:

"The firing altogether didn't occupy more than 25 seconds, during which time fully 30 shots were fired. After the fight was over, Billy Clanton, who, with wonderful vitality, survived his wounds for fully an hour, was carried into a house near where he lay, and everything possible done to make his last moments easy. He was game to the last, never uttering a word of complaint, and just before breathing his last he said, 'Goodbye boys; go away and let me die....'"

That evening Phin Clanton, brother of Billy and Ike, came to town, and placing himself under the guard of the sheriff, visited the morgue to see the remains of his brother, and then passed the night in jail in company with the other brother.

"At the morgue the bodies of the three slain cowboys lay side by side, covered with a sheet. Very little blood appeared on their clothing, and only on the face of young Billy Clanton was there any distortion of the features or evidence of pain in dying. The features of the two McLowery [sic] boys looked as calm and placid in death as if they had died peaceably. No unkind remarks were made by anyone, but a feeling of unusual sorrow seemed to prevail..."[41]

The next day the funeral of Billy Clanton and the two McLaury brothers was held. The *Nugget* had this account of it under the heading:

An Imposing Funeral
The Burial of the Dead Cowboys—An Immense Procession, Etc.

"While it was not entirely expected, the funeral of Billy Clanton and Thomas and Frank McLowry, yesterday, was the largest ever witnessed in Tombstone. It was advertised to take place at 3 o'clock, but it was about 4 o'clock before the cortege moved, yet a large number had gathered at the undertaker's long before the first time mentioned. The bodies of the three men, neatly and tastefully dressed, were placed in handsome caskets with heavy silver trimmings. Upon each was a silver plate bearing the name, age, birthplace and date of the death of each. A short time before the funeral, photographs were taken of the dead. The procession was headed by the Tombstone brass band playing the solemn and touching march of the dead. The first wagon contained the body of Billy Clanton, followed by those of the McLowry boys. A few carriages came next in which were near friends and relatives of the deceased, among

whom were Ike and Phin Clanton. After these were about three hundred people on foot, twenty-two carriages and buggies and one four-
horse stage, and the horsemen, making a line of nearly two blocks
in length. The two brothers were buried in one grave, and young
Clanton close by those who were his friends in life and companions
in death. The inscription upon the plates of the caskets stated that
Thomas McLowry was 25 years of age, Frank McLowry 29 years of
age, both natives of Mississippi, and that William H. Clanton was
19 years of age and a native of Texas. 'Yet a little sleep, a little
slumber, a little fading of the hands to sleep.'"[42]

Originally Billy's grave was surrounded by a neat wooden fence
of rustic design and his headstone read, "Sacred to the Memory of
William Clanton Who Was Murdered October 26, 1881. Age 19
Years."[43] The grave appears very different today. The fence and
headstone are gone and a small marker reads simply "Billy Clanton
killed Oct. 26, 1881."

An inquest was held, but the jury's verdict that the three cowboys
came to their deaths by gunshot wounds satisfied no one. The
Nugget made sarcastic comment in an article headed "Glad to
Know":

"The people of the community are deeply, indebted to the twelve
intelligent men who composed the coroners jury for the valuable
information that the three persons who were killed last Wednesday
were shot. Some thirty or forty shots were fired, and the whole
affair was witnessed by perhaps a dozen people, and we have a faint
recollection of hearing someone say the dead men were shot, but
people are liable to be mistaken and the verdict reassures us. We
might have thought they had been struck by lightning or stung to
death by hornets and we never could have told whether they were in
the way of the lightning or the lightning was in their way."[44]

Warrants were sworn out for the arrest of the Earps and Doc
Holliday on a murder charge and a hearing was held before Justice
of the Peace Wells Spicer. This hearing lasted thirty days and
though several witnesses testified that Ike Clanton and Tom
McLaury were unarmed and that Billy Clanton and Frank McLaury
were mortally wounded before they drew their pistols, Justice
Spicer's "opinion" was that the Earps acted in self-defense, though
he did say that he felt that Virgil Earp "committed an injudicious
and censurable act" in calling upon Wyatt Earp and J.H. Holliday to

assist him in arresting and disarming the Clantons and McLaurys.[45]

Shortly after this, Virgil Earp was wounded from ambush and in the middle of January, 1882, Wyatt and a posse attempted to arrest Phin and Ike Clanton on a charge of assault with intent to murder. The Clantons repeatedly sent word that they were ready and willing to answer to the charges, but would not surrender to the Earps for fear of being killed. When John H. Jackson was given a duplicate warrant to serve, and a strong posse was sent out under the command of Charlie Bartholomew and Peter Spencer, they willingly surrendered. Upon their arrival in Tombstone, Judge Stilwell adjourned his court that he might sit as an examining magistrate.[46] The evidence against the Clantons seems to have consisted mainly of Sherman McMaster's statement that he heard Ike Clanton say that he "Would have to go up and do the job over again." Seven men testified that Ike was in Charleston on the night of the attempted murder and the case was dismissed.[47]

Ike Clanton then had the Earps and Holliday arrested again on a charge of murdering Billy Clanton, but they were released on a writ of habeas corpus and no further examination was made.[48]

By 1883 Ike and Phin had moved their ranching operations to Apache County. They each acquired one-hundred and sixty acres in the area known as Cienega Amarilla.[49] Here they joined their sister Mary Elsie and her second husband Eben Stanley, a former school teacher. In July of 1883 a grand jury indicted Phin Clanton and Eben Stanley on five counts of improper branding and marking of calves and at least one trial was had, but the outcome is unknown.[50]

On the morning of June 1, 1887, Detective J.V. Brighton and Deputy Sheriff Miller, who had warrants for Ike Clanton and others on charges of cattle rustling, were at Wilson's ranch on the Blue River. Ike Clanton rode up and when he recognized them, turned to ride away, at the same time drawing his Winchester rifle from its scabbard. They commanded Ike to halt and when he did not, Brighton fired, killing him instantly.[51]

Phin Clanton and Eben Stanley were arrested and though there was conflicting testimony, Phin was found guilty and sentenced to ten years in Yuma prison. Because Eben Stanley had borne a good reputation and was at one time marshal in the Territory, he was not prosecuted, on condition that he leave the Territory within sixty days.[52] He and his family moved to New Mexico, where they lived for many years. Mary Elsie died in 1916 and is buried in the Lowell Evergreen cemetery near Bisbee, Arizona.[53]

On March 15, 1889, after serving one year and five months in prison, Phin was pardoned by Governor Meyer Zulick. According to his pardon, "Testimony has been produced which goes to establish the fact that the evidence upon which said Clanton was convicted was false and the result of a conspiracy to receive a reward of $250.00 which had been offered for the larceny of stock, the property of the Apache County Stockgrowers Association, which facts are certified in a petition requesting pardon of said Clanton by all of the trial jurors who passed upon his case, the District Attorney of Apache County and other county officials, endorsed also by the Board of Prison Commissioners."[54]

Upon his release Phin took up a ranch in Gila County near Globe, where it is said he raised goats and worked in the mines. He later owned shares of several mines.[55] In 1891 he had the interesting experience of reading about his own death. The *Globe Silver Belt* commented in this article:

"Says a Clifton dispatch: Advises [sic] from Apache County state that Phin Clanton was shot and killed by Ballard Pearson at St. Johns. No particulars.

"The foregoing announcement will be news to many people, and to no one is it more of a surprise than to Phin, himself, who is here in Globe and relishes three square meals a day and an occasional 11 p.m. lunch, but notwithstanding, in his case food does not seem to have fructified; he is still as thin as a shad after spawning time...."[56]

After being a bachelor for many years, Phin married Laura Jane Neal, a divorcee with a young son. In September, 1905, the *Silver Belt* described an accident in which Phin and his wife were injured:

"Mr. and Mrs. Phin Clanton were badly hurt in a runaway accident near Black Warrior last Monday forenoon while on their way to Globe from their ranch.

"Coming down the grade above the Black Warrior office building the horse which Mr. Clanton was driving became unmanageable and ran for a distance of a hundred yards or more when the cart was overturned and Mr. and Mrs. Clanton were thrown violently to the ground. Mrs. Clanton was severely bruised on the head, side, and arm while Mr. Clanton suffered a contusion on the head and had his right ear painfully lacerated.

"Supt. E.M. White and others went to the relief of Mr. and Mrs. Clanton who are still at Black Warrior, and improving under the care of Mrs. Baldridge."[57]

Three months later Phin suffered exposure in a severe snow storm and died January 5, 1906, of "congestive chills and fever."[58] He is buried in the Globe cemetery.[59] The son of his step-son still carries on the ranching operations, but raising cattle instead of goats.

John Wesley Clanton and his family were living in Mariposa, California, in 1900 where he and his son William W. worked as teamsters.[60] He died in Santa Rosa on April 19, 1916, after an illness of four days. Contributing causes were senility and overexertion.[61] His widow, Nancy Kelsey Clanton, outlived him by more than thirty years. Well into her nineties, she was living with a grandson in Fresno, California when she fell and suffered a broken hip. She died three weeks later, on May 19, 1948.[62]

Perhaps I should mention the perplexing puzzle of Peter Clanton. It seems that a young man named "Pete" was mixed up with some horse thieves preying on the people around St. Johns, Arizona, and was killed by a citizens committee in 1877. In newspaper accounts of the "trouble on the Little Colorado," Pete's surname is variously mentioned several times.[63] Though some writers believe that "Pete" is a son of Newman Clanton, I have been unable to make a connection between the two. St. Johns was then part of Yavapai County and it appears that the Clanton family was living in Pima County at this time. Newman and sons John Wesley, Phin, and Ike—the only male members of the family of voting age—are listed in the *Pima County Great Register* for 1876 through 1880.[64] There was, however, another family by the name of Clanton living in Yavapai County about this time.[65]

The only son of Newman Clanton who is unaccounted for is Alonzo, who is listed as one year old in the 1860 census.[66] I have not yet located him in subsequent censuses nor seen any further mention of him. Though there is the remote possibility that "Pete" might be Alonzo, there is still the question of the brother named Sam who was also killed. While I don't believe that "Pete" was a member of the Newman Clanton family, for the time being he remains a mystery.

References

1 Stewart Holbrook, "Wyatt Earp Rides Again," *Woman's Day*, January, 1956.

2 William McLeod Raine, "Wyatt Earp: Man Versus Myth" *Riders West* New York: Dell Publishing Co. 1956.

3 Microfiche Records, LDS Church Genealogy Library, Annandale, Virginia.

4 Ibid.

5 Ibid.

6 Personal Correspondence with Mrs. F.M. Gossurn, Jr.

7 Marriage License, Book B: Page 40, Callaway County Recorder of Deeds, Fulton, Missouri.

8 U.S. Census, 1850, Callaway County, Missouri, National Archives, Washington, D.C.

9 U.S. Census. 1860, Dallas County, Texas, 1908 Census, Sierra County, New Mexico, National Archives, Washington D.C.

10 Ad Valorern Tax Rolls, Dallas County, 1854-60, Genealogy Section, Texas State Library, Austin, Texas.

11 1860 Census, Dallas County.

12 Confederate Muster Roll Index, Texas State Library.

13 Compiled Military Service Records, Record Group 109, War Department Collection of Confederate Records, National Archives, D C.

14 "Proceedings of the Court Martial the Case of John W. Clanton, Company "B" Parson's Regt. Cavalry" Record Group 109, National Archives, Washington D.C.

15 Ibid.

16 Ibid.

17 Confederate Muster Roll Index, Texas State Library.

18 Both Poll Tax Rolls 1861-64 and Confederate Muster Rolls indicate the family was living in Hamilton County at this time.

19 Compiled Military Service Records, National Archives, D.C.

20 Ibid.

21 Personal Correspondence with Mrs. Helen Hill and Mrs. F.M. Gossum, Jr.

22 U.S. Census, 1870, Inyo County, California, National Archives, Washington D.C.

23 U.S. Census, 1880. Apache County, Arizona Territory, National Archives. Washington, D.C.

24 Tucson *Arizona Citizen*, Dec. 13. 1873.

25 Ibid., Sept. 12, 1874.

26 Lloyd and Rose Hamill, *Tombstone Picture Gallery*, Glendale, California, Western Americana Press 1960.

27 "Territory of Arizona vs. Morgan Earp, Wyatt Earp, and J.H. Holliday,"

Document 94, Dept. of Library, Archives, and Public Records, Phoenix, Arizona, Deposition of Ike Clanton.

28 Letter from W.R. McLaury to D.D. Applegate, Nov. 9, 1881, Arizona Historical Society.

29 Tucson *Arizona Daily Star,* March 26, 1882.

30 Tucson *Arizona Weekly Star,* August 25, 1881; *Arizona Daily Star,* Sept. 1, 1881.

31 Tucson *Arizona Daily Star,* March 26, 1882.

32 Doc. 94, Deposition of Ike Clanton.

33 Ibid., Deposition of A. Bauer.

34 Ibid., Deposition of William Allen.

35 Ibid., Deposition of William Claiborn.

36 Ibid., Deposition of Ike Clanton.

37 Ibid.

38 Ibid., Deposition of Wesley Fuller.

39 Ibid., Deposition of John H. Behan.

40 Ibid., Deposition of Thomas Keefe.

41 Joseph Miller, *Arizona: The Last Frontier,* New York: Hastings House, 1956.

42 *Tombstone Nugget,* October 27, 1881.

43 Tucson *Arizona Daily Star,* August 31, 1895.

44 *Tombstone Nugget,* October 30, 1881.

45 Doc. 94, Opinion of Justice Wells Spicer.

46 *Tombstone Nugget,* January 31, 1882.

47 Tucson *Arizona Daily Star,* February 4, 1882.

48 *Tombstone Nugget,* February 16, 1882.

49 Cash Entry #249 Prescott, AZ., Homestead Final certificate #98, Prescott, AZ, Record Group 49, Records of the Bureau of Land Management, Nation Archives, Washington, D.C.

50 Alford E. Turner, "The Clantons of Apache County", *Real West,* Vol. 22, March, 1979.

51 *Phoenix Weekly Herald,* June 16, 1887.

52 *Phoenix Daily Herald,* September 22, 1887.

53 *Arizona Death Records,* Tucson: Arizona State Genealogical Society, 1976.

54 Pardon of Phineas F. Clanton. March 15, 1889, Department of Library and Archives, Phoenix. AZ.

55 Records of the Probate Court, Gila County. AZ.

56 Florence *Arizona Enterprise,* April 25, 1891.

57 Globe *Arizona Silver Belt,* September 28, 1905.

58 Ibid., January 11,1906.

59 Personal Correspondence with William Bohme.

60 U.S. Census, 1900 Mariposa County, California, National Archives. Washington D.C.

61 Death Certificate, Dept. of Health Services. State of California.

62 Death Certificate, County of Fresno, State of California.

63 Prescott *Arizona Weekly Miner*, Nov. 23, 1877; Nov. 29, 1878.

64 *Pima County Great Register*, Dept. of Library and Archives, Phoenix, AZ.

65 U.S. Census, Yavapai County, AZ, National Archives, Washington, D.C.

Nellie Snyder Yost

Born June 20, 1905, in a sod house near North Platte, Nebraska, Nellie Yost was graduated from Maxwell high school in 1923. Her first book, *Pinnacle Jake*, a biography of her father, was published in 1951 to wide acclaim. She authored more than ten books and numerous magazine articles, most of them dealing with the Nebraska plains that she loved. She was recognized as a leading authority on North Platte's most famous resident, William F. "Buffalo Bill" Cody. In addition to NOLA, she held membership in the Western Writers of America, the Little Big Horn Association, and the Cody Corral of the Westerners. She was secretary-treasurer of WWA for eight years. That organization honored her with both its Golden Spur and Golden Saddleman awards. She also received the Mari Sandoz award for excellence in nonfiction Western writing and the Cowboy Hall of Fame Wrangler Award. She held many offices, including presidency of the Nebraska State Historical Society and the Nebraska Writers Guild, and directorship of the Westerners International. She held the rank of colonel in the Cody Scouts and the Nebraska National Guard. Married twice, she had one child, a son. Nellie Yost died at North Platte January 16, 1992.

BUFFALO BILL CODY:
OUTLAW, LAWMAN, SHOWMAN
•

By Nellie Snyder Yost
NOLA *Quarterly*, Winter 1983-84

Although more famous as a showman, William F. "Buffalo
Bill" Cody was both a lawman and outlaw. He was born
in Scott County, Iowa, in 1846 to pioneer farm parents. In
1854 the family moved to Kansas, near Leavenworth, where Cody's
father, Issac, became involved in abolitionist arguments, was
wounded in an altercation and, in 1857, died from the effect of the
wound. Eleven-year-old Bill, the only boy in the family, then
became the man of the house, helping his mother provide for his
several sisters.

The lad first worked for a neighbor for fifty cents a day, then as a
messenger boy for Russell, Majors and Waddell, the great freight-
ing firm.

At fourteen he was riding a Pony Express stretch west of
Julesburg, Colorado.

Then followed several adventurous years as a scout and volunteer
with various segments of Civil War troops, mainly the Seventh
Kansas Cavalry.

After a few months as an Overland Stage driver between Fort
Kearny and Plum Creek (Lexington) in Nebraska, he married
Louisa Frederici of St. Louis in 1866.

Soon thereafter he was scouting for the Army in Indian country,
where he quickly built a reputation as an excellent tracker and
hunter, resulting in the Goddard Brothers employing him to furnish

buffalo to feed the Kansas Pacific railroad crews, then laying track westward across Kansas.

After eight months, during which he killed 4,280 buffalo, the railroad was terminated at Sheridan, in western Kansas, in May, 1868. It was during that period that Cody was given his title of "Buffalo Bill," the name he was to make famous around the world.

Cody then went back to scouting for the army. He came to the favorable attention of General Phil Sheridan and was delegated chief scout for the Duke Alexis buffalo hunt on the Red Willow in Nebraska.

It was also during this period that he had a run-in with the law and spent a night under arrest.

In May, 1869, Cody went to Fort McPherson with General Eugene A. Carr's Fifth Cavalry and played a prominent part in the Battle of Summit Springs, just over the border in Colorado. From then on his fame built rapidly.

He served a brief stint as a justice of the peace at Fort McPherson, then deserted the plains for the stage. After ten years as one of the country's most popular actors, he put together his own production, his great Wild West show, and traveled much of the world with it.

In addition, he developed mines in Arizona, pioneered in huge irrigation projects in Nebraska and Wyoming (the Big Horn Basin and Cody Dam development) and the town of Cody, Wyoming, which was named for him and where he built his famous Irma Hotel.

During this time he put together his show place, Scout's Rest Ranch at North Platte, and his TE Ranch near Cody. The Nebraska ranch buildings, now fully restored, are a popular tourist stop.

An unsurpassed showman to the end, he died in Denver on January 10, 1917, and a nation, as well as much of the world, mourned his passing. He was buried on Lookout Mountain, above Denver, where hundreds of thousands visit his grave.

In 1869 Cody was on the army payroll, by Special Order No. 46, Headquarters, Expedition from Fort Lyon, Colorado Territory, commanded by Lieutenant Edward M. Hayes, quartermaster of the Fifth Cavalry, as scout at $125 per month.

Early in the year Cody asked for one month's leave of absence to visit his family. The leave was granted and he set off for St. Louis, Missouri, to see his wife and baby daughter.

Lieutenant Hayes allowed Cody to take a horse to ride and a mule on which to pack his belongings. With this outfit he proceeded from Fort Lyon to the end-of-track at Sheridan, with instructions to leave the animals at the quartermaster's corral at nearby Fort Wallace in Kansas. Instead of following orders, Cody left them with a Mr. Perry, a hotel keeper in Sheridan, to be sent out to the Fort.

When Cody returned to Sheridan by train he learned that a quartermaster's agent at the Fort had reported the animals stolen by Cody, who had then sold them to the hotel keeper and left the country. The horse and mule had then been seized as government property and taken to Fort Wallace, where the scout should have taken them in the first place.

Righteously indignant, Bill went at once to the Fort and beat up the quartermaster's agent. He then demanded the animals, since he was responsible to Lieutenant Hayes for them. The commanding officer, General Henry C. Bankhead, and also Captain Samuel C. Lauffer, ordered him off the reservation. So Bill went back to town, found the quartermaster's agent and beat him up again.

That night he was arrested by soldiers from the Thirty-eighth Infantry, under Captain Israel Ezekial, an old friend. Cody observed that Ezekial could have arrested him *without* bringing the Negro regiment with him, to which the captain replied that, in view of Cody's treatment of the quartermaster's agent, he wasn't sure how Cody would react to his arrest. Although Cody was taken to the guardhouse, he was not locked in a cell but allowed to sleep in a sergeant's bunk.

The matter was soon resolved, Cody was exonerated and on his way again; but he did spend a night under arrest, thus placing him briefly outside the pale of the law abiding.

Cody first served in the capacity of a "lawman" while still in Colorado Territory. Some horses and mules were stolen from Fort Lyon and he was, according to his own biography, commissioned a "United States detective" to recover them. Other scouts had followed the trail of the stolen stock for some distance, then lost it in tall grass. Cody picked it up again and, by means of some super-sleuthing, followed it to Sand Creek where he, too, lost it.

By then, however, they were near enough to Denver that Cody was convinced they could find the animals at the Saturday auction in that city. They did, and arrested the thieves and recovered the stolen government property.

Buffalo Bill again took up his lawman career in Nebraska in 1871, some two years after being transferred to Fort McPherson in that state. The army has little jurisdiction beyond the limits of its own military grounds. Consequently outlaws and sharpers of various sorts soon began to hang around the fringes of the reservations, preying upon soldiers, settlers and travelers.

At Fort McPherson crooked gambling and stealing of government property had become so prevalent that the commanding officer, General W.H. Emory, deciding something had to be done, recommended the appointment of W.F. Cody as justice of the peace at Cottonwood Springs, the village beside the post.

General Emory figured that someone who was sympathetic to the army's side of such matters would be more helpful than an ordinary civilian, and anyway Cody's log house was located in Cottonwood Springs, just off the reservation.

In 1866 old Shorter County (first title given the vast expanse of territory that constituted what is now the western half of Nebraska and part of Wyoming) was reorganized and named Lincoln County. The following year the county seat was removed from Cottonwood Springs to the new town of North Platte, eighteen miles farther west.

There is no existing record of Cody's appointment as a justice of the peace, but convincing evidence that he actually served in that office is found in the minutes of the county commissioners' court for June, 1872, in an entry noting his resignation as a justice of the peace at Cottonwood Springs.

Cody insisted that he didn't "know any more about law than a government mule does about book-keeping," but nevertheless he served capably for at least a little over six months. Shortly after his appointment, as he tells it, "A man came rushing up to my house and stated that he wanted to get out a writ of replevin to recover possession of his horse which a stranger was taking out of the country." Bill says he had no blank forms for such an action.

Whether that was the reason he didn't make out one, or whether be didn't yet know how to go about it, is not known. At any rate all he did was to saddle his horse and pick up his "old reliable gun, Lucretia," the best "writ of replevin" he knew of, and set off after the stranger. Upon overtaking the man and his herd of horses, Cody informed him he was an officer of the law and had an attachment for the horse, which had been described to him by the real owner.

The would-be thief asked Cody what he proposed to do about it, and Cody told him he proposed to take the horse back to its owner. The rustler, taking Lucretia into account, told him he could take the horse but that he, himself, didn't have time to go back. The new justice of the peace told him he would have to "take the time' or pay the cost here and now." When informed the costs were twenty dollars, he pulled out a twenty and handed it to Cody, who thereupon "released him from custody," took the horse and went home. Not bad for an embryo officer of the law.

The main event of Cody's brief term as a J.P. appears to have been the occasion on which he was called upon to perform a marriage. Cody biographers have had a field day with this bit. It has been told and retold a thousand times. Cody states that it was his most frightening experience, since he couldn't remember how the ritual went, nor could he find any help in the State of Nebraska, so he made up a ceremony and went ahead. It ended with the famous words, "whomsoever God and Buffalo Bill have joined together let no man put asunder. "

Since no evidence of the celebrated wedding seemed to exist, historians have long wondered if it really happened, or if it was just another tall tale; until January, 1983, when the original marriage license came to light in a file of hundreds of Lincoln County marriage licenses, long stored away in the state files in Lincoln, Nebraska.

According to the 113-year-old document, on December 31, 1870, Peter C. Peterson thirty-three years old and born in Denmark but now residing at Fort McPherson, applied for a license to wed Mary Jane Short, age thirty, also residing at Fort McPherson. On January 2, 1871, in the presence of Mr. and Mrs. John B. Stevens, both of Fort McPherson, Peter Peterson and Mary Jane Short were married at the Fort. The paper is signed by W.F. Cody, Justice of the Peace. Whether or not he actually uttered his famous "last words" we shall probably never know—but I'm betting that he did.

INDEX